SO-CCJ-236

Fodor's InFocus

CAYMAN ISLANDS

Fodor's Travel Publications New York, Toronto, London, Sydney, Auckland
www.fodors.com

Excerpted from Fodor's Caribbean 2013

14
TOP EXPERIENCES

The Cayman Islands offer terrific experiences that should be on every traveler's list. Here are Fodor's top picks for a memorable trip.

1 Seven Mile Beach

Those who love long, broad, uninterrupted sweeps of champagne-hued sand will be thrilled with Grand Cayman's longest beach. *(Ch. 6)*

2 Bird-watching on the Sister Islands

The Booby Pond on Little Cayman and the Brac's Parrot Preserve are just two of the gorgeous areas set aside for communing with nature. (Ch. 7 & 8)

3 Buying Crafts, Cayman Brac

Some of the best local craftspeople, including Annalee Ebanks (thatch-weaving) and Tenson Scott (caymanite carving), are found on the Brac. (Ch. 7)

4 George Town, Grand Cayman

In addition to dynamite duty-free shopping, the handsome waterfront capital hosts the historic Cayman Islands National Museum. *(Ch. 2)*

5 Pirates Point, Little Cayman

The dinners here aren't quite as elegant or complex as what you might find at one of Grand Cayman's top spots, but the bon mots and bonhomie are unmatched. *(Ch. 8)*

6 Queen Elizabeth II Botanic Garden

Critically endangered blue iguanas have found a home at this park, where you learn about their life cycles, then stroll the peaceful, gorgeously laid-out gardens. *(Ch. 2)*

7 Stingray City, Grand Cayman

You can interact with gracefully balletic, silken stingrays, so "tame" you can feed them as they beg for handouts on this shallow sandbar in the North Sound. *(Ch. 6)*

8 Diving Bloody Bay Wall

One of the top dive sites in the world plunges from 18 feet to more than a mile into the Cayman Trench; the visibility is remarkable. *(Ch. 6)*

9 Barefoot Man at the Reef Resort

Head to Pelican's Reef on the East End of Grand Cayman to hear the blond Calypsonian, Barefoot Man (née George Nowak), a beloved island icon. *(Ch. 5)*

10 Happy Hour, Grand Cayman

Such popular waterfront spots as Rackam's and The Wharf serve creative cocktails and reel in the revelers for sunset tarpon feeding. *(Ch. 5)*

11 Owen Island, off Little Cayman

Easily accessible by kayak from Little Cayman's "mainland," Owen Island appeals to snorkelers and romantics, who have their choice of captivating coves. *(Ch. 8)*

12 Local Food, Grand Cayman

Sample mouth- and eye-watering jerk chicken from a roadside stall or George Town shack. A few local chefs even serve meals in their homes. *(Ch. 3)*

13 Blue by Eric Ripert, at the Ritz-Carlton

The wine-pairing menu at Le Bernardin chef Eric Ripert's only Caribbean restaurant is the kind of epicurean experience that comes along once in a blue moon. *(Ch. 3)*

14 Underwater Sculpture, Cayman Brac

Nature's artistry is matched by the world's largest (and still growing) underwater installation, the sculptor Foots's gorgeously imagined, impressively engineered Lost City of Atlantis. *(Ch. 7)*

CONTENTS

ABOUT THIS GUIDE

Fodor's Ratings

Everything in this guide is worth doing—we don't cover what isn't—but exceptional sights, hotels, and restaurants are recognized with additional accolades. **Fodor's Choice ★** indicates our top recommendations; ★ highlights places we deem highly recommended. Care to nominate a new place? Visit Fodors.com/contact-us.

Trip Costs

We list prices wherever possible to help you budget well. Hotel and restaurant price categories from **$** to **$$$$** are noted alongside each recommendation. For hotels, we include the lowest cost of a standard double room in high season. For restaurants, we cite the average price of a main course at dinner or, if dinner isn't served, at lunch. For attractions, we always list adult admission fees; discounts are usu-

ally available for children, students, and senior citizens.

Hotels

Our local writers vet every hotel to recommend the best overnights in each price category, from budget to expensive. Unless otherwise specified, you can expect private bath, phone, and TV in your room. For expanded hotel reviews, facilities, and deals visit Fodors.com.

Restaurants

Unless we state otherwise, restaurants are open for lunch and dinner daily. We mention dress code only when there's a specific requirement and reservations only when they're essential or not accepted. To make restaurant reservations, visit Fodors.com.

Credit Cards

The hotels and restaurants in this guide typically accept credit cards. If not, we'll say so.

Ratings
★ Fodor's Choice
★ Highly recommended
☾ Family-friendly

Listings
⊠ Address
⊠ Branch address
🕮 Mailing address
☎ Telephone
🖷 Fax
⊕ Website

✎ E-mail
🎟 Admission fee
☉ Open/closed times
Ⓜ Subway
✛ Directions or Map coordinates

Hotels & Restaurants
🏨 Hotel
🛏 Number of rooms
🍽 Meal plans

✕ Restaurant
🍴 Reservations
👔 Dress code
🖃 No credit cards
💲 Price

Other
⇨ See also
☞ Take note
⛳ Golf facilities

DID YOU KNOW?

The endangered Lesser Cayman's iguana that is endemic to Little Cayman and Cayman Brac was recently introduced in Grand Cayman.

Experience
the Cayman
Islands

WHAT'S WHERE

C a r i b b e a n   S e a

LITTLE CAYMAN

DISTANCE ON MAP
IS COMPRESSED

Jacksons **3**
Pt.
Gov.
Anchorage   Gore Bird
Bay   South   Sanctuary
Town   South Ho
West End Point   Sound

**Edward Bodden
Airfield**

Head of
Barkers

Hell

MARINE PARK

Rum Point

Seven Mile Beach

Water Cay

Cayman Kai   Old Man Bay   A3

A4

**West
Bay**   A1   Malportas
Booby   HUTLAND   Pond   OLD
Cay   MAN
BAY

Owen Roberts   *North*   GRAND CAYMAN
International   *Sound*
Airport

George   HALF
Town   PEASE   MOON
BAY   BREAKERS   BAY
A4
NORTH   **1**   A3
SOUND   *Pease*
ESTATES   BELFORD   A3   *Bay*   Ironshore
NEWLANDS   ESTATES   Point
A2   Bodden Town
SAVANNAH   A2
Bodden
A5   *Bay*

Southweat
Point

1 **Grand Cayman.** The Cayman Islands' main island offers the longest, liveliest sandy strand (Seven Mile Beach), great diving, fine dining, upscale resorts, surprisingly varied nightlife, and an attractive waterfront capital with duty-free shopping in George Town. Despite the development and congestion around Seven Mile Beach and George Town, the neighborhoods of West Bay and East End are mellow and filled with natural wonders.

2 **Cayman Brac.** The archipelago's most rugged, dramatically scenic island is known for its bullying bluff, which vaults 140 feet. The bird-watching, caving, hiking, and rock climbing (experienced only with your own gear) are phenomenal, and the island is just as spectacular underwater for divers and snorkelers. The Brac is laid-back, friendly, and cheap, with good villa values and small inns and resorts.

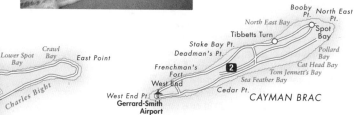

Booby Pt. North East Pt.
North East Bay
Spot Bay
Tibbetts Turn
Crawl Bay
Lower Spot Bay   East Point
Stake Bay Pt.
Deadman's Pt.
Pollard Bay
Frenchman's Fort
Cat Head Bay
Tom Jennett's Bay
West End
Sea Feather Bay
Charles Bight
West End Pt.
Gerrard-Smith Airport
Cedar Pt.
CAYMAN BRAC

2

Spotter Bay
COLLIERS
Colliers Bay
EAST END
Lower Bay

The Bahamas   ATLANTIC OCEAN
Cuba
Haiti   Dominican Republic
Caribbean Sea
COLOMBIA   VENEZUELA
Caribbean

3 **Little Cayman.** The smallest
of the Cayman Islands is the least
developed, most unspoiled in the
chain. Ecotourists can get back
to nature (but not the basics) at
splendid little resorts catering to
divers and birders. You'll find world-
famous dive sites like Bloody Bay
Marine Park, equally fantastic fishing
(especially light-tackle), secluded
beaches, and fabulous bird-watching
along the shore and wetlands covering nearly half the island.

CAYMAN ISLANDS PLANNER

Island Activities	Logistics
Diving is a major draw; the Bloody Bay Wall, off the coast of Little Cayman, is one of the Caribbean's top dive destinations, but there are many sites convenient to Grand Cayman where shore diving is also good.	**Getting to the Islands:** There are plenty of nonstop flights to Grand Cayman (GCM) from the United States; then you can hop over to the Brac (CYB) and Little Cayman (LYB) on a small plane.
On Grand Cayman, a dive or snorkeling trip to **Stingray City** is very popular. There's good off-the-beach snorkeling in West Bay Cemetery, at Rum Point, and at Smith's Cove in Grand Cayman.	**Hassle Factor:** Low for Grand Cayman; medium to high for Little Cayman and Cayman Brac.
On land, Grand Cayman has the most to offer, with plenty of tours and activities, including **semisubmersible tours** of the bay.	**Nonstops:** You can fly nonstop to Grand Cayman from Atlanta (Delta), Boston (US Airways and JetBlue once weekly), Charlotte (US Airways), Detroit (Northwest once weekly), Fort Lauderdale (Cayman Airways), Houston (Continental once weekly), Miami (American, Cayman Airways), Minneapolis (Northwest once weekly), New York–JFK (Cayman Airways daily, JetBlue three times weekly), New York–Newark (Continental once weekly), Philadelphia (US Airways once weekly), and Tampa (Cayman Airways).
Grand Cayman's **Seven Mile Beach** is one of the Caribbean's finest long stretches of sand. Little Cayman has the best beaches of the Sister Islands, especially Owen Island and Point o' Sand.	**On the Ground:** In Grand Cayman you must take a taxi or rent a car at the airport, since most hotels are not permitted to offer airport shuttles. Hotel pickup is more readily available on Cayman Brac and Little Cayman.
Rock climbers have now discovered the Brac's limestone bluff.	**Renting a Car:** It's possible to get by without a car on Grand Cayman if you are staying in the Seven Mile Beach area. If you want to explore the rest of the island—or if you are staying elsewhere—you'll need a car. Though less necessary on Cayman Brac or Little Cayman, cars are available on both islands. Driving is on the left, and you need a local driving permit, available at the car-rental office for US$7.50.

Where to Stay

Grand Cayman is expensive during the high season but offers the widest range of resorts, restaurants, and activities. Both Little Cayman and Cayman Brac are more geared toward serving the needs of divers, who compose the majority of visitors. The smaller islands are cheaper than Grand Cayman, but with the extra cost of transportation, the overall savings are minimized.

Grand Cayman: Grand Cayman has plenty of medium-size resorts as well as the Ritz-Carlton, a large seven-story resort on Seven Mile Beach. The island also has a wide range of condos and villas, many in resortlike compounds on or near Seven Mile Beach and the Cayman Kai area. There are even a few small guesthouses for budget-minded visitors.

The Sister Islands: Cayman Brac has mostly intimate resorts and family-run inns. Little Cayman has a mix of small resorts and condos, most appealing to divers.

Hotel and Restaurant Costs

Prices in the restaurant reviews are the average cost of a main course at dinner or, if dinner is not served, at lunch; taxes and service charges are generally included. Prices in the hotel reviews are the lowest cost of a standard double room in high season, excluding taxes, service charges, and meal plans (except at all-inclusives). Prices for rentals are the lowest per-night cost for a one-bedroom unit in high season.

Tips for Travelers

All visitors must have a valid passport and a return or ongoing ticket to enter the Cayman Islands.

The minimum legal drinking age in the Cayman Islands is 18.

Electricity is reliable and is the same as in the United States (110 volts/60 cycles). U.S. electrical appliances will work just as if at home.

You should not need to change money in Grand Cayman, since U.S. dollars are readily accepted. ATMs generally offer the option of U.S. or Cayman dollars. The Cayman dollar is pegged to the U.S. dollar at the rate of approximately CI$1.25 to $1. Be sure you know which currency is being quoted when making a purchase.

IF YOU LIKE

Getting Away from It All

Though Grand Cayman's Seven Mile Beach is completely developed, other areas of the island still offer respite from the crowds as do the Sister Islands. Here are some ideas for romantic R&R:

Cotton Tree, Grand Cayman. This serene West Bay sanctuary artfully combines Cayman heritage with a gaggle of the latest gadgets and other luxe amenities.

Pirates Point and The Southern Cross Club, Little Cayman. You can't go wrong with either of Little Cayman's upscale yet down-home intimate beachfront resorts.

Lighthouse Point, Grand Cayman. This eco-centric hideaway recycles practically everything, allowing guests to get back to nature but not the basics.

Cayman Breakers, Cayman Brac. Tucked away at the remotest point on the Brac, this condo complex satisfies any desire for seclusion; the owners are building an even more elegant complex next door.

The Reef, Grand Cayman. If you crave activity and facilities galore, yet still value privacy, this midsize resort fits the bill on Grand Cayman's East End.

Great Eating

Foodies can savor a smorgasbord of gastronomic goodies, from sophisticated fusion fare to fiery local cuisine—and everything in between. Try these special spots:

Blue by Eric Ripert, Grand Cayman. Ripert's great NYC seafood-centric eatery, Le Bernardin, goes coastal with shipshape results.

Michael's Genuine Food & Drink, Grand Cayman. James Beard Award–winning chef Michael Schwartz delectably adapts his Miami outpost's "slow food" philosophy.

Ortanique, Grand Cayman. Celebrity chef Cindy Hutson and her partner Delius Shirley make waves with this outpost of their Floribbean sensation.

Agua, Grand Cayman. Go for the superlative ceviches, stay for the sublime pastas at this civilized eatery.

Morgan's Harbour, Grand Cayman. Enjoy the stellar views of fishing dinghies and pleasure craft cruising the North Sound alongside pub grub elevated to an art form.

Cimboco, Grand Cayman. Everything about this spot is creative, from the boldly colored decor to the innovative takes on Caribbean cuisine.

Pirate's Point, Little Cayman. It's practically worth a day trip from Grand Cayman to enjoy the food

and conversation at Gladys Howard's lovely retreat.

The Water

Bloody Bay and Stingray City are the showcase attractions in Cayman, but here are some suggestions for other stellar sites as well as aquatic activities aplenty:

Wreck Diving, Grand Cayman and Cayman Brac. The Cayman Islands government sank the decommissioned 251-foot USS *Kittiwake* to create another artificial reef, while the Brac counters with the 330-foot *Capt. Keith Tibbetts*, a virtual fireworks display of reel life.

Shore Diving, Grand Cayman. Silverside minnows swarm in the grottoes at Eden Rock, forming liquid silver lamé curtains of fish; its neighbor, the Devil's Grotto resembles an abstract marine painting.

Kayaking, Grand Cayman. Glide through protected mangrove wetlands teeming with a unique ecosystem; the Bio Bay tour on moonless nights is unforgettable.

Deep See Cayman, Grand Cayman. To explore the underwater world without getting your feet wet, Deep See Cayman uses a robot to plumb the depths up to 2,400 feet, transmitting live feed as you watch on a yacht.

Sportfishing, Cayman Brac and Little Cayman. Both Sister Islands offer sensational bonefishing in the flats, as well as deep-sea fishing for marlin, wahoo and sushi-grade tuna.

Shopping

It's fun to bring home a memento for yourself and souvenirs for your friends and family. Here are some suggestions:

Caymanian Crafts, Grand Cayman and Cayman Brac. The Cayman Craft Market and fun funky stores like Pure Art sell everything from local preserves to paintings, while Tenson Scott on the Brac is famed for his Caymanite creations.

Rum and More Rum, Grand Cayman. Cayman's own Seven Fathoms Rum produces a mellow spirit via a unique underwater aging process, while Tortuga Rum is celebrated for its rum-soaked cakes in many flavors.

Art, Grand Cayman. Find original paintings and sculptures by Cayman artists, including Al Ebanks, Luelan Bodden, Gordon Solomon, Nickola McCoy-Snell, and Randy and Nasaria Suckoo Cholette.

Jewelry, Grand Cayman. Downtown George Town is practically one giant duty-free shopping center, highlighting numerous name brands and individual jewelers, while conspicuous consumption continues in the malls along Seven Mile Beach.

WHEN TO GO

The high season in the Cayman Islands is traditionally winter—from December 15 to April 15—when northern weather is at its worst. It's the most fashionable, the most expensive, and the most popular time to visit—and most resorts are heavily booked. You must make reservations at least two or three months in advance for the very best places (sometimes a year in advance for the most exclusive spots). Hotel prices drop 20%–50% after April 15; airfares and cruise prices also fall. Saving money isn't the only reason to visit the Cayman Islands during the off-season. In summer the sea is even calmer (ideal for diving—except when tropical storms roil the waters), and things move at a slower pace. The water is clearer for snorkeling and smoother for sailing in May, June, and July, when the big game fish, though abundant year-round, really run riot.

Climate

The average daily temperature is about 80°F, and there isn't much variation from the coolest to the warmest months, including the water temperature. Rainfall averages 50 to 60 inches per year (less in the more arid Sister Islands and Grand Cayman's East End). But in the tropics, rainstorms tend to be sudden and brief, often erupting early in the morning and at dusk.

Toward the end of summer, hurricane season begins in earnest. Starting in June, islanders pay close attention to the tropical waves as they form and travel across the Atlantic from Africa. In an odd paradox, tropical storms passing by leave behind the sunniest and clearest days you'll ever see.

Festivals and Events

January gets the Cayman calendar literally cooking with the celebrity-heavy **Cayman Cookout** co-organized by top toque Eric Ripert. February usually celebrates Cayman culture in the **Arts Festival.** Cayman explodes with color every April with its take on Carnival called **Batabano.** May's **Cayman Islands International Fishing Tournament** lures anglers from around the world. November's **GimmiSTORY** celebrates Cayman's rich oral storytelling tradition. But the big blockbuster is November's **Pirates Week Festival,** when Grand Cayman turns into one giant 11-day party, featuring parades, costume competitions, street dances, Heritage Days, mock pirate invasions, sporting events, fireworks, and delicious local grub.

GREAT ITINERARIES

It's a shame that so few visitors (other than divers) spend time on more than one island in a single trip. If you have more than a week, you can certainly spend some quality time on both Grand Cayman and one of its Sister Islands.

If You Have 3 Days

Ensconce yourself at a resort along Grand Cayman's **Seven Mile Beach,** spending your first day luxuriating on the sand. On Day 2, get your feet wet, if you snorkel or dive, at **Stingray City and Sandbar** in West Bay, where you can feed the alien-looking gliders by hand. Splurge for a great dinner on your second night, perhaps at **Blue by Eric Ripert.** On your last day, head into **George Town** for some shopping. Have lunch with scintillating harbor views at **Breezes by the Bay** or **Casanova** before soaking up some last rays of sun.

If You Have 7 Days

Since divers need to decompress before their return flight, the last day should be spent sightseeing on Grand Cayman. **Boatswain's Beach,** the expensive but exceptional marine theme park, is a fine destination. On the East End you could hike the pristine **Mastic Trail,** then stroll through the gorgeous grounds at **Queen Elizabeth II Botanic Park.** Spend your final morning in George Town (perhaps snorkeling **Eden Rock**). Non-divers, too, should explore a bit farther afield instead of spending all their time at Seven Mile Beach. A full day around West Bay, perhaps beachcombing at savagely beautiful **Barkers,** is a good choice. If you have a car, explore the East End natural attractions, lunching at the **Lighthouse.** Head east another day to visit historic **Pedro St. James Castle;** drive through the original capital, **Bodden Town;** then spend the afternoon (lunch, swimming, and water sports) at **Cayman Kai/ Rum Point.**

If You Have 10 Days

With 10 days, you can spend time on two or even all three islands. Begin on Cayman Brac; after diving the **north coast** walls, **MV Capt. Keith Tibbetts,** and the **Lost City of Atlantis** (or just lying on the beach), save a morning to hike through the **Parrot Reserve,** perhaps out to the **East End Lighthouse** for its sensational views (or climb the Lighthouse Steps, peeking into **Peter's Cave**). On Little Cayman, chill out picnicking on **Owen Island,** and don't miss the **Booby Pond Nature Reserve.** Spend at least two nights on Grand Cayman.

WEDDINGS AND HONEYMOONS

There's no question that the Cayman Islands, especially Grand Cayman, are one of the Caribbean's foremost honeymoon destinations. Destination weddings are also particularly popular on Grand Cayman, where the larger resorts have wedding planners to help you with the paperwork and details.

The Big Day

Choosing the Perfect Place. When choosing a location, remember that you really have two choices to make: the ceremony location and the reception location. For the former, there are beaches, bluffs overlooking beaches, gardens, private residences, historic buildings, resort lawns, and, of course, places of worship (after which you can trot away to your life together in a horse-drawn carriage). Most couples choose to say their vows on lovely Seven Mile Beach, with the sun setting into the azure sea as their picture-perfect backdrop. Underwater weddings in full scuba gear with schools of fish as impromptu witnesses are also possible (kissing with mask on optional). Cathy Church can photograph your underwater wedding *(see ⇨ Shopping in Chapter 2).* You can literally leave things up in the air, getting hitched while hovering in a helicopter ("I do; Roger and out," responded one blushing bride over the propeller noise). As for the reception, you can opt for most of the same choices, as well as restaurants. If you decide to go outdoors, remember the seasons—yes, the Caribbean has seasons. If you're planning a wedding outdoors, be sure you have a backup plan in case it rains. Also, if you're planning an outdoor wedding at sunset—which is very popular—be sure you match the time of your ceremony to the time the sun sets at that time of year.

Finding a Wedding Planner. If you're planning to invite more than a minister and your loved one to your wedding ceremony, seriously consider an on-island wedding planner, who can help select a location, help design the floral scheme and recommend a florist as well as a photographer, help plan the menu, and suggest any local traditions to incorporate into your ceremony.

Of course, all the larger resorts have their own wedding planners on-site. If you're planning a resort wedding, work with the on-site wedding coordinator to prepare a detailed list of the exact services he or she will provide. If your idea of your wedding doesn't match the resort's services, try a different resort. Or look for independent wedding planners, who do not work directly for resorts.

Legal Requirements. Documentation can be prepared ahead of time or in one day while on the

island. A minimal residency waiting period, blood test, and shots aren't required.

You need to supply a Cayman Islands international embarkation/disembarkation card, as well as proof of identity (a passport or certified copy of your birth certificate signed by a notary public), and age (those under 18 must provide parental consent). If you've been married before, you must provide proof of divorce with the original or certified copy of the divorce decree if applicable or a copy of the death certificate if your previous spouse died. You must list a marriage officer on the application, and you need at least two witnesses; if you haven't come with friends or family, the marriage officer can help you with that, too. A marriage license costs CI$200 (US$250).

Wedding Attire. In the Caribbean, basically anything goes, from long, formal dresses with trains to white bikinis. Floral sundresses are fine, too. Men can wear tuxedos or a simple pair of solid-color slacks with a nice white linen shirt. If you want formal dress and tuxedo, it's usually better to bring your formal attire with you.

Photographs. Deciding whether to use the photographer supplied by your resort or an independent photographer is an important choice. Resorts that host a lot of weddings usually have their own photographers, but you can also find independent, professional island-based photographers, and an independent wedding planner will know the best in the area. Look at the portfolio (many photographers now have websites), and decide if this person can give you the kind of memories you are looking for. If you're satisfied with the photographer that your resort uses, make sure you see proofs and order prints before you leave the island.

The Honeymoon

Do you want champagne and strawberries delivered to your room each morning? A maze of a swimming pool in which to float? A five-star restaurant in which to dine? Then a resort is the way to go, and Grand Cayman offers options in different price ranges. Whether you want a luxurious experience or a more modest one, you'll certainly find someplace romantic to which you can escape. You can usually stay on at the resort where your wedding was held. On the other hand, maybe you want your own private home in which to romp naked— or maybe your own kitchen in which to whip up a gourmet meal for your loved one. In that case, a private vacation-rental home or condo is the answer.

KIDS AND FAMILIES

Grand Cayman and, to a much lesser extent, Cayman Brac jump with activities and attractions that will keep children of all ages (and their parents) happily occupied. Some resorts and hotels welcome children, others do not, and still others restrict kids to off-season visits. All but the fanciest (and most expensive) restaurants are kid-friendly.

Family-Friendly Resorts

The **Ritz-Carlton,** the biggest and most fashionable of the island's resorts, welcomes children at any time with "edu-tainment" programs for all ages, including Jean-Michel Cousteau's Ambassadors of the Environment initiative introducing Cayman's culture and ecology. Less pricey is **Grand Cayman Marriott Beach Resort** on Seven Mile Beach with children's programs and a fine stretch of beach. Many of the condo complexes toward the northern end of Seven Mile Beach, such as **Christopher Columbus** and **Discovery Point Club** offer good value and a wide rock-free strand. On Cayman Brac, the **Brac Reef Beach Resort** is best equipped for families. Little Cayman is too quiet for most kids, but the **Little Cayman Beach Resort** can keep children occupied while their parents dive.

Family-Friendly Dining and Activities

Dining out with the family is not an issue, as Grand Cayman has more restaurants than you can count serving a virtual United Nations of cuisines. The Sister Islands are much more limited in their offerings, though the friendly locals will do their utmost to please finicky palates. **Camana Bay** is definitely family-friendly, from climbing the Observation Tower for smashing panoramas to splashing in the fountains and watching the frequent street performers. Most of the islands' water-based activities cater to kids, including **Deep See Cayman, the Atlantis semisubmersible, Stingray City snorkeling tours and the Dolphin Discovery.** The attractions at the **Cayman Turtle Farm,** including the predator reef and breeding facility, mesmerize all ages, as will learning about blue iguanas at their habitat in the **Queen Elizabeth II Botanical Garden.** Pipes, ramps, and rails galore, not to mention a wave-surf machine, have kids screaming while doing wheelies at the **Black Pearl Skate & Surf Park.**

Exploring Grand Cayman

WITH SHOPPING

WORD OF MOUTH

"We . . . stopped at the [Queen Elizabeth II] Botanic [Park] on the way [back to our resort] which was wonderful. Blue iguanas and lots of lush foliage made it a stop worth doing."

—starfish1

By Jordan
Simon

THOUGH GRAND CAYMAN IS MOST celebrated for its aquatic activities, there's no shortage of diversions to please landlubbers, history buffs, the eco-centric, and families, from turtle and butterfly farms to ruined fortifications. It's just as alluring on land as underwater, gleaming with a ravishing dryness. Though not lush, the surrounding scenery can spiral from arid semidesert to tropical hardwood forests that pierce the sky like cathedral spires. Many attractions admirably attempt to foster greater understanding of the environment and the importance of responsible stewardship of our resources.

Window-shopping in the captivating capital, George Town, ranks as many visitors' favorite form of recreation and sightseeing. Not only will you find no additional sales tax, but there's duty-free merchandise aplenty. And though most people's image of Grand Cayman is bustling Seven Mile Beach, there are downright rural, pastoral pockets where if time doesn't stand still, it slows to a turtle's steady crawl. This is where travelers can experience the "real" Cayman, including craft traditions such as thatch weaving that have nearly vanished.

EXPLORING GRAND CAYMAN

The historic capital of George Town, on the southeast corner of Grand Cayman, is easy to explore on foot. If you're a shopper, you can spend days here; otherwise, an hour will suffice for a tour of the downtown area. To see the rest of the island, rent a car or scooter or take a guided tour. The portion of the island called West Bay is noted for its jumble of neighborhoods, many featuring ornate Edwardian homes built by seafarers, nautical tour companies (and real fishing fleet) at Morgan's Harbour, and a few attractions. When traffic is heavy, it's about a half hour to West Bay from George Town, even with the newer bypass road that runs parallel to West Bay Road. The less-developed North Side and East End have natural attractions from blowholes to botanical gardens, as well as the remains of the island's original settlements. Plan on at least 45 minutes for the drive out from George Town (more than an hour during rush hours). You need a day to explore the entire island—including a stop at a beach for a picnic or swim.

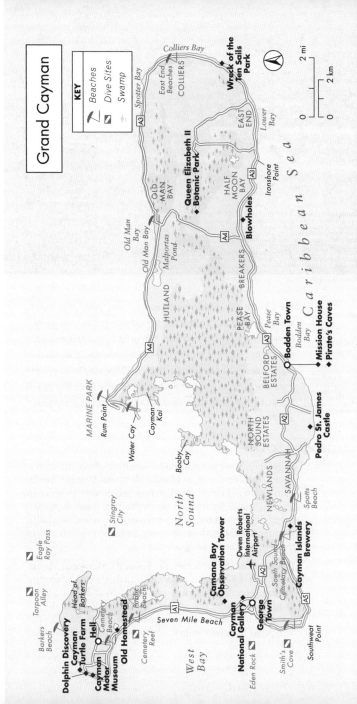

Grand Cayman

KEY

- Beaches
- Dive Sites
- Swamp

Colliers Bay

Spotter Bay

East End Beaches

COLLIERS

Wreck of the Ten Sails Park

A3

EAST END

Lower Bay

Queen Elizabeth II Botanic Park

Old Man Bay

OLD MAN BAY

HALF MOON BAY

Blowholes

A3

Ironshore Point

Old Man Bay

Malportas Pond

A4

HUTLAND

BREAKERS

Pease Bay

Bodden Bay

Bodden Town

Mission House

Pirate's Caves

BELFORD ESTATES

C a r i b b e a n S e a

MARINE PARK

Rum Point

Water Cay

Cayman Kai

Booby Cay

NORTH SOUND ESTATES

NEWLANDS

A2

SAVANNAH

Pedro St. James Castle

Stingray City

North Sound

Spotts Beach

Owen Roberts International Airport

Camana Bay Observation Tower

A2

South Sound

Cemetery Beach

Cayman Islands Brewery

A5

Eagle Ray Pass

Tarpoon Alley

Barkers Beach

Head of Barkers

Dolphin Discovery

Cayman Turtle Farm

Hell

Cayman Motor Museum

Old Homestead

Cemetery Beach

Public Beach

A1

Cemetery Reef

Seven Mile Beach

West Bay

Cayman National Gallery

George Town

Eden Rock

Smith's Cove

Southwest Point

0 2 mi

0 2 km

An aerial view of West Bay

CRUISE CRUSH. On certain days George Town, Seven Mile Beach, and even West Bay's attractions crawl with cruise-ship hordes. Check the Cayman Island Port Authority (⊕ *www.caymanport. com/schedule.htm*) for the latest schedule and plan accordingly, unless you like being trampled. There may be anywhere from one to three ships at anchor off George Town any day of the week, but more ships tend to call on Tuesday, Wednesday, and Thursday.

GEORGE TOWN

Begin exploring the capital by strolling along the waterfront, Harbour Drive, to **Elmslie Memorial United Church,** named after the first Presbyterian missionary to serve in the Caymans. Its vaulted timber ceiling (built from salvaged wreck material in the shape of an upside-down hull), wooden arches, mahogany pews, and tranquil nave reflect the island's deeply religious nature.

Just north near Fort Street, the **Seamen's Memorial Monument** lists 153 names on an old navigational beacon; a bronze piece by Canadian sculptor Simon Morris, titled *Tradition,* honors the almost 500 Caymanians who have lost their lives at sea. Dive-industry pioneer Bob Soto, wife Suzy, and daughter-in-law Leslie Bergstrom spearheaded

BEST BETS

■ **Feeling Blue.** Visiting the endangered blue iguana compound at the glorious Queen Elizabeth II Botanic Park.

■ **Petting a Turtle.** Though it's hideously expensive, Boatswain's Beach encapsulates everything that makes Cayman special. And admission to its world-class turtle research center/farm, true edu-tainment, is cheaper.

■ **Getting Touched by History.** Pedro St. James Castle bears eloquent testimony to Caymanian struggles for democracy, freedom, and survival against the elements.

■ **National Trust–worthy.** The National Trust is an admirable institution dedicated to preserving the Caymanian environment and culture. If you're on island when they're running a tour (perhaps to the bat caves or historic homes) or a demonstration (cooking, thatch weaving), go!

■ **Whatta Guy.** When he's not off adventuring, acclaimed marine biologist-artist Guy Harvey is usually in his amazing gallery-shop; buy a print, ask him to sign it, and converse on conservation.

the project, which Prince Edward unveiled during the 2003 quincentennial celebrations.

A few steps away lie the scant remains of **Fort George,** constructed in 1790 to repel plundering pirates; it also functioned as a watch post during World War II to scan for German subs.

In front of the court building, in the center of town, names of influential Caymanians are inscribed on the **Wall of History,** which also commemorates the islands' quincentennial. Across the street is the Cayman Islands **Legislative Assembly Building,** next door to the **1919 Peace Memorial Building.** A block south is the horseshoe-shaped **General Post Office,** built in 1939 at the tail end of the art deco period. Let the kids pet the big blue iguana statues.

★ Fodor's Choice **Cayman Islands National Museum.** Built in 1833, ☾ the historically significant clapboard home of the national museum has had several different incarnations over the years, serving as courthouse, jail, post office, and dance hall. It features an ongoing archaeological excavation of the Old Gaol and excellent 3-D bathymetric displays, murals, dioramas, and videos that illustrate local geology, flora and fauna, and island history. The first floor focuses on natural

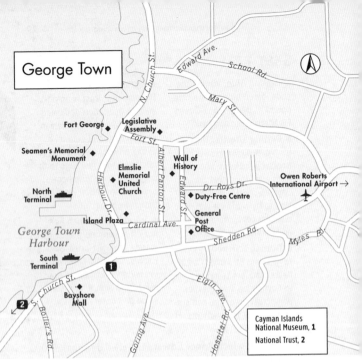

history, including a microcosm of Cayman ecosystems, from beaches to dry woodlands and swamps, and offers such interactive elements as a simulated sub. Upstairs, the cultural exhibit features renovated murals, video history reenactments, and 3-D back panels in display cases holding thousands of artifacts ranging from a 14-foot catboat with animatronic captain to old coins and rare documents painting a portrait of daily life and past industries such as shipbuilding and turtling, stressing Caymanians' resilience when they had little contact with the outside world. There are also temporary exhibits focusing on aspects of Caymanian culture, a local art collection, and interactive displays for kids. ⊠ *Harbour Dr., George Town, Grand Cayman* ☏ *345/949–8368* ⊕ *www.museum.ky* ☜ *$8* ⊗ *Weekdays 9–5, Sat. 9–1.*

NEED A BREAK? **Full of Beans Cafe.** On the surprisingly large, eclectic, Asian-tinged menu using ultrafresh ingredients, standouts include homemade carrot cake, mango smoothies, a curried chicken-cucumber wrap, cranberry-Brie-pecan salad, and a rosemary-roasted portobello panini. Owner Cindy Butler fash-

Maritime Heritage Trail

The National Trust for the Cayman Islands, National Museum, National Archive, Sister Islands Nature Tourism Project, and Department of the Environment have collaborated on a series of land-based sightseeing trails on Grand Cayman and the Sister Islands that commemorate the country's maritime heritage. Shoreside signs around the islands denote points of access and explain their historic or natural significance, from shipwreck sites to shorebird-sighting spots, chandlers' warehouses to lighthouses.

Brochures and posters are available at the National Trust and tourism offices on each island, as well as at many hotels. They provide additional information on turtling, ship-building, salvaging, fishing, and other sea-based economies. The project provides visitors with interactive edu-tainment as they explore the islands.

---

ions a feast for weary eyes as well, with rotating artworks and stylish mosaic mirrors contrasting with faux-brick walls and vintage hardwood tables. ⊠ *Pasadora Place, Smith Rd., George Town, Grand Cayman* ☎ *345/943–2326, 345/814–0157.*

National Trust. For a wonderful map of the historic and natural attractions, go to the office of the National Trust. The Trust sells books and guides to Cayman. The fabulous website has more than 50 information sheets on cultural and natural topics from iguanas to schoolhouses. Take advantage of the regularly scheduled activities, from boat tours through the forests of the Central Mangrove Wetlands to cooking classes with local chefs to morning walking tours of historic George Town. Stop here first before you tour the island. Be forewarned: though the office is walkable from George Town, it's an often-hot 20-minute hike from downtown. ⊠ *Dart Park, 558 S. Church St., George Town, Grand Cayman* ☎ *345/749–1121* ⊕ *nationaltrust. org.ky* ☉ *Weekdays 9–5:30.*

SEVEN MILE BEACH

★ **Camana Bay Observation Tower.** This 75-foot structure pro-
☾ vides striking 360-degree panoramas of otherwise flat Grand Cayman, sweeping from George Town and Seven Mile Beach to the North Sound. The double-helix staircase is impressive in its own right. Running alongside the steps (though an elevator is also available), a floor-to-ceiling

A traditional Cayman cottage at Boatswain's Beach

mosaic replicates the look and feel of a dive from seabed to surface. Constructed of countless tiles in 114 different colors, it's one of the world's largest marine-themed mosaic installations. Benches and lookout points encourage you to take your time and take in the views as you ascend. Afterward you can enjoy 500-acre Camana Bay's gardens, waterfront boardwalk, and pedestrian paths lined with shops and restaurants, or frequent live entertainment. ✉ *Extending between Seven Mile Beach and North Sound, 2 miles (3 km) north of George Town, Camana Bay, Grand Cayman* ☎ *345/640–3500* ⊕ *www.camanabay.com* ✍ *Free* ☉ *Sunrise–10 pm.*

★ **National Gallery.** A worthy nonprofit organization, the museum was established in 1996 to display and promote the range of Caymanian artists and craftspeople, both established and grassroots. The gallery coordinates a wealth of first-rate outreach programs for everyone from infants to inmates. It usually mounts six major exhibitions a year, including three large-scale retrospectives or thematic shows and multimedia installations. Director Natalie Coleman also brings in international shows that somehow relate to the island, often inviting local artists for stimulating dialogue. The gallery hosts public slide shows, a lunchtime lecture series running in conjunction with current exhibits, Art Flix (video presentations on art history, introduced with a short lecture and followed by a discussion led by

CLOSE UP

Camana Bay

Dubbed a "new town" (in all senses of the term), ambitious in scope and philosophy, the mixed-use, master-planned Camana Bay stretches along 500 acres from Seven Mile Beach to the North Sound. It's a sustainable, traditionally, and colorfully Caribbean—yet technologically cutting-edge—design, and ecologically sensitive to boot. Specifically designed by more than 100 consultants from several leading local and global firms as a gathering center to live, work, and play, Camana Bay has been carefully developed in three phases (the final phase is expected to be completed by 2016 and will include hotels and a marina, alongside residential and office development).

The four residential-office-retail courtyards feature unique feels and color schemes unifying native flora with surrounding walls, walks, and mosaics.

Streets were aligned to mitigate heat and to capture breezes. Plants were carefully chosen to attract birds and butterflies, and the development has green space galore, including artificial islands and harbors, as well as water features like canals and fountains.

The pedestrianized main street, called the Paseo, is lined with mostly high-end shops that are open late, restaurants, and entertainment (including a weekly farmers' market and a movie theater complex). The Paseo culminates in the Crescent, a waterfront plaza with restaurants, more gardens, interactive fountains, an esplanade, amphitheater, and public venues for fireworks to festivals. There are also jogging/biking trails, pocket parks, open spaces, and a beach. Residents and visitors are encouraged to park their cars and stroll (enhancing the green lifestyle) or just hang out.

curators or artists), and a CineClub (movie night). The gallery has also developed an Artist Trail Map with the Department of Tourism and can facilitate studio tours. The gallery's large new quarters near Seven Mile Beach on Harquail Bypass opened in early 2012. ⊠ *Esterly Tibbetts Highway at Harquail Bypass, Seven Mile Beach, Grand Cayman* ☎ *345/945–8111* ⊕ *www.nationalgallery.org.ky* ☜ *Free* ⊘ *Weekdays 9–5, Sat. 11–2.*

WEST BAY

★ Fodor'sChoice **Cayman Turtle Farm.** Cayman's premier attrac-
♻ tion, the Turtle Farm, has been rebranded and transformed
into a marine theme park. The expanded complex now has
several souvenir shops and restaurants. Still, the turtles
remain a central attraction, and you can tour ponds in
the original research–breeding facility with thousands in
various stages of growth, some up to 600 pounds and
more than 70 years old. Turtles can be picked up from
the tanks, a real treat for children and adults as the little
creatures flap their fins and splash the water. Four areas—
three aquatic and one dry—cover 23 acres; different-color
bracelets determine access (the steep full-pass admission
includes snorkeling gear). The park helps promote conservation, encouraging interaction (a tidal pool houses
invertebrates such as starfish and crabs) and observation.
Animal Program events include Keeper Talks, where you
might feed birds or iguanas, and biologists speaking about
conservation and their importance to the ecosystem. The
freshwater **Breaker's Lagoon,** replete with cascades plunging over moss-carpeted rocks evoking Cayman Brac, is the
islands' largest pool. The saltwater **Boatswain's Lagoon,**
replicating all the Cayman Islands and the Trench, teems
with 14,000 denizens of the deep milling about a cannily
designed synthetic reef. You can snorkel here (lessons and
guided tours are available). Both lagoons have underwater
4-inch-thick acrylic panels that look directly into **Predator Reef,** home to six brown sharks, four nurse sharks,
and other predatory fish such as tarpons, eels, and jacks.
These predators can also be viewed from terra (or terror,
as one guide jokes) firma. Make sure you check out feeding times! The free-flight **Aviary,** designed by consultants
from Disney's Animal Kingdom, is a riot of color and noise
as feathered friends represent the entire Caribbean basin,
doubling as a rehabilitation center for Cayman Wildlife and
Rescue. A winding interpretive **nature trail** culminates in the
Blue Hole, a collapsed cave once filled with water. Audio
tours are available with different focuses, from butterflies to
bush medicine. The last stop is the living museum, **Cayman
Street,** complete with facades duplicating different types of
vernacular architecture; an herb and fruit garden; porch-
side artisans, musicians, and storytellers; model catboats;
live cooking on an old-fashioned caboose (outside kitchen)
oven; and interactive craft demonstrations from painting mahogany to thatch weaving. ✉ *825 Northwest Point*

Rd., Box 812, West Bay, Grand Cayman ☎ *345/949–3894*
⊕ *www.turtle.ky* ✉ *Comprehensive ticket $45; Turtle Farm
only, $30* ⊙ *Daily 8:30–4:30.*

Cayman Motor Museum. This unexpected collection documents the magnificent obsession of one man, Norwegian
magnate Andreas Ugland. More than 80 vehicles, preening
like supermodels, gleam in ranks. Holy $%&, it's one of
the three original Batmobiles from the TV series. There's
the world's first produced auto, an 1886 Benz! Tiers of
classic Ferraris, Jags, Corvettes, BMWs, and more date
back nearly a century, including such unique collectibles as
Elton John's Bentley, the 1930 Phantom driven in the film
Yellow Rolls Royce, and Queen Elizabeth II's first limo.
You can go hog wild over Harleys and other bad-ass bikes.
And well, just because, coffee grinders. This isn't actually
mere kitchen kitsch: Peugeot started producing mills and
grinders in the mid-19th century. An avid sailor, Mr. Ugland
wants to start a boat museum as well. That might be fun
but it likely won't capture the unlikely charm of this Cayman oddity. ✉ *864 North West Point Rd., West Bay, Grand
Cayman* ☎ *345/947–7741* ⊕ *www.caymanmotormuseum.
com* ✉ *$15* ⊙ *Mon.–Sat. 9–5.*

Ⓒ **Dolphin Discovery.** If you ever dreamed of frolicking with
Flipper, here's your (photo) opportunity, as the organizers
of this global business promise a "touching experience."
There are three main options essentially depending on time
spent splashing in the enormous pool with the dolphins
and stingrays. They range in price from $99 to $169 (kids
receive a discount but must swim with an adult). The pre-
mium is the Royal Swim, which includes a dorsal tow and
foot push, showcasing the amazing strength, speed, and
agility of these majestic marine mammals. Other options
offer a handshake, kiss, even a belly ride. All participants
receive free entrance to the Turtle Farm across the street,
taking some of the sting out of the high prices. ✉ *Northwest
Point Rd., West Bay, Grand Cayman* ☎ *345/769–7946,
866/393–5158 toll-free from U.S., 345/949–7946* ⊕ *www.
dolphindiscovery.com/grand-cayman.*

Hell. Quite literally the tourist trap from Hell, especially
when overrun by cruise-ship passengers, this attraction does
offer free admission, fun photo ops, and sublime surrealism.
Its name refers to the quarter-acre of menacing shards of
charred brimstone thrusting up like vengeful spirits (actually blackened and "sculpted" by acid-secreting algae and

fungi over millennia). The eerie lunarscape is now cordoned off, but you can prove you had a helluva time by taking a photo from the observation deck. The attractions are the small post office and a gift shop where you can get cards and letters postmarked from Hell, not to mention wonderfully silly postcards titled "When Hell Freezes Over" (depicting bathing beauties on the beach), "The Devil Made Me Do It" bumper stickers, Scotch bonnet–based Hell sauce, and "The coolest shop in Hell" T-shirts. Ivan Farrington, the owner of the Devil's Hang-Out store, cavorts in a devil's costume (horn, cape, and tails), regaling you with demonically bad jokes. ⊠ *Hell Rd., West Bay, Grand Cayman* ☎ *345/949–3358* ☜ *Free* ☉ *Daily 9–6.*

EAST END AND NORTH SIDE

The Tourism Attraction Board and 14 leading eastern-district businesses (from Ocean Frontiers dive shop to Kaibo Beach Bar) and attractions developed the **"Discover the East" Adventure Card** to encourage visitors (and locals) to experience the beauty, culture, and heritage of Grand Cayman's eastern districts. The $16 card provides free admission to the Queen Elizabeth II Botanic Park and to Pedro St. James (normally $10 each), as well as gifts and discounts throughout Bodden Town, Cayman Kai, North Side, and the East End, from free desserts with dinner to $20 off diving.

ⓒ **Blowholes.** When the easterly trade winds blow hard, crashing waves force water into caverns and send impressive geysers shooting up as much as 20 feet through the ironshore. The blowholes were partially filled during Hurricane Ivan in 2004, so the water must be rough to recapture their former elemental drama. ⊠ *Frank Sound Rd., roughly 10 miles (16 km) east of Bodden Town, near East End, Grand Cayman.*

Bodden Town. In the island's original south-shore capital you can find an old cemetery on the shore side of the road. Graves with A-frame structures are said to contain the remains of pirates. There are also the ruins of a fort and a wall erected by slaves in the 19th century. The National Trust runs tours of the restored 1840s Mission House. A curio shop serves as the entrance to what's called the Pirate's Caves ($8), partially underground natural formations that are more hokey (decked out with fake treasure chests and mannequins in pirate garb, with an outdoor petting zoo) than spooky. ⊠ *Grand Cayman.*

DID YOU KNOW?

The blowholes on Grand Cayman's south shore were formed when waves pushed seawater through the ceilings of caves under the ironshore, sending the spray up into the air.

Cayman House and Garden

The few original Caymanian cottages that exist represent a unique architectural vernacular cannily adapted to the climate and available resources. Foundation posts and floors were constructed from durable, termite-resistant ironwood. Wattle-and-daub walls were fashioned from basket-woven sticks plastered on both sides with lime daub (extracted coral burned with various woods). The earliest roofs were thatched with woven palm fronds (later shingled or topped with corrugated zinc); their peaks helped cool houses, as hot air rises. The kitchen was separate, usu-ally just a "caboose" stove for cooking.

The other unusual custom, "backing sand," originated as a Christmas tradition, then be-came a year-round decorative statement. Women and children would tote woven-thatch baskets by moonlight to the beach, bringing "back" glittering white sand to cover their front yards. They'd rake intricate patterns and adorn the sand with sinu-ous conch-shell paths. The yard was also swept Saturdays so it would look well tended after Sunday services. A side benefit was that it helped reduce in-sect infestation.

Cayman Islands Brewery. This brewery occupies the former Stingray facility; free tours are available on the hour (you must call first). Caybrew is a full-bodied yet light lager with a crisp hop finish. The guide will explain the iconic imagery of the bottle and label, and the nearly three-week process: seven days' fermentation, 10 days' lagering (storage), and one day in the bottling tank. The brewery's eco-friendly features are also championed: local farmers receive the spent grains used to produce the beer to serve as cattle feed at no charge, while waste liquid is channeled into one of the Caribbean's most advanced water-treatment systems. Then enjoy your complimentary tasting with the knowledge that you're helping the local environment and economy. ✉ *366 Shamrock Rd., Red Bay, Grand Cayman* ☏ *345/947–6699* ⊕ *www.cib.ky* ✇ *Free* ☉ *Weekdays 9–5, Sat. 10–5.*

Mission House. The Mission House is a classic gabled two-story Caymanian home on wooden posts, with wattle-and-daub accents, dating to the 1840s and restored by the National Trust. The building earned its sobriquet thanks to early missionaries, teachers, and families who lived here while helping establish the Presbyterian ministry and school in Bodden Town. Shards of 19th-century glass and

Pedro St. James Castle

ceramics found on-site and period furnishings are on display. The posted opening hours are irregular, especially during the off-season. ⊠ *63 Gun Square Rd., Bodden Town, Grand Cayman* ☎ *345/749–1132* ⊕ *www.nationaltrust.org. ky* ⊠ *CI$5* ⊙ *Wed.–Sat. 9–5:30.*

★ **Fodor's Choice Pedro St. James Castle.** Built in 1780, the great house is Cayman's oldest stone structure and the only remaining late-18th-century residence on the island. In its capacity as courthouse and jail, it was the birthplace of Caymanian democracy, where in December 1831 the first elected parliament was organized and in 1835 the Slavery Abolition Act signed. The structure still has original or historically accurate replicas of sweeping verandahs, mahogany floors, rough-hewn wide-beam ceilings, outside louvers, stone and oxblood- or mustard-color lime-wash-painted walls, brass fixtures, and Georgian furnishings (from tea caddies to canopy beds to commodes). Paying obsessive attention to detail, the curators even fill glasses with faux wine. The mini museum also includes a hodgepodge of displays from slave emancipation to old stamps. The buildings are surrounded by 8 acres of natural parks and woodlands. You can stroll through landscaping of native Caymanian flora and experience one of the most spectacular views on the island from atop the dramatic Great Pedro Bluff. First watch the impressive multimedia theater show, complete with smoking pots, misting rains, and two film screens where the story of Pedro's Castle is presented on the hour. The poignant Hurricane Ivan Memorial outside uses text, images, and symbols to represent important aspects of that horrific 2004 natural disaster. ⊠ *Pedro Castle Rd., Box 305, Savannah, Grand Cayman* ☎ *345/947–3329* ⊕ *www. pedrostjames.ky* ⊠ *$10* ☉ *Daily 9–5.*

Pirate's Caves. You enter the Pirate's Caves through a surprisingly good curio shop (the owner is noted for jewelry fashioned from doubloons). Outside, ceramic "skulls" embedded into banyan trees and mini gravestones enhance the supposed spookiness. Younger kids should adore the playground and mini zoo with freshwater Brazilian stingrays, turtles, parrots, macaws, iguanas, agoutis (a large rodent), mountain goats, and farm animals like chickens, the pig Percy, and the horse Spirit. The caves themselves are pure yo-ho-hokum, tricked up with more faux "skeletons," swords jutting from limestone formations, and other rusted artifacts of dubious authenticity (such as fake treasure chests), lanterns, and conch shells, as well as an authentic fossilized bone or two. Beware the steep descent (with only rope handrails). Very informative sheets on history and the native plants are provided, as well as good interpretive signage within the grounds. ⊠ *South Shore Rd., Bodden Town, Grand Cayman* ☎ *345/947–3122* ⊠ *$8* ☉ *Daily 9–6.*

★ Fodor's Choice **Queen Elizabeth II Botanic Park.** This 65-acre wilderness preserve showcases a wide range of indigenous and nonindigenous tropical vegetation, approximately 2,000 species in total. Splendid sections include numerous water features from limpid lily ponds to cascades; a Heritage Garden with a traditional cottage and "caboose" (outside kitchen) that includes crops that might have been planted on Cayman a century ago; and a Floral Colour Garden arranged by color, the walkway wandering through sections of pink, red, orange, yellow, white, blue, mauve, lavender, and purple. A 2-acre lake and adjacent wetlands includes three islets that provide a habitat and breeding ground for native birds just as showy as the floral displays: green herons, black-necked stilts, American coots, blue-winged teal, cattle egrets, and rare West Indian whistling ducks. The nearly mile-long Woodland Trail encompasses every Cayman ecosystem from wetland to cactus thicket, buttonwood swamp to lofty woodland with imposing mahogany trees. You'll encounter birds, lizards, turtles, agoutis, and more, but the park's star residents are the

Queen Elizabeth II Botanic Park

protected endemic blue iguanas, found only in Grand Cayman. The world's most endangered iguana, they're the focus of the National Trust's Blue Iguana Recovery Program, a captive breeding and reintroduction facility. This section of the park is usually closed to the general public, though released "blue dragons" hang out in the vicinity. The Trust conducts 90-minute behind-the-scenes safaris Monday–Saturday at 11 am for $30. ✉ *367 Botanic Rd., Grand Cayman* ☎ *345/947–9462* ⊕ *www.botanic-park.ky* 🔖 *$10* ⊙ *Apr.–Sept., daily 9–6:30; Oct.–Mar., daily 9–5:30; last admission 1 hr before closing.*

Wreck of the Ten Sails Park. This lonely, lovely park on Grand Cayman's windswept eastern tip commemorates the island's most (in)famous shipwreck. On February 8, 1794, the *Cordelia*, heading a convoy of 58 square-rigged merchant vessels en route from Jamaica to England, foundered on one of the treacherous East End reefs. Its warning cannon fire was tragically misconstrued as a call to band more closely together due to imminent pirate attack, and nine more ships ran aground. The local sailors, who knew those rough seas, demonstrated great bravery in rescuing all 400-odd seamen. Popular legend claims (romantically but inaccurately) that King George III granted the islands an eternal tax exemption. Queen Elizabeth II dedicated the park's plaque in 1994. Interpretive signs document the historic details. The ironically peaceful headland provides magnificent views of

Blue Dragons

Co-sponsored by the Botanic Park and the National Trust, the **Blue Iguana Recovery Program** (⊕ www.blueiguana.ky) is a model captive breeding plan for the remarkable reptiles that only two decades ago faced total extinction. The Grand Cayman blue iguana lived on the island for millennia until man arrived, its only natural predator the racer snake. Until recently they were the world's most critically endangered species, functionally extinct with only 25 remaining in the wild. BIRP has released more than 200 into the Salina Reserve, with an ultimate repopulation goal of 1,000 if they can breed successfully in the wild.

The National Trust conducts safaris six mornings a week, giving you a chance to see hatchlings in the cages, camouflaged toddlers, and breeding-age adults like Mad Max and Blue Blue. Most of the iguanas raised here are released at two years by the Wildlife Conservation Society with a microchip implant tag for radio tracking and color-coded beading ("their navel rings," jokes a guide) for unique identification. Tones fluctuate according to light-ing and season, brightening to azure during the April–May breeding period. Guides explain the gestation and incubation periods and the pairing of potential mates ("some are too dominant, and we don't want inbreeding like Appalachian hillbillies, leading to potential mutations or sterility").

If you can't make it to the park, look for the 15 larger-than-life, one-of-a-kind outdoor sculptures commissioned from local artists scattered around the island. You can download maps of the Blue Dragon Trail from the BIRP, National Trust, and Botanic Park sites. Many hotels also stock leaflets with maps and fun facts (the iguanas live up to 70 years, grow to 6 feet in length, and weigh 25 pounds). You can even purchase custom blue iguana products (helping fund research), such as Joel Friesch's limited-edition hand-painted bobbleheads (blues bob their heads rapidly as a territorial warning) packaged in a bright yellow hard cardboard box. You can also volunteer for a working vacation (or longer field-work study stint) online.

---

the reef (including more recent shipwrecks); bird-watching is superb from here half a mile south along the coast to the Lighthouse Park, perched on a craggy bluff. ⊠ *Gun Bay, East End, Grand Cayman* ☎ *345/949–0121 (National Trust)* ☜ *Free* ☾ *Daily.*

SHOPPING

On Grand Cayman the good news is that there's no sales tax *and* plenty of duty-free merchandise including jewelry, china, crystal, perfumes, and cameras. Savings on luxury goods, though rarely as great as good sales in big cities or at outlet malls in the United States, range between 10% and 25%. Notable exceptions are liquor, which is available minus that tariff only at specially designated shops, and haute couture (though the ritzier resort shops stock some designer labels). "Brand Cayman" is the local nickname for the glamorous shops along Cardinal Avenue, the local answer to New York's Madison Avenue and Beverly Hills's Rodeo Drive. Esteemed names include Waterford and Wedgwood, Cartier, and Cayman's own Bernard K. Passman.

Worthy local items include woven thatch mats and baskets, jewelry made from a marblelike stone called caymanite (from Cayman Brac's cliffs, a striated amalgam of several metals), and authentic sunken treasure often fashioned into jewelry, though the last is never cheap (request a certificate of authenticity if one isn't offered). You'll also find individual artists' ateliers and small, colorful craft shops whose owners often love discussing the old days and traditions. Bear in mind that most major attractions feature extensive and/or intriguing gift shops, whether Boatswain's Beach or the National Gallery.

Local palate pleasers include treats made by the Tortuga Rum Company (both the famed cakes and the actual distilled spirit, including a sublime 12-year-old rum), Cayman Honey, Cayman Taffy, and Cayman Sea Salt (from the eco-friendly "farm" of the same name). Seven Fathoms is the first working distillery actually in Cayman itself, its award-winning rums aged underwater (hence the name). Also seek out such gastronomic goodies as jams, sauces, and vinegars from Hawley Haven and Whistling Duck Farms on the eastern half of the island. Cigar lovers, take note: Some shops carry famed Cuban brands, but you must enjoy them on the island; bringing them back to the United States is illegal.

An almost unbroken line of strip malls runs from George Town through Seven Mile Beach, most of them presenting shopping and dining options galore. The ongoing Camana Bay mega-development already glitters with glam shops, including Island Companies' largest and grandest store offering the hautest name-brand jewelry, watches, and duty-free goods.

Words and Music

Local books and CDs make wonderful gifts and souvenirs. Recapture the flavor of your stay with *Miss Cleo's Cayman Kitchen*—subtitled "Treasured Recipes from the East End"—by Cleopatra Conolly, or *Cook' in Little Cayman*, by irrepressible Gladys Howard, a longtime resort owner who studied under James Beard and Julia Child. Plunge into *Diary of a Dirtbag Divemaster* by Little Cayman's Terry Thompson; it's a fact-inspired fiction recounting the escapades of six dive instructors working on a small Caribbean island. Another Little Cayman expat, Gay Morse, relates her own amusing behind-the-scenes anecdotes about teaching scuba and helping operate a small resort, *So You Want to Live on an Island?* H. George "Barefoot Man" Nowak's *Which Way to the Islands?* is another hilarious collection of only-in-the-Caribbean stories. Noted artist Nasaria Suckoo-Chollette pens poems and short stories based on local culture and folklore, including *Story Telling Rundown.* On a more serious note, celebrated photographer Courtney Platt documented the devastation wrought by Hurricane Ivan in the 330 striking images composing *Paradise Interrupted.*

Sway back home to soca, reggae, calypso, and Carib-country beats. Grand Cayman has several recording studios, including the state-of-the-art Hopscotch, whose Platinum label records both Lammie and MOJ. Garden Studios is owned by popular group Hi Tide. C and B Studio records exclusively for Sea and B—Earl la Pierre and Barefoot Man (the latter alone has 28 CDs and counting). Other worthwhile local recording artists include jazz masters Gary Ebanks and Intransit, hard rockers Ratskyn and Cloudburst, and sultry soulster Karen Edie.

GEORGE TOWN

SHOPPING CENTERS

Bayshore Mall. Optimally located downtown and one of the newest shopaholics' targets (you can't miss the cotton-candy colors), this mall contains a Kirk Freeport department-store branch (Tag Heuer to Herend porcelain, Mikimoto to Mont Blanc), swank Lalique and Lladró boutiques, La Parfumerie (which often offers makeovers and carries 450 beauty brands), and other usual luxury culprits. ⊠ *South Church St., George Town, Grand Cayman.*

Cayside Courtyard. This small courtyard shopping center is noted for its specialty jewelers and antiques dealers. ⊠ *Harbour Dr., George Town, Grand Cayman.*

Duty Free Plaza. This mall caters to more casual shoppers with the T-shirt Factory, Island Treasures, Havana Cigars, Blackbeard's Rumcake Bakery, and the Surf Shop. It also contains a kid-pleasing 12,000-gallon saltwater aquarium with sharks, eels, and stingrays. ⊠ *S. Church St., George Town, Grand Cayman.*

Island Plaza. Here you'll find 15 duty- and tax-free stores, including Swarovski Boutique, Island Jewellers, and Churchill's Cigars (with bars to de-stress in after binge shopping). ⊠ *Harbour Dr., George Town, Grand Cayman.*

★ **Kirk Freeport Plaza.** This downtown shopping center, home to the Kirk Freeport flagship department store, is ground zero for couture; it's also known for its boutiques selling fine watches and jewelry, china, crystal, leather, perfumes, and cosmetics, from Baccarat to Bulgari, Raymond Weil to Waterford and Wedgwood (the last two share their own autonomous boutique). Just keep walking—there's plenty of eye-catching, mind-boggling consumerism in all directions: Boucheron, Cartier (with its own mini boutique), Chanel, Clinique, Christian Dior, Clarins, Estée Lauder, Fendi, Guerlain, Lancôme, Yves Saint Laurent, Issey Miyake, Jean Paul Gaultier, Nina Ricci, Rolex, Roberto Coin, Rosenthal and Royal Doulton china, and more. ⊠ *Cardinal Ave., George Town, Grand Cayman.*

Landmark. Stores in the Landmark sell perfumes, treasure coins, and upscale beachwear; Breezes by the Bay restaurant is upstairs. ⊠ *Harbour Dr., George Town, Grand Cayman.*

ART GALLERIES

The art scene has exploded in the past decade, moving away from typical Caribbean motifs and "primitive" styles. Cayman's most famous artist had been the late Gladwyn Bush, fondly known as Miss Lassie, who died in 2003. She began painting her intuitive religious subjects after a "vision" when she was 62. She also decorated the facade, interior walls, furnishings, even appliances of her home (which at this writing was being converted into a museum and workshop space, at the junction of South Shore Road and Walkers Road). Bush was awarded the MBE (Most Excellent Order of the British Empire) in 1997, and her work is found in collections from Paris to Baltimore (whose American Visionary Art Museum owns several canvases). Bendel Hydes is another widely respected local (who moved to SoHo more than two decades ago yet still paints Caymanian-inspired works that capture the islands' elemental colors and dynamic movement). Leading expat artists include Joanne Sibley and Charles Long, both of whom create more figurative Cayman-theme art from luminous landscapes and shining portraits to pyrotechnically hued flora. Several artists' home-studios double as galleries, including the internationally known Al Ebanks, the controversial Luelan Bodden, and fanciful sculptor Horacio Esteban; the National Gallery has a list.

★ **Al Ebanks Studio Gallery.** This gallery shows the eponymous artist's versatile, always provocative work in various media. Since you're walking into his home as well as atelier, everything is on display. Clever movable panels maximize space "like Art Murphy beds." His work, while inspired by his home, could never be labeled traditional Caribbean art, exhibiting vigorous movement through abstract swirls of color and textural contrasts. Though nonrepresentational (save for his equally intriguing sculpture and ceramics), the focal subject from carnivals to iguanas is always subtly apparent. Ask him about the Native Sons art movement he co-founded. ⊠ *186B Shedden Rd., George Town, Grand Cayman* ☎ *345/927–5365, 345/949–0693.*

Artifacts. On the George Town waterfront, Artifacts sells Spanish pieces of eight, doubloons, and Halcyon Days enamels (hand-painted collectible pillboxes made in England), as well as antique maps and other collectibles. ⊠ *Cayside Courtyard, Harbour Dr., George Town, Grand Cayman* ☎ *345/949–2442* ⊕ *www.artifacts.com.ky.*

★ **Cathy Church's Underwater Photo Centre and Gallery.** Come see a collection of the acclaimed underwater shutterbug's spectacular color and limited-edition black-and-white underwater photos. Have Cathy autograph her latest coffee-table book and regale you with anecdotes of her globe-trotting adventures. The store also carries the latest marine camera equipment, and she'll schedule private underwater photography instruction as well on her own dive boat outfitted with special graphics-oriented computers to critique your work. She also does wedding photography, both above and underwater. ⊠ *S. Church St., George Town, Grand Cayman* ☎ *345/949–7415* ⊕ *www.cathychurch.com.*

Goin Native Sons

In 1995 three artists founded a collaborative called Native Sons, adding a fourth in 1996, and currently featuring 10 members. Their primary goal is to develop and promote Caymanian artists. Though they work in different mediums and styles, the group resists facile characterization and challenges conventions as to what characterizes "Caribbean" art. One of the core members, Al Ebanks, has achieved major international success, but he admits that the islands can be provincial: "Cayman doesn't always recognize talent unless you're signed to a gallery overseas."

Though the National Gallery and the Cayman National Cultural Foundation both vigorously support the movement and are committed to sponsoring local artists, some Native Sons members feel their agendas can be too safe, betraying the bureaucratic, corporate mentality they admit is often necessary to raise funds for nonprofit institutions. They have also felt subtle pressure to conform commercially and an inherent bias toward expat artists, whose work often depicts the literally sunnier side of Caymanian life, and resent what they perceived to be censorship of rawer, edgier works, including depictions of nudity in arch-conservative Cayman.

They have sought to push the boundaries for both institutions and private galleries. "Yes, art is art and shouldn't be grounded in national stereotypes, though my country inspires my work.... We just want balance," Ebanks says. "People look at more challenging work and ask 'Where's the boats?' We live that scene!"

Obviously this is a hot-button topic on a tiny island. Chris Christian, who originally achieved success through representational beach scenes but wanted to expand and experiment, uses the Cayman term "crabs in a bucket," describing how "artists in a small pool scratch and scramble over each other, succeeding by badmouthing others." Which is why the support structure and philosophy of Native Sons is so vital: They help each other negotiate "that constant balance between commercial success and artistic integrity."

Other members include cofounder Wray Banker, Randy Chollette, Nasaria Suckoo-Chollette, Gordon Solomon, Horacio Esteban, and Nickola McCoy. These native sons and daughters all passionately believe art isn't merely about pretty pictures and uncompromisingly believe in preserving Caymanian culture and freedom of expression.

2

★ **Guy Harvey's Gallery and Shoppe.** This is where world-renowned marine biologist, conservationist, and artist Guy Harvey showcases his aquatic-inspired action-packed art in nearly every conceivable medium, branded tableware, and sportswear (even logo soccer balls and Zippos). The soaring, two-story 4,000-square-foot space is almost more theme park than store, with monitors playing his sport-fishing videos, wood floors inlaid with tile duplicating rippling water, dangling catboats "attacked" by lifelike shark models, and life-size murals honoring such classics as Hemingway's *Old Man and the Sea.* Original paintings, sculpture, and drawings are expensive, but there's something (tile art, prints, lithographs, and photos) in most price ranges. ⊠ *49 S. Church St., George Town, Grand Cayman* ☏ *345/943–4891.*

Island Glassblowing Studio. The studio is run by the Zawistowski family of designers, who offer free demonstrations of their incredible skills as they almost acrobatically gather red-hot molten glass with long steel rods from a 2,000°F furnace, then roll it in vibrantly colored powders. Figurines (dolphins to elephants) to functional art (vases, platters) to fetching jewelry that captures the light all glow in cobalt to coral colors that rival nature's creativity. ⊠ *189 N. Church St., George Town, Grand Cayman* ☏ *345/946–1483* ⊕ *www. islandglassblowing.com.*

★ **Pure Art.** About 1½ miles (2½ km) south of George Town, Pure Art purveys wit, warmth, and whimsy right from the wildly colored front steps. Its warren of rooms resembles a garage sale run amok or a quirky grandmother's attic spilling over with unexpected finds, from foodstuffs to functional art. ⊠ *S. Church St., George Town, Grand Cayman* ☏ *345/949–9133* ⊕ *www.pureart.ky.*

Seven Fathoms Rum. Surprisingly, this growing company, established in 2008, is Cayman's first distillery. It has already garnered medals in prestigious international competitions for its artisanal small-batch rums. You can stop by for a tasting and self-guided tour, learning how they age the rum at 7 fathoms (42 feet) deep; supposedly the natural kinetic motion of the currents enables the rum to maximize contact with the oak, extracting its rich flavors and enhancing complexity. Based on the results, it's not just yo-ho-hokum. ⊠ *Waterfront, next to Hammerhead's, George Town, Grand Cayman* ☏ *345/925–5379, 345/926–8186* ⊕ *www.sevenfathomsrum.com.*

CAMERAS

★ **Camera Store.** The Camera Store has friendly and knowledgeable service, lots of duty-free digital cameras, accessories, and fast photo printing from self-service kiosks. ⌧ *Waterfront Centre, N. Church St., George Town, Grand Cayman* ☎ *345/949–4551.*

CIGARS

Given Cayman's proximity to Cuba, the banned but tempting panatelas and robustos are readily available at reasonable prices. They are still considered contraband in the United States until the embargo is lifted.

Churchill's Cigars. A cigar-store Indian points the way into this tobacco emporium, which sells the island's largest selection of authentic Cubanos (and other imports), including such names as Upmann, Romeo y Julieta, and Cohiba, almost fetishistically displayed in the dark, clubby surroundings. The enthusiastic staff will advise on drink pairings (bold older rum for a Montecristo No. 2, cognac for smaller Partagas Shorts, a single-malt scotch such as Glenmorangie for the Bolivar Belicoso Fino). There's a small airport branch as well. ⌧ *Island Plaza, Harbour Dr., George Town, Grand Cayman* ☎ *345/945–6141.*

CLOTHING

Arabus. The store carries primarily classy, classic ready-to-wear and knockoffs—though not at rip-off prices—for both sexes, casual to dressy, in flowing silk and cushy cashmere (for back home). ⌧ *West Wind Bldg., 8 Fort St., George Town, Grand Cayman* ☎ *345/949–4620.*

Blue Wave. Your adrenalin starts pumping as soon as you enter this so-called lifestyle wear-surf shop. All the accoutrements you need to play the Big Kahuna are handsomely displayed, from sandals to sunglasses, Billabong plaid shirts to Quicksilver shorts, surfboards to eco-sensitive Olukai footwear (talk to the clerks and you're ready to sign up for Greenpeace). ⌧ *10 Shedden Rd., George Town, Grand Cayman* ☎ *345/949–8166.*

FOODSTUFFS

There are seven modern, U.S.-style supermarkets (three of them have full-service pharmacies) on Grand Cayman. Ask for the one nearest you. Together, they will spoil you for choices of fresh fruit and vegetables, a wide selection of groceries, and a good selection of meats, poultry, and fish. All have deli counters serving hot meals, salads, sandwiches,

DID YOU KNOW?

At popular Stingray Sandbar in Grand Cayman, the rays come right up to the excursion boats and will eat out of your hand.

Not Just a Guy Thing

Guy Harvey is a man of many hats. He has a PhD in marine biology and is also a world-class angler, renowned aquatic wildlife artist, cinematographer, TV producer, presenter of a weekly TV program titled *Portraits from the Deep*, clothing designer, and dedicated environmentalist.

Anyone passing through the Fort Lauderdale airport has seen his dramatic three-story mural (a smaller mural adorns Grand Cayman's Owen Roberts Airport). His art features meticulous composition and vibrant color, capturing the adrenaline-pumping action. "I try to humanize them, give them character in my paintings," Harvey says, though hardly in dewy, Disney-esque fashion.

Growing up a 10th-generation Jamaican, he loved fishing and diving with his father from an early age. Obsessed by all things aquatic, Harvey first gained notice in art circles with a 1985 Kingston exhibit of pen-and-ink drawings based on Hemingway's *Old Man and the Sea*, a recurring theme: man and animal bonding and exhibiting grace under pressure in their struggle for survival.

He moved to Cayman during Jamaica's political upheaval in the late 1970s. He liked Cayman's similar culture and cuisine, British heritage, and proximity to both Jamaica and Florida. Harvey has used his high profile synergistically as an artist, angler, author, and documentarian to strike merchandising deals, creating apparel and houseware lines and restaurants, pouring many of the profits back into research. He still travels the world on interactive marine programs such as following tagged sharks from Belize to Brazil. These expeditions serve a dual purpose: "...saving the environment while inspiring me artistically."

Harvey has consistently supported "catch and release" ethics for game fish around the world. He works closely with many conservation organizations to help protect global fishery resources and was appointed a trustee of the International Game Fish Association in 1992; six years later he was voted the IGFA's first-ever "Lifetime Achievement Award" from the World Fishing Awards Committee. The nonprofit Guy Harvey Research Institute was established with the Oceanographic Center of Nova Southeastern University in 1999 to support effective conservation and restoration of fish resources and biodiversity. His views can be controversial. Commenting on dolphin swim programs, he has said: "Dolphin safety is one of the biggest lies foisted on the public."

cold cuts, and cheeses. Kirk Supermarket carries a wide range of international foods from the Caribbean, Europe, and Asia. The biggest difference you'll find between these and supermarkets on the mainland is the prices, which are about 25%–30% more than at home.

Foster's Food Fair-IGA. The island's biggest supermarket chain has five stores. The Airport Centre and Strand stores have full-service pharmacies. These stores are open from Monday through Saturday, 7 am to 11 pm. ✉ *Airport Centre, 63 Dorcy Dr., George Town, Grand Cayman* ☎ *345/949–5155* ⊕ *www.fosters-iga.com.*

✉ *Strand Shopping Center, 46A Canal Point Dr., off West Bay Rd., Seven Mile Beach, Grand Cayman* ☎ *345/945–4748* ⊕ *www.fosters-iga.com.*

✉ *Republix Plaza, 2373 Willie Farrington Dr., Seven Mile Beach, Grand Cayman* ☎ *345/949–3214* ⊕ *www.fosters-iga.com.*

✉ *Morritt's Shopping Centre, 2206 Queens Hwy., East End, Grand Cayman* ☎ *345/947–2826* ⊕ *www.fosters-iga.com.*

✉ *Countryside Shopping Center, 33 Hirst Rd., Savannah, Grand Cayman* ☎ *345/943–5155* ⊕ *www.fosters-iga.com.*

Kirk Supermarket and Pharmacy. This store is open Monday through Thursday from 7 am to 10 pm (until 11 pm Friday and Saturday) and is a particularly good source for traditional Caymanian fast food (oxtail, curried goat) and beverages at the juice bar. It also carries the largest selection of organic and special dietary products; the pharmacy stocks various homeopathic and herbal remedies. ✉ *Eastern Ave. near intersection with West Bay Rd., George Town, Grand Cayman* ☎ *345/949–7022.*

Tortuga Rum Company. This company bakes, then vacuum-seals, more than 10,000 of its world-famous rum cakes daily, adhering to the original "secret" century-old recipe. There are eight flavors, from banana to Blue Mountain coffee. The 12-year-old rum, blended from private stock though actually distilled in Guyana, is a connoisseur's delight for after-dinner sipping. You can buy a fresh rum cake at the airport on the way home at the same prices as at the factory store. ✉ *N. Sound Rd., Industrial Park, George Town, Grand Cayman* ☎ *345/949–7701* ⊕ *www. tortugarumcakes.com.*

CLOSE UP

Cayman Craft Market

This open-air marketplace run by the Tourism Attraction Board at Hog Sty Bay, smack in the middle of George Town, is artists' central, helping maintain old-time Caymanian skills. The vendors offer locally made leather, thatch, wood, and shell items. You'll also find dolls, hats, carved parrots, bead and seed jewelry, hand-painted thatch bags and bonnets, and hand-carved waurie (also spelled warri) boards—an ancient African game using seeds (or the more modern marbles).

Also available here are Sea Salt (and their luxury bath product);

Hawley Haven Farm products (Mrs. Laurie Hawley's delectable papaya, tamarind, and guava jams; spicy mango chutney; thyme vinegar; Cayman honey; and jerk sauce; as well as her painted folkloric characters on handmade sun-dried paper made with native flowers, leaves, and herbs); the Cayman Tropicals line of fragrant fruit-based hair and skin-care products; and North Side's Whistling Duck Farm specialties from soursop to sea grape jams and jellies. Every month highlights a different area of the Cayman Islands, from Cayman Brac to Bodden Town.

HANDICRAFTS AND SOUVENIRS

Pirate's Grotto. The Grotto is a cute store with duty-free liquor and cigars (including Cubans) as well as Cayman Islands souvenirs. ⊠ *Harbour Dr., basement level, below Landmark Shopping Center, George Town, Grand Cayman* ☎ *345/945–0244.*

JEWELRY

Although you can find black-coral products in Grand Cayman, they're controversial. Most of the coral sold here comes from Belize and Honduras; Cayman Islands marine law prohibits the removal of live coral from its own sea. Black coral grows at a glacial rate (3 inches per decade) and is an endangered species. Cayman, however, is famed for artisans working with the material; shops are recommended, but let your conscience dictate your purchases.

Balaclava Jewellers. This shop is the domain of Martina and Philip Cadien, who studied at Germany's prestigious Pforzheim Goldsmithing School. The showroom sparkles appropriately, with breathtaking handcrafted pieces—usually naturally colored diamonds set in platinum or 18K white, yellow, and rose gold—framed and lovingly, almost sensuously lit. Although there are simpler strands, this is a place where flash holds sway; the prices take your breath away, but the gems are flawless. ✉ *Governors Square, West Bay Rd., Seven Mile Beach, Grand Cayman* ☎ *345/945–5788* ⊕ *www.balaclava-jewellers.com.*

★ **Bernard Passman.** The black-coral creations of Bernard Passman have won the approval of the British royal family, who chose him to create a wedding present for Prince Charles and Princess Diana. His fabulous flatware and fanciful candelabras would stand out in the Addams Family manse. He even creates three-dimensional bas-relief scenes with cavorting dolphins, as well as mermaids with glittering gold gilt tails and golfers (each movement of the swing depicted by a dozen clubs in 18K gold). ✉ *Cardinal Ave., George Town, Grand Cayman* ☎ *345/949–0123.*

Island Time. Locals appreciate Island Time for its affordable line of watches, especially top-notch Swiss brands, from Movado to Maurice Lacroix. ✉ *Island Plaza, Cardinal Ave., George Town, Grand Cayman* ☎ *345/946–2333.*

Landmark Jewellers. Landmark proffers sparkling savings on unique gemstone jewelry by such respected designers as Mark Henry, as well as both loose and set rubies, emeralds, sapphires, and tanzanite. The watch selection astounds, with Switzerland alone clocking in with the likes of DOXA, Ball, Frédérique Constant, Oris, and Krieger. ✉ *Landmark Bldg., Harbour Dr. and Cardinal Ave., George Town, Grand Cayman* ☎ *345/945–0204.*

Magnum Jewelers. Befitting its name, Magnum Jewelers traffics in high-caliber pieces by the elite likes of Girard-Perregeaux and Harry Winston for a high-powered clientele. President Harry Chandi travels the world, his keen eye sourcing distinctive contemporary watches and bijoux (especially increasingly rare colored diamonds) for his equally glittery celebrity clientele, who also appreciate a bargain like the rest of us. Smaller spenders might appreciate the whimsical items such as pendants with hand-painted enamel sandals or crystal-encrusted purses. ✉ *Cardinal Plaza, Cardinal Ave., George Town, Grand Cayman* ☎ *345/946–9199* ⊕ *www.magnumjewelers.com.*

SEVEN MILE BEACH

SHOPPING CENTERS

Galleria Plaza. Nicknamed Blue Plaza for its azure hue, Galleria Plaza features several galleries and exotic home-accessories stores dealing in Oriental rugs or Indonesian furnishings, as well as more moderate souvenir shops hawking T-shirts and swimwear. ⊠ *West Bay Rd., Seven Mile Beach, Grand Cayman.*

The Strand Shopping Centre. This mall has branches of Tortuga Rum and Blackbeard's Liquor, and banks galore—the better to withdraw cash for shops with cachet like Polo Ralph Lauren and another Kirk Freeport (this branch particularly noteworthy for china and crystal, from Kosta Boda to Baccarat, as well as a second La Parfumerie). ⊠ *West Bay Rd., Seven Mile Beach, Grand Cayman.*

West Shore Shopping Centre. Dubbed Pink Plaza for reasons that become obvious upon approach, West Shore offers upscale boutiques and galleries (tenants range from Sotheby's International Realty to the Body Shop). ⊠ *West Bay Rd., Seven Mile Beach, Grand Cayman.*

ART GALLERIES

Ritz-Carlton Gallery. This gallery more than fulfilled one of the resort's conditions upon securing rights to build, which was to commission local arts and artisans to help decorate the public spaces. The corridor-cum-bridge spanning West Bay Road became a gallery where Chris Christian of Cayman Traditional Arts curates quarterly exhibitions of Cayman's finest (there are also themed shows devoted to photography and local kids' art). Each piece is for sale; CTA or the hotel will mediate in the negotiations between artist and buyer at a favorable commission. ⊠ *Ritz-Carlton Grand Cayman, West Bay Rd., Seven Mile Beach, Grand Cayman* ☎ *345/943–9000.*

BOOKS

Books & Books. The Miami independent bookseller operates this outlet in Grand Cayman. Regular events include author readings and "Floetry," when poets and performers express themselves at the open mike. ⊠ *45 Market St., Camana Bay, Grand Cayman* ☎ *345/640–2665.*

CIGARS

Havana Club Cigars. This store is the brainchild of Raglan Roper, who sailed from Florida to Cayman two decades ago, stopping in Cuba en route. Immediately hooked on the cigars, cuisine, and culture, he eventually opened a Cayman shop, then expanded (he also owns a Cuban restaurant). In addition to the famed brands, the attraction is the irresistible in-house *torcedor* (cigar roller), Jesus Lara Perez, who rotates demonstrations between the stores. Jesus started working at 14 in the Cuban cigar factory La Isolina in Santa Clara, eventually becoming chief cigar roller for other leading brands. ⊠ *508 West Bay Rd., Seven Mile Beach, Grand Cayman* ☎ *345/946–0523* ⊕ *www.havanaclub-cigars.com.*

FOODSTUFFS

☼ **Cayman Taffy.** Visitors to this genial candy store can satisfy their curiosity along with their taste buds by viewing the candy-making process in restored vintage equipment dating back to the early 20th century. Then sample saltwater taffy, caramel corn, and brittle in such exotic flavors as banana, coconut, mango, and Jamaican rum. The packaging, in coconut shells or boldly painted boxes, is almost as delectable. ⊠ *West Bay Rd., Seven Mile Beach, Grand Cayman* ☎ *345/943–2333* ⊕ *www.caymantaffy.net.*

JEWELRY

★ **Mitzi's Fine Jewelry.** Mitzi's is a treasure trove of salvaged 18th-century coins, silver, caymanite pieces, and black coral; the store also carries Italian porcelain and the Carrera y Carrera line of jewelry and sculptures. Self-taught, vivacious proprietor Mitzi Callan, who specializes in handmade pieces, is usually on hand to help. ⊠ *5 Bay Harbour Centre, West Bay Rd., Seven Mile Beach, Grand Cayman* ☎ *345/945–5014.*

★ **24K-Mon Jewelers.** This store sells works of art from many jewelers, including Wyland, Merry-Lee Rae, and Stephen Douglas, as well as designs courtesy of owner-goldsmith Gale Tibbetts and her friends, incorporating everything from Swarovski crystals to Spanish doubloons. Most pieces are inspired by the sea. The adjacent gallery is one of the few commercial outlets for local artists such as Miguel Powery. ⊠ *Buckingham Sq., Seven Mile Beach, Grand Cayman* ☎ *345/949–1499* ⊕ *www.24k-monjewelers.com.*

WEST BAY

HANDICRAFTS AND SOUVENIRS

Bed Buddies. The name of this store refers to husband-wife team Bonnie and Fernando Thompson, who fashion lovely jewelry, bags, and baubles from local materials, including whelk shells, coconut husks, tree resin, and distinctive seeds from cat's claw to Cayman red apple. ✉ *Hell Rd., West Bay, Grand Cayman* ☎ *345/917–1182* ⊕ *www.bed-buddiescreation.com.*

EAST END AND NORTH SIDE

ART GALLERIES

Bodden Town Art Shop. This shop purveys a grab bag of goodies, from homemade jellies to giclee prints, woven thatch handbags to hardwood and bronze sculpture. Top local and expat artists such as Randy Chollette and Avril Ward also exhibit here. ✉ *293 Bodden Town Rd., next to Pirate Caves, Bodden Town, Grand Cayman* ☎ *345/943–2827* ⊕ *www.btartshopcayman.com.*

★ **NasArt.** At the home-studio of Luelan Bodden, virtually every surface is painted with wild images and hues. One of Cayman's most exciting, controversial artists, he works in various media and is deliberately provocative with a sociopolitical slant. ✉ *Crewe Rd., Red Bay, Grand Cayman* ☎ *345/945–8278.*

FOODSTUFFS

★ **Hurley's Marketplace.** Hurley's is open Monday through Saturday from 7 am to 11 pm. ✉ *Grand Harbour Shopping Centre, 1053 Crewe Rd., Red Bay, Grand Cayman* ☎ *345/947–8488.*

Where to Eat in Grand Cayman

WORD OF MOUTH

"[W]e usually eat breakfast and lunch in our condo (oceanfront) and go out for dinner. Yes, it costs more than where we live in the U.S., but LOTS less than our trip to Europe this fall. It's relative."

—luvtotravl

By Jordan
Simon

NO INDIGENOUS PEOPLES OR GAGGLE of contentious colonial powers left much of an imprint on Grand Cayman cuisine, as was the case on many other islands. Until recently, the strongest culinary contributions to Cayman cuisine came from nearby Jamaica and, to a lesser extent, Cuba, though the worst of the British pub tradition lingered in pasties and heavy puddings. Fortunately, since the boom of the late 1970s, chefs from around the world (and the need to offer familiar ingredients and dishes to expats from as far afield as Beijing and Berlin) have seasoned a once-bland dining scene.

Today, despite its small size, comparative isolation, and British colonial trappings, Grand Cayman offers a smorgasbord of gastronomic goodies. With more than 100 eateries, something should suit and sate every palate and pocketbook (especially once you factor in fast-food franchises sweeping the islandscape like tumbleweed and stalls dispensing local specialties).

The term *melting pot* describes both the majority of menus and the multicultural population. It's not uncommon to find "American" dishes at an otherwise Caribbean restaurant, Indian fare at an Italian eatery (and vice versa). The sheer range of dining options from Middle Eastern to Mexican reflects the island's cosmopolitan, discriminating clientele. Imported ingredients reflect the United Nations, with chefs sourcing salmon from Norway, foie gras from Périgord, and lamb from New Zealand. Wine lists can be equally global in scope (often receiving awards from such oeno-bibles as *Wine Spectator*). Don't be surprised to find both Czech and Chilean staffers at a remote East End restaurant.

As one restaurateur quipped, "Cayman is the ultimate culture-shock absorber."

WHERE TO EAT

Grand Cayman dining is casual (even shorts are okay, at least for lunch, but *not* beachwear and tank tops). More upscale restaurants usually require slacks for dinner. Mosquitoes can be pesky when you dine outdoors, especially at sunset, so plan ahead or ask for repellent. Winter can be chilly enough to warrant a light sweater. You should make reservations at all but the most casual places, particularly during the high season.

Eat Like a Local

Caymanian cuisine evolved from whatever could be coaxed from the sea and eked out from the poor, porous soil. Farmers cultivated carb-rich crops that could remain fresh without refrigeration and furnish energy for the heavy labor typical of the islanders' hardscrabble existence. Hence pumpkins, coconuts, plantains, breadfruit, sweet potatoes, yams, and other "provisions" (root vegetables) became staple ingredients. Turtle (now farm-raised), the traditional specialty, can be served in soup or stew and as a steak. Conch, the meat of a large pink mollusk, is prepared in stews, chowders, and fritters and pan-fried (cracked). Fish—including snapper, tuna, wahoo, grouper, and marlin—is served baked, broiled, steamed, or "Cayman-style" (as an escoveitch with peppers, onions, and tomatoes).

"Rundown" is another classic: Fish (marinated with fresh lime juice, scallions, and fiery Scotch bonnet peppers) is steamed in coconut milk with breadfruit, pumpkin dumplings, and/ or cassava. Fish tea boils and bubbles similar ingredients for hours—even days—until it thickens into gravy. The traditional dessert, heavy cake, earned its name because excluding scarce flour and eggs made it incredibly dense: Coconut, sugar, spices, and butter are boiled, mixed with seasonal binders (cassava, yam, pumpkin), and baked.

Jamaican influence is seen in oxtail, goat stew, jerk chicken and pork, salt cod, and ackee (a red tree fruit resembling scrambled eggs in flavor and texture when cooked), and manish water (a lusty goat-head stew with garlic, thyme, scallion, green banana [i.e., plaintain], yam, potato, and other tubers).

Since nearly everything must be imported, prices average about 25% higher than those in a major U.S. city. Many restaurants add a 10%–15% service charge to the bill; be sure to check before leaving a tip (waiters usually receive only a small portion of any included gratuities, so leave something extra at your discretion for good service). Alcohol can send your meal tab skyrocketing. Buy liquor duty-free, either at the airport before your flight to the Cayman Islands or in one of the duty-free liquor stores that can be found in almost every strip mall on Grand Cayman, and enjoy a cocktail or nightcap from the comfort of your room or balcony. Cayman customs limits you to two bottles per person. Lunch often offers the same or similar dishes at a

BEST BETS

Fodor's Choice ★
Blue by Eric Ripert, Michael's
Genuine, Ortanique

BEST VIEWS
Cracked Conch, Grand
Old House, Luca, Morgan's
Harbour, Osetra Bay, Over the
Edge, Reef Grill at
Royal Palms

BEST FOR ROMANCE
Blue by Eric Ripert, Casa
Havana, Grand Old House,
Reef Grill at Royal Palms

BEST FOR FAMILIES
Al La Kebab, Chicken!
Chicken!, Cimboco, Eats Café

BEST FOR LOCAL CUISINE
Chicken! Chicken!, Cimboco,
Over the Edge

MOST POPULAR
Agua, Al La Kebab, Guy
Harvey's Island Grill, Eats Café,
Morgan's Harbour, Ragazzi,
Yoshi Sushi

considerable discount. Finally, when you are figuring your dining budget, remember that the Cayman dollar is worth 25% more than the U.S. dollar, and virtually all menus are priced in Cayman dollars.

RESTAURANT PRICES
Prices in the restaurant reviews are the average cost of a main course at dinner or, if dinner is not served, at lunch; taxes and service charges are generally included.

GEORGE TOWN AND ENVIRONS

You'll find a fair number of restaurants in George Town, including such standbys as Guy Harvey's and Casanova, not to mention the splurge-worthy Grand Old House.

$$$$ ✕ **The Brasserie.** *Eclectic.* Actuaries, bankers, and CEOs frequent this contemporary throwback to a colonial country club for lunch and "attitude adjustment" happy hours for cocktails and complimentary canapés. Inviting fusion cuisine, emphasizing local ingredients whenever possible (the restaurant even has its own boat), includes terrific bar tapas like the "Mini Argentinian" (skirt steak, house-made chorizo, chimichurri sauce), or melted Brie with white truffle–and–mango marmalade. Several evenings, you can get a five- or eight-course market-driven "Random Acts of Cooking" blind tasting. Dishes deftly balance flavors and textures without sensory overload: this is serious food with a sense of playfulness. Save room for desserts, from an arti-

Ortanique

sanal cheese plate to an ice-cream-and-sorbet tasting menu to elaborate architectural confections. Lunch is more reasonably priced but equally creative; the adjacent Market excels at takeout, and the wine list is well considered. ⑤ *Average main: $31* ✉ *171 Elgin Ave., Cricket Sq., George Town, Grand Cayman* ☎ *345/945–1815* ⊕ *www.brasseriecayman. com* ⌥ *Reservations essential* ⊘ *Closed weekends.*

$$ ✕ **Breezes by the Bay.** *Caribbean.* There isn't a bad seat in the house at this nonstop feel-good fiesta festooned with tiny paper lanterns, Christmas lights, ship murals, model boats, and Mardi Gras beads (you're "lei'd" upon entering). Wrap-around balconies take in a dazzling panorama from South Sound to Seven Mile Beach. It's a joyous nonstop happy hour all day every day, especially at Countdown to Sunset. Signs promise "the good kind of hurricanes," referring to the 23-ounce signature "category 15" cocktails with fresh garnishes; rum aficionados will find 48 varieties (flights available). Equally fresh food at bargain prices, including home-made baked goods and ice creams, isn't an afterthought. Chunky, velvety conch chowder served in a bread bowl or near-definitive conch fritters are meals in themselves. Hefty sandwiches are slathered with yummy jerk mayo or garlicky aioli. Signature standouts include meltingly moist whole fish escoveitch, curry chicken, popcorn shrimp, jerk-glazed pork chops, and any pie from the new pizza station. ⑤ *Average main: $19* ✉ *Harbor Dr., George Town, Grand Cayman* ☎ *345/943–8439* ⊕ *www.breezesbythebay.com.*

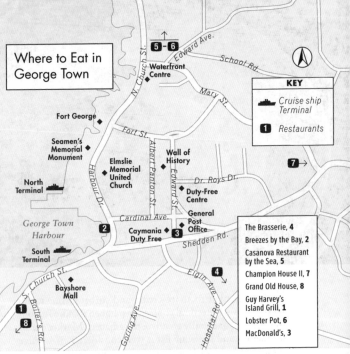

Where to Eat in George Town

KEY

🚢 Cruise ship Terminal

1 Restaurants

The Brasserie, **4**

Breezes by the Bay, **2**

Casanova Restaurant by the Sea, **5**

Champion House II, **7**

Grand Old House, **8**

Guy Harvey's Island Grill, **1**

Lobster Pot, **6**

MacDonald's, **3**

FREELOADING UP. Competition is fierce between Grand Cayman's many bars and restaurants. In addition to entertainment (from fish feeding to fire eating), even upscale joints host happy hours offering free hors d'oeuvres and/or drinks.

$$$$ ✕ **Casanova Restaurant by the Sea.** *Italian.* Owner Tony Crescente and younger brother–maitre d' Carlo offer a genuinely simpatico dining experience, practically exhorting you to *mangia,* and sending you off with a chorus of ciaos (photos of happy diners cover one wall). There's a bit of decorative *formaggio*: murals of Calabria, grape clusters, and chubby cherubs cavorting; paintings of the Amalfi Coast; "una finestra sul mare" ("window to the sea") stenciled redundantly over arches opening onto the harbor. But the kitsch doesn't extend to the kitchen, with such sterling Italian favorites as salmon marinated in citrus, olive oil, and basil; lovely lemony veal piccata; pappardelle *del brigante* (with rosemary-scented lamb ragout); or seafood grill in parsley-garlic-lemon sauce. Enjoy grappa at the marble bar of Il Bacio lounge, which is lined with wooden wine racks (the impressive selection isn't overly Italian-centric). The patio juts over the harbor; the moonlight

(abetted by a soundtrack of Bocelli to Bennett) would transform any amorous coward into a Casanova. ⑤ *Average main: $31* ⊠ *65 N. Church St., George Town, Grand Cayman* ☏ *345/949–7633* ⊕ *www.casanova.ky* ⚓ *Reservations essential.*

WORD OF MOUTH. "[Grand Cayman] is not a cheap place, but it is one of our favorite islands to eat on. When we were there, we grabbed a free *What's Hot* magazine. It tells you what's going on when you're on the island—and every once in awhile you might find a restaurant that has a deal. We absolutely love Casanova's. The Reef Grill also has a good menu and food.—Knowing.

$$ ✕ **Champion House II.** *Caribbean.* Ads trumpet that this restaurant is "where the islanders dine." Indeed they have since the Robinson family started selling takeout from its kitchen in 1965. This favorite overlooks a garden with a cheery tropic motif. The West Indies breakfast and themed lunch buffets are legendary spreads. Local food (curried goat, oxtail with broad beans, turtle soup, and heavy cake) is authentic, hearty, and cheap. Pricier global dishes range from fine Indian vegetarian options like samosas and *masala dal* (lentils simmered with green chilies) to Eisenhower-era standards like bacon-wrapped filet mignon in red wine sauce and scallops braised with sweet peppers in brandy. ⑤ *Average main: $20* ⊠ *43 Eastern Ave., George Town, Grand Cayman* ☏ *345/949–7882* ⊕ *www.championhouse.ky.*

$$$$ ✕ **Grand Old House.** *European.* Built in 1908 as the Petra Plantation House and transformed into the island's first upscale establishment decades ago, this grande dame is that rare restaurant that genuinely transports diners to a gracious era of bygone grandeur sans pretension. The interior rooms, awash in crystal and mahogany, recall its plantation-house origins. Classical and jazz pianists enhance the period ambience, but outside, hundreds of sparkling lights adorn the gazebos to compete with the starry sky. Rumors of a charming blond ghost trailing white chiffon complete the picture: this is a place to propose or let someone down easily. You'll find such expertly executed classics as butter-poached lobster with saffron risotto and fennel-parsnip purée or beef tenderloin with a choice of five sauces, but the increasingly innovative menu has adopted Asian and even Southwestern influences. Pistachio-and-herb-crusted chicken is spiced by apple mole, and grilled jumbo shrimp and bacon-wrapped smoked wahoo swim in ginger-plum sauce with roasted pumpkin and asparagus. The subtle yet

complex flavor interactions, stellar service, and encyclopedic if stratospherically priced wine list ensure legendary landmark status. ⑤ *Average main: $51* ✉ *648 S. Church St., George Town, Grand Cayman* ☎ *345/949–9333* ⊕ *www.grandoldhouse.com* ⚓ *Reservations essential* ⊗ *Closed Sept. No lunch weekends.*

$$$$ ✕ **Guy Harvey's Island Grill.** *Seafood.* This stylish, sporty, upstairs bistro celebrates the sea, from decor to cuisine. You half expect to find Hemingway regaling fellow barflies in the clubby interior with mahogany furnishings, ship's lanterns, porthole windows, whirring ceiling fans, fishing rods, and Harvey's action-packed marine art. The cool blues echo the sea and sky on display from the inviting balcony. Seafood is carefully chosen to exclude overexploited and threatened species. Seasonally changing dishes are peppered with Caribbean influences but puréed through the French chef's formal training. Hence, silken lobster bisque is served with puff pastry, scallops Rockefeller with spinach and béarnaise sauce, and the signature crab cakes with roasted-red-pepper aioli. You can select your fish baked, pan-sautéed, or grilled with any of eight sauces. Carnivores needn't despair, with rack of lamb in balsamic glaze or an intensely flavored filet mignon Roquefort (frites optional). Many specialties are cheaper at lunch. Nightly specials for CI$9.99 and the four-course CI$30 dinner reel in savvy locals. ⑤ *Average main: $35* ✉ *Aquaworld Duty-Free Mall, 55 S. Church St., George Town, Grand Cayman* ☎ *345/946–9000* ⊕ *www.guyharveysgrill.com.*

$$$$ ✕ **Lobster Pot.** *Seafood.* The nondescript building belies the lovely marine-motif decor and luscious seafood at the intimate, second-story restaurant overlooking the harbor. No surprise that fish seem to jump from the plate (or to it, as fishermen cruise up to the dock downstairs). Enjoy lobster prepared a half-dozen ways along with reasonably priced wine, which you can sample by the glass (particularly fine Austrian selections) in the cozy bar. The two musts are the Cayman Trio (lobster tail, grilled mahimahi, and garlic shrimp), and the Pot (lobster, giant prawns, and crab), but the kitchen can happily provide reduced-oil and -fat alternatives to most dishes. The balcony offers a breathtaking view of the sunset tarpon feeding. Lobster is market price and can be as much as $60; other entrées are less expensive. ⑤ *Average main: $47* ✉ *245 N. Church St., George Town, Grand Cayman* ☎ *345/949–2736* ⊕ *www.lobsterpot.ky* ⊗ *No lunch weekends.*

Farm Fresh

A joint initiative of the Cayman Islands Agricultural Society, the Ministry of Agriculture, the Department of Agriculture, and local vendors-purveyors, the **Market at the Grounds** is a jambalaya of sights, sounds, and smells held every Saturday from 7 AM at the Stacy Watler Agricultural Pavilion in Lower Valley (East End). Local growers, fishers, home gardeners and chefs (dispensing scrumptious, cheap cuisine), and artisans display their wares in a tranquil green setting. To preserve Caymanian flavor, everything must be 100% locally grown. Participating craftspeople and artists, from couturiers to musicians, must use local designs and materials whenever possible. The market fosters a renewed spirit of community, providing literal feedback into the production process, while the interaction with visitors promotes understanding of island culture.

3

$ ✕**MacDonald's.** *Caribbean.* One of the locals' favorite burger joints—not a fast-food outlet—MacDonald's does a brisk lunch business in stick-to-your ribs basics like rotisserie chicken and fish escoveitch. Yellows and pinks predominate, with appetizing posters of food, but decor is an afterthought to the politicos, housewives in curlers, and cops flirting shyly with the waitresses. ⑤ *Average main: $11* ⊠ *99 Shedden Rd., George Town, Grand Cayman* ☏ *345/949–4640* ⌀ *Reservations not accepted.*

SEVEN MILE BEACH

The lion's share of Grand Cayman restaurants is to be found along Seven Mile Beach, where most of the island's resorts are also located. Some are in the strip malls on the east side of West Bay Road, but many are in the resorts themselves.

$$$$ ✕**Agua.** *Italian.* This quietly hip, happening hot spot plays
★ up an aquatic theme, from black-and-white photos of bridges and waterfalls to indigo glass fixtures and cobalt-and-white walls subtly recalling foamy waves. The team of young, international chefs likewise emphasize seafood, preparing typical regional dishes from around the globe with a Caymanian slant. Thai ceviche with kaffir lime and coconut milk and tuna *tiradito* (similar to carpaccio) with avocado tamarind sauce burst with flavor. Superlative pastas include buffalo mozzarella tortelli in basil butter and lobster-shiitake ravioli with potato mascarpone sauce. Presentation is painterly throughout, and even side dishes

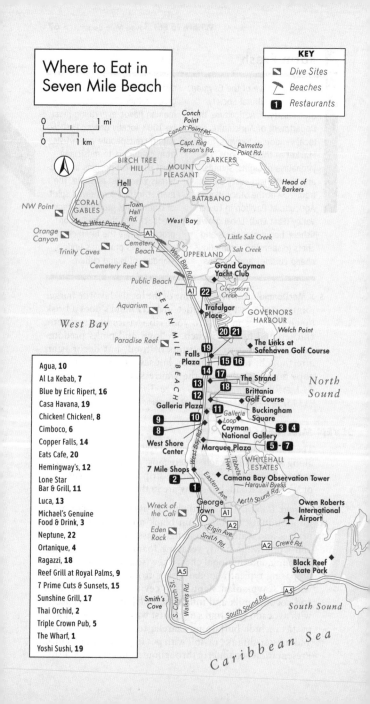

Where to Eat in Seven Mile Beach

KEY

- Dive Sites
- Beaches
- 1 Restaurants

0 ——— 1 mi
0 ——— 1 km

Agua, **10**

Al La Kebab, **7**

Blue by Eric Ripert, **16**

Casa Havana, **19**

Chicken! Chicken!, **8**

Cimboco, **6**

Copper Falls, **14**

Eats Cafe, **20**

Hemingway's, **12**

Lone Star Bar & Grill, **11**

Luca, **13**

Michael's Genuine Food & Drink, **3**

Neptune, **22**

Ortanique, **4**

Ragazzi, **18**

Reef Grill at Royal Palms, **9**

7 Prime Cuts & Sunsets, **15**

Sunshine Grill, **17**

Thai Orchid, **2**

Triple Crown Pub, **5**

The Wharf, **1**

Yoshi Sushi, **19**

such as potato croquettes masterfully counterpoint taste and texture. Don't miss the authentic gelatos to cap your meal. The admirable wine list brings in unusual offerings from lesser-known regions that often represent good value, with 20 offered by the glass. Happy-hour free tapas and the CI$15.95 three-course menu, as well as late-night appetizer discounts, are steals. ⑤ *Average main: $46* ⊠ *Galleria Plaza, Seven Mile Beach, Grand Cayman* ☎ *345/949–2482* ⊕ *www.agua.ky.*

$ ✕ **Al La Kebab.** *Middle Eastern.* Alan and Laura Silverman (he's Canadian, she's German) loved *shawarma* growing up and craved it after moving to Cayman. Their eatery works miracles out of two makeshift lean-tos splashed in vibrant colors and wall-to-wall stainless-steel appliances. They started by serving late-night kebabs and gyros. They remain open until 4 am weeknights and 2 am weekends "to keep the roads safe," but do a brisk lunch trade as construction workers line up with government ministers. Alan calls it a building-block menu, where you can modify the bread and sauce—a dozen varieties, including several curries, peanut satay, mango *raita* (yogurt, tomatoes, chutney), tahini, garlic cream, even gravy as Mom used to make. The menu romps from Malaysia through the Mediterranean to Mexico: spicy chicken tikka, Thai chicken-lemongrass soup, and tzatziki share the stage with unusual salads (try the fabulous Lebanese *fattoush*—toasted bread, mint, and parsley) and creative sides (addictive jalapeño-cheddar salsa for fries). There's also a George Town outpost. ⑤ *Average main: $9* ⊠ *Marquee Plaza, West Bay Rd., Seven Mile Beach, Grand Cayman* ☎ *345/943–4343* ⊕ *www.kebab.ky* ⌨ *Reservations not accepted.*

★ Fodor's Choice ✕ **Blue by Eric Ripert.** *Seafood.* *Top Chef* judge Eric
$$$$ Ripert consulted on every aspect of the first outpost bearing his name, from decor to dishware. His trademark ethereal seafood (executed by his handpicked brigade), flawless but not fawning service, swish setting, and soothing sophistication sans pretension make this one of the Caribbean's finest restaurants. Choose from a regular three-course or the chef's hedonistic tasting menu (with or without wine pairing). Many dishes are clever improvisational riffs on the mother restaurant (New York's celebrated Le Bernardin), using the island's natural bounty (the tribute to the great Bernardin tuna foie gras adds Cayman sea salt). The sensuous counterpoint of flavors, textures, even colors is unimpeachable, as in sautéed kingklip with avocado-coconut cream, sunflower sprouts, and lime sauce *vierge*; sautéed

Blue by Eric Ripert

ocean yellowtail in bourbon-lime–guajillo-pepper broth with mango-jalapeño salad; or melt-in-your-mouth chocolate mousse with caramelized banana, mango-saffron sauce, and cocoa sorbet. The vast wine list offers big names but also showcases hot new regions and lesser-known varietals that offer quality and comparative value. $ *Average main:* *$111* ⊠ *Ritz-Carlton Grand Cayman, West Bay Rd., Seven Mile Beach, Grand Cayman* ☎ *345/943–9000* ⚓ *Reservations essential* ⊘ *Closed Sun. and Mon. No lunch.*

$$$$ ✕ **Casa Havana.** *Eclectic.* This refined eatery glamorously channels prerevolution Cuba with crystal chandeliers, mahogany furnishings, burgundy walls, gold damask curtains, exquisite art naïf and still-life paintings, and picture windows. Yves Lafond's artfully prepared and presented Asian-Cuban cuisine adds Eastern flair to Floribbean fare, with sophisticated flavor and texture counterpoints. The velvety "Thai" lobster bisque is the gustatory equivalent of a Victoria's Secret silk negligee. Other stunning starters include seared diver scallops with cashew-and-pumpkin purée, and rooibos smoked eel and chorizo with pasilla pepper, wakame, and seasonal greens in sake-orange emulsion. For a teasing taste, choose from the tapestry of tapas: four for CI$17. The must-eat entrée is macadamia-nut-crusted sea bass floating in shiitake tea with white truffle essence. Incredible island-inspired desserts include mango-banana napoleon with gingered raspberry coulis. Wine Master dinners pair several courses with wines (Marchese

di Barolo to Gosset Champagne), often introduced by the guest winemakers or owners from as far afield as Tuscany, Australia, Napa, and Chile. ⑤ *Average main: $42* ⊠ *Westin Casuarina, West Bay Rd., Seven Mile Beach, Grand Cayman* ☎ 345/945–3800 ⊕ *www.westincasuarina.net* ⌖ *Reservations essential* ⊘ *No lunch Mon.–Sat.*

$ ✕ **Chicken! Chicken!** *Caribbean.* Chicken! Chicken! Devotees
☾ would probably award four exclamation points to the marvelously moist chicken, slow-roasted on a hardwood open-hearth rotisserie. Most customers grab takeout, but the decor is appealing for a fast-food joint; the clever interior replicates an old-time Cayman cottage. Bright smiles and home cooking completely from scratch enhance the authentic vibe. Hearty but (mostly) healthful heaping helpings of sides include scrumptious Cayman-style corn bread, honey-rum beans, jicama coleslaw, and spinach-pesto pasta. ⑤ *Average main: $12* ⊠ *West Shore Centre, West Bay Rd., Seven Mile Beach, Grand Cayman* ☎ 345/945–2290 ⊕ *www. chicken2.com.*

$$ ✕ **Cimboco.** *Eclectic.* This animated celebration of all things
★ fun, funky, and Caribbean is saturated in psychedelic colors: orange, lemon, and lavender walls; cobalt glass fixtures; paintings of musicians in fevered Fauvist hues; a mosaic of flames dancing up the exhibition kitchen's huge wood-burning oven. History buffs may be interested to know that the *Cimboco* was the first motorized sailing ship built in Cayman (in 1927) and for 20 years the main connection—lifeline to the outside world; National Archive photographs and old newspapers invest the space with still more character. Everything from breads (superlative bruschetta and jalapeño corn bread) to ice creams is made from scratch. Artisanal pizzas betray a (Wolfgang) Puck-ish sensibility with such toppings as balsamic-roasted eggplant, pine nuts, pesto, and feta; or curried chicken with pineapple and spinach. Signature items include banana-leaf-roasted snapper, fire-roasted bacon-wrapped shrimp, and mahimahi ceviche salad, but the daily specials are also inspired. The popular breakfast and brunch are equally creative. Amazingly good desserts start with a moist, intensely rich brownie. The small but well-considered wine list features more than a dozen by the glass. ⑤ *Average main: $19* ⊠ *The Marquee, West Bay Rd. at Harquail Bypass, Seven Mile Beach, Grand Cayman* ☎ 345/947–2782 ⊕ *www.cimboco.com.*

$$$$ ✕ **Copper Falls.** *Steakhouse.* The restaurant's tagline, "A
★ Rare Steakhouse, Very Well Done," is only a touch hyperbolic. The brashly contemporary look (copper-clad water-

falls and hand-painted metal bas relief contrasting with century-old Douglas fir wainscoting and high-back suede booths) screams corporate takeover in progress. Hand-cut 28-day aged Angus cuts, from 8-ounce filet mignon to 28-ounce porterhouse, certify its Grade A status, attracting a demanding business clientele. Lighter options run from red snapper topped with lobster and mushrooms in sun-dried tomato sauce to Parmesan-Dijon mustard-crusted chicken with garlic demi-glace. There's a choice of five starches (including scrumptious garlic mashed potatoes), three vegetables, and six sauces. Best of all, every entrée includes a complimentary beer or cocktail (the martinis would stir 007), helping make Copper Falls pure gold for steak-house purists. $ *Average main: $50 ⊠ 43 Canal Point Rd., The Strand, Seven Mile Beach, Grand Cayman ☎ 345/945–4755 ⊕ www.copperfallssteakhouse.com* ⌂ *Reservations essential* ☉ *No lunch.*

$$ ✕ **Eats Cafe.** *Eclectic.* This happy, hopping hangout is more
☼ eclectic and stylish than any diner, with dramatic decor (crimson booths and walls, flat-screen TVs lining the counter, pendant steel lamps, an exhibition kitchen, gigantic flower paintings, and Andy Warhol reproductions) and vast menu (Cajun to Chinese), including smashing breakfasts. The 15 burgers alone (Rasta Mon Jerkya to Cajun Peppercorn to I'm Sooo Bleu, as well as fish and veggie versions) could satisfy almost any craving, but you could also get a Caesar salad or sushi, Philly cheese steak or chicken chimichangas. It's noisy, busy, buzzing, and hip—but not aggressively so. $ *Average main: $20 ⊠ Falls Plaza, West Bay Rd., Seven Mile Beach, Grand Cayman ☎ 345/943–3287 ⊕ www.eats.ky.*

$$$$ ✕ **Hemingway's.** *Eclectic.* Willowy palms, hardwood furnishings, a churchlike profusion of candles and torches, whirring paddle fans, wicker, lacquered bamboo, and picture windows opening onto Seven Mile Beach pay tribute to Hemingway's tropical travels. Specialties are described earnestly with their Hemingway significance: lobster (perhaps swimming in lemongrass butter sauce) because Papa often feasted on it in Key West, paella because bullfighters fascinated him, rum-and-coconut shrimp with tamarind drizzle since Ernest founded the Royal Order of Shrimp Eaters in Havana. The key lime pie does justice to the restaurant's namesake. $ *Average main: $32 ⊠ Grand Cayman Beach Suites, West Bay Rd., Seven Mile Beach, Grand Cayman ☎ 345/945–5700, 345/949–1234 ⊕ www.grand-cayman-beach-suites.com* ⌂ *Reservations essential.*

Casa Havana

$$$ ✕ **Lone Star Bar and Grill.** *Southwestern.* This temple to sports and the cowboy lifestyle serves a Texas-size welcome and portions. If it can be barbecued, deep-fried, jerked, pulled, or nacho-ized, it's probably on the menu. Many locals swear the burgers are Cayman's best (the Death Burger topped with jalapeño peppers, guacamole, and Swiss cheese should jolt your taste buds). Such Tex-Mex standards as shrimp fajitas are appropriately mouth and eye watering, and regulars lick their chops at the reasonable prices, especially on theme nights like Monday, when you can get all-you-can-eat fajitas and Budweiser bucket specials. $ *Average main: $22 ⊠ 686 West Bay Rd., Seven Mile Beach, Grand Cayman ☎ 345/945–5175 ⊕ www.lonestarcayman.com.*

$$$$ ✕ **Luca.** *Italian.* Owners Paolo Polloni and Andi Marcher spared no expense in realizing their vision of a smart (in every sense) beachfront trattoria that wouldn't be out of place in L.A. Everything was painstakingly handpicked, from the wine "wall" dramatically displaying more than 3,000 bottles from around the globe to the Murano glass fixtures, blown-up photographs in glossy, glassy frames, leather banquettes, and a curving onyx-top bar. Chef Frederico Destro delights in unorthodox pairings, all gorgeously presented. Spicy tuna tartare is served with satiny pepper sauce and crunchy alfalfa sprouts. Hudson Valley foie gras knits spinach sauce with Anjou pear or caramelized pineapple. His homemade pastas shine, particularly the pumpkin ravioli in drawn thyme butter and fantastically fluffy spinach gnocchi tossed with shrimp and asparagus in pesto and poppy seeds. Entrées are invariably solid; the standout is whole Mediterranean striped bass baked in salt crust. His wit and whimsy truly inform the desserts, which are more ambitious and intellectual than successful (chocolate-aubergine mousse or chocolate pappardelle in coriander sauce with pistachio ice cream), yet stimulate the palate and conversation. ⑤ *Average main: $37* ⊠ *Caribbean Club, 871 West Bay Rd., Seven Mile Beach, Grand Cayman* ☎ *345/623–4550* ⚓ *Reservations essential* ⊘ *No lunch Sun.*

★ **Fodor's**Choice × **Michael's Genuine Food & Drink.** *Eclectic.* James
$$$$ Beard Award–winning chef Michael Schwartz and hand-picked executive chef Thomas Tennant have successfully imported the Slow Food philosophy of the groundbreaking original Michael's Genuine in Miami, using seasonal, locally sourced produce that travels short distances from the on-site garden and carefully chosen Cayman farmers, fishermen, and ranchers. The results live up to the Schwartz mantra of "fresh, simple, pure": honest, uncluttered food that sings with color and flavor right down to the homemade sodas. Lunch offers a more traditional but lengthy selection, whereas dinner dishes are divided into small, medium, large, and extra-large portions to encourage family-style sharing and exploration. Sublime staples on the ever-changing menu include burrata (look for such seasonal standouts as heirloom tomato or breadfruit) and sweet-and-sour pork belly (juxtaposing crunchy kimchi with crisp yet unctuously fatty meat). You can't go wrong with any wood-oven-roasted dish, whether pizza, snapper (memorably accented by roasted fennel, grilled lemon, and smoked Cayman sea salt), or *poulet rouge* chicken. The well-considered wine list offers occasional bargains; the menu suggests creative pairings from the vast beer selection. Tennant has also devised an inspired solution to the invasive lionfish population: look for it as a menu special, and if you dive, ask about the Lionfish Safari. ⑤ *Average main: $34* ⊠ *47 Forum La., Canella Court, Camana Bay, Grand Cayman* ☎ *345/640–6433* ⊕ *www.michaelsgenuine.com* ⊘ *No lunch Sun.*

$$$ × **Neptune.** *Italian.* Despite pretensions toward decorative dash (faux stone arches to mermaid murals), Neptune thrives precisely because the food eschews fancy frills, stressing tried-and-true preparations that incorporate fresh (and easily obtained) ingredients. The greatest Italian hits menu ranges from *insalata Caprese* to carpaccio, lasagna to linguine *fra diavolo*. Although seafood reigns supreme, you'll find standout steaks as well. There's a bias toward

cream in the sauces, which some find heavenly, others merely heavy. But personable co-owner–chef Raj Kumar gladly accommodates special dietary requirements, including oil- and salt-free options, as well as such off-the-menu items as salmon Provençal. The likes of Ramazzotti and Rossini provide soothing background music, but avoid Saturday, when karaoke takes over. ⑤ *Average main: $29* ✉ *Trafalgar Place, West Bay Rd., Seven Mile Beach, Grand Cayman* ☎ *345/946–8709.*

★ **Fodor's** Choice ✕ **Ortanique.** *Eclectic.* The original Miami

$$$$ Ortanique—a royal marriage between celebrity chef Cindy Hutson and Delius Shirley, son of Jamaican doyenne of cooking Norma Shirley—helped revolutionize Floribbean fusion fare, and the vibrant food at their Cayman outpost lives up to the nickname "Cuisine of the Sun." Even the interior gleams in rich yellows and oranges that subtly recall plantation living, though prize seating is on the inviting patio, shaded by sea grape trees overlooking a small islet. Cuisine of the Sun emphasizes Caribbean and South American gastronomy infused with Asian inspirations. Seemingly disparate, they share similar landscapes and ingredients. Executive Chef Sara Mair, a semifinalist on *Top Chef,* reinvents classics with an island twist: witness jerk-rubbed foie gras, cooled by burnt-orange marmalade, or plump Mediterranean mussels in Red Stripe broth with shallots, Scotch bonnet peppers, tomatoes, and Jamaican thyme. Or try the signature jerked double pork chop, its fire tamed by guava-spiced rum glaze. Save room for such decadent desserts as a deceptively airy Cloud of Coconut Joy or rum-soaked banana fritters. ⑤ *Average main: $40* ✉ *47 Forum La., The Crescent, Camana Bay, Grand Cayman* ☎ *345/640–7710* ⊕ *www.ortaniquerestaurants.com.*

$$$ ✕ **Ragazzi.** *Italian.* The name means "good buddies," and this
★ strip-mall jewel offers simpatico ambience indeed, always percolating with conversation and good strong espresso. The airy space is convivial: blond woods, periwinkle walls and columns, and handsome artworks of beach scenes, sailboats, and palm trees (against a striking yellow sky) with the scenes extended onto the frame. Chef Adriano Usini turns out magnificent, meticulously prepared standards (the antipasto alone is worth a visit, as are the homemade breadsticks and focaccia, and definitive carpaccio and insalata Caprese). The shellfish linguine (shrimp, scallops, and mussels in a light, silken tomato sauce, with cherry-tomato skins pulled back and crisped) and gnocchi in four-cheese sauce with brandy and pistachios will please any pasta perfec-

tionist. Two dozen first-rate pizzas emerge from the wood-burning oven, and meat and seafood mains are beautifully done, never overcooked. The wine list is notable (400-odd choices) for a casual eatery, showcasing great range and affordability even on high-ticket, hard-to-find heavy hitters such as Biondi Santi Brunello, Jermann Pinot Grigio, and Giacosa Barbaresco; the affable, knowledgeable staff will gladly suggest pairings, including unusual finds. ⑤ *Average main: $29* ⊠ *Buckingham Sq., West Bay Rd., Seven Mile Beach, Grand Cayman* ☎ *345/945–3484* ⊕ *www.ragazzi.ky.*

$$$ ✕**Reef Grill at Royal Palms.** *Eclectic.* This class act appeals to a casually suave crowd, many of them regulars, who appreciate its consistent quality, attentive yet unobtrusive service, soothing seaside setting, top-notch entertainment, and surprisingly reasonable prices. The space is cannily divided into four areas, each with its own look and feel. Co-owner–chef George Dahlstrom gives his perfectly prepared, familiar items just enough twist to satisfy jaded palates: calamari is fried in arborio rice batter with lemon aioli; toasted, sesame-crusted, seared tuna kicks with kimchi; melt-in-your-mouth braised short ribs, one of the smaller "lite bites" (think megatapas), come with blue cheese-peppercorn poutine (fries covered with cheese curds and gravy); and sea scallops are pan-seared with a creamy roasted corn–smoked bacon mash. Dance the calories off to the estimable reggae, calypso, and soca sounds of Coco Red or really sweat it out during Chill Wednesdays, and then adjourn to the cozy lounge for an aged rum or single malt. It's equally enticing at lunch, when it exudes a soigné beach bar ambience. ⑤ *Average main: $28* ⊠ *537 West Bay Rd., Seven Mile Beach, Grand Cayman* ☎ *345/945–6358* ⊕ *www.reefgrill.com* ⊘ *No dinner Sun. May–Nov.*

$$$$ ✕**7 Prime Cuts/Sunsets.** *Steakhouse.* The Ritz-Carlton's all-purpose dining room transforms from a bustling breakfast buffet (and appealing lunch spot with simpler menus) into an elegant eatery come evening. Tall potted palms, terrazzo floors, red and black columns, and the tiered pool just outside are lighted to strategically stylish effect. Sinatra and Ella keep the sultry beat while the kitchen jazzes standard meat-and-potatoes dishes with inventive seasonings and eye-catching presentations. Splendid aged steaks come with four sauces, from Madagascar green peppercorn jus to béarnaise. The Kobe beef and foie gras burger and such sides as truffled mac-and-cheese redefine divine decadence. The calorie- and cholesterol-conscious can savor melt-in-your-mouth tuna tartare with wasabi mayo or impeccably

cooked catch of the day with a choice of several sauces. Then, just surrender to such confections as "Volcano" chocolate cake with malted-milk ice cream and strawberry sauce *dulce de leche* (caramelized sweetened milk). Ⓢ *Average main: $54* ⊠ *Ritz-Carlton Grand Cayman, West Bay Rd., Seven Mile Beach, Grand Cayman* ☎ *345/943–9000* ⊕ *www.ritzcarlton.com.*

$$ ╳ **Sunshine Grill.** *Caribbean.* This cheerful, cherished locals'
☖ secret serves haute comfort food at bargain-basement prices. Even the chattel-style poolside building, painted a delectable lemon with lime shutters, whets the appetite. Sunshine ranks high in the island's greatest burger debate, while the jerk chicken egg rolls and fabulous fish and Cuban chicken tacos elevate pub grub to an art form. Wash it down with one of the many signature libations, like the Painkiller. Take advantage of affordably priced nightly dinner specials such as Thai chili salmon, red snapper amandine, and Cuban pork loin with *sofrito* (a dip of cilantro, garlic, onions, tomatoes, and oregano). Ⓢ *Average main: $17* ⊠ *Sunshine Suites, West Bay Rd., Seven Mile Beach, Grand Cayman* ☎ *345/949–3000.*

$$$ ╳ **Thai Orchid.** *Thai.* East meets West at this elegant eatery, and the combination makes for a tasty meal. The look juxtaposes some Thai crafts and black-lacquer accents with track lighting, blue-pomegranate-and-mango sponge-painted walls, gilt-trim flower paintings, and bold artworks of semi-abstract beach scenes and decidedly Western cupids. The Thai chefs turn out splendid classics like *yum nuer* (sliced char-grilled strip loin tossed with green salad in lime dressing); the standout signature entrée is boneless duck sautéed with basil and bell peppers in chili sauce. Seafood lovers can opt for the fresh sushi, and plentiful vegetarian options include curries perfumed with lemongrass. Sunday's Thai–sushi buffet (just CI$13.95) is a superb bargain. Desserts return west, besting most Asian restaurants: dark-and-white-chocolate mousse cake with *crème anglaise* and raspberry coulis is a standout. Ⓢ *Average main: $29* ⊠ *Queens Court, West Bay Rd., Seven Mile Beach, Grand Cayman* ☎ *345/949–7955* ⊕ *www.thaiorchid.ky.*

$$ ╳ **Triple Crown Pub.** *British.* This mate-y pub lures lonely London-to-Limerick lads and lasses with a lengthy list of draft beers and fittings and furnishings sourced throughout the United Kingdom. Popular British standbys include a beef-and-ale pie that should be packaged for supermarkets, as well as the odd fancy effort, such as homemade fish goujons (fried and breaded strips of fish) with curried mayo.

Smoke-eating machines efficiently minimize haze; big-screen TVs blast major British and occasionally even U.S. sporting events (forget Manchester United, this is Arsenal territory). The bar menu is served until midnight. Prices are generally low—the Sunday all-you-can-eat carvery is only CI$16.25, and Thursday night steak dinners are CI$10–12. Entertainment encompasses raucous trivia and bingo competitions, karaoke, DJ Fridays, and occasional live bands. ⑤ *Average main: $15* ⊠ *Marquee Plaza, Seven Mile Rd., Seven Mile Beach, Grand Cayman* ☎ *345/943–7821.*

$$$$ ✕ **The Wharf.** *Seafood.* The popularity of this large restaurant often leads to impersonal service and mediocre food. But the location, a series of elevated decks and Victorian-style gazebos in blue and white hugging the sea, is enviable and helps to explain its enduring appeal (wedding parties have their own pavilion, but celebrations of all sorts can overrun the place, including Boogie Nights Fridays). The Ports of Call bar is a splendid place for sunset fanciers, and tarpon feeding off the deck is a nightly (9 pm) spectacle. Stick to simpler fare (creole-style marinated conch fritters, the signature basil-and-pistachio-crusted sea bass in champagne cream) and avoid anything sounding too pretentious. Chef Christian Reiter is Austrian and patriotic, so save room for dessert: warm toffee banana pudding or chocolate-hazelnut tart baked with caramel and topped with orange jelly and bittersweet chocolate mousse don't disappoint. ⑤ *Average main: $40* ⊠ *43 West Bay Rd., Seven Mile Beach, Grand Cayman* ☎ *345/949–2231, 345/814–0179* ⊕ *www.wharf. ky* ⚓ *Reservations essential* ⊙ *No lunch.*

$$$ ✕ **Yoshi Sushi.** *Japanese.* The superlative sushi's fresh—and
★ the clientele sometimes even fresher—at this modish, modern locals' lair. Scarlet cushions, cherry pendant blown-glass lamps, leather-and-bamboo accents, and maroon walls help create a sensuous, even charged vibe in the main room. The backlit bar sees its share of carefree customers trying to manipulate their chopsticks after a few kamikaze sake bomber missions (plunging hot cups of sake into frosty Kirin beer). Savvy diners literally leave themselves in Yoshi's hands (the rolls and nightly special sushi "pizzas" are particularly creative), and the raw-phobic can choose from fine cooked items, from beef tataki to tempura to teriyaki. The congenial staff recommends intriguing sake and beer pairings, though the wine list and martini selection are also admirable for an Asian eatery. ⑤ *Average main: $24* ⊠ *Falls Plaza, West Bay Rd., Seven Mile Beach, Grand Cayman* ☎ *345/943–9674* ⊕ *www.eats.ky* ⚓ *Reservations essential.*

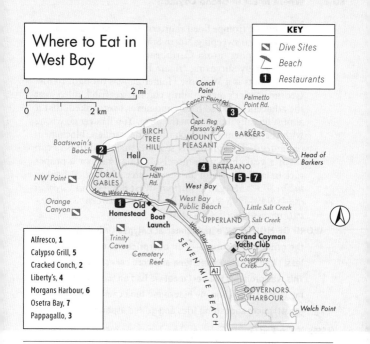

KEY

Dive Sites
Beach
Restaurants

Where to Eat in West Bay

Alfresco, **1**
Calypso Grill, **5**
Cracked Conch, **2**
Liberty's, **4**
Morgans Harbour, **6**
Osetra Bay, **7**
Pappagallo, **3**

WEST BAY

There are fewer restaurant choices in West Bay, but there are some spots that are worth the trip. Be sure to have good driving directions when heading out into this area.

$$$ ✕ **Alfresco.** *Caribbean.* This ultrafriendly locals' insider spot, straddling the unofficial "border" between Seven Mile Beach and West Bay, resembles a little neighborhood diner transported to the ocean. Enjoy equally fresh sea breezes and food on the waterfront wood deck (built over a former parking lot) under one of the mismatched umbrellas. The co-owner is a longtime fisherman, and the fish-and-chips would make any Londoner proud. Other savvy seafood selections run from fiery Scotch bonnet shrimp to specials such as lobster ravioli in gossamer pumpkin-cream sauce. Indeed, the menu is as much Capri as Cayman, with yummy pizzas and fried calamari served with both jerk mayo and marinara sauce. ⑤ *Average main: $21 ⊠ 53 Town Hall Rd., West Bay, Grand Cayman* ☎ *345/947–2525.*

$$$$ ✕ **Calypso Grill.** *Eclectic.* Shack chic describes this inviting split-level space splashed in Dr. Seuss primary colors that contrast with brick walls, hardwood furnishings, terra-

cotta floors, trompe l'oeil shutters, and (real) French doors opening onto sweeping North Sound views. If the interior is like stepping into a Caribbean painting, the outdoor deck serenely surveying frigate birds watchfully circling fishing boats is a Winslow Homer canvas brought to life. George Fowler's menu rightly emphasizes fish hauled in at the adjacent dock, so fresh (and never overcooked) that it almost literally jumps from the plate. You'll never go wrong with the unvarnished catch of the day grilled, blackened, or sautéed. Though this is seafood turf, landlubbers can savor a veal chop with morel-Marsala sauce or a proper rack of lamb. End with the sticky toffee pudding. ⑤ *Average main: $43* ⊠ *Morgan's Harbour, West Bay, Grand Cayman* ☎ *345/949–3948* ⊕ *www.calypsogrillcayman.com* ⊜ *Reservations essential* ⊗ *Closed Mon.*

WORD OF MOUTH. "We had dinner at Calypso Grill—my wife had the grilled tiger shrimp—a bit overpriced but good nonetheless. I had the blackened tuna and crab cakes as an appetizer. This was probably the best meal we had on the island. . . . Both my wife's shrimp and my blackened tuna came with the same (great) micro shoestring fries and grilled asparagus." —DKG50

$$$$ ✕ **Cracked Conch.** *Eclectic.* This longtime institution, rebuilt after Hurricane Ivan, effortlessly blends upscale and downhome. The interior gleams from the elaborate light-and-water sculpture at the gorgeous mosaic-and-mahogany entrance bar to the plush booths with subtly embedded lighting. You can drink in the remarkable water views through large shutters, but for maximum impact, dine on the multitiered patio. Executive Chef Gilbert Cavallaro similarly revitalized the kitchen with dazzling juxtapositions of color, taste, and texture. Newfangled variations on old-fashioned cuisine include honey-jerk-glazed tuna with tomato sorbet, crispy calamari with cardamom-marinated carrots and chipotle sauce, and crab cakes with red-pepper reduction and passion-fruit demi-glace. Sample stellar signature items include the definitive conch chowder or ceviche, silken short rib ravioli with truffles and Parmesan foam, and mahimahi poached *sous vide* over cannellini emulsion drizzled with truffle oil. Desserts delight, from a gossamer vanilla crème brûlée with pineapple-bergamot salsa to a miraculously moist guava-glazed bread-and-butter pudding. Locals flock to Sunday brunch or Monday's all-you-can-eat barbecue bash, or they just hang out at the dockside Macabuca tiki bar (fab sunsets, sunset-hued libations), which lives up to its mellow name, indigenous Taíno for "What does it matter?" ⑤ *Average main: $44* ⊠ *Northwest Point Rd., West Bay, Grand Cayman* ☎ *345/945–5217* ⊕ *www.crackedconch.com.ky.*

$$ ✕ **Liberty's.** *Caribbean.* Just follow the boisterous laughter and pulsating Caribbean tunes to this hard-to-find mint-green Caymanian cottage, where you feel as if you've been invited to a family reunion. The Sunday Caribbean buffet attracts hordes of hungry churchgoers (call ahead to ensure they're open that week), but every day offers authentic turtle steak, oxtail, jerk, and delectable fried snapper with sassy salsas that liberate your taste buds from the humdrum. There's also a George Town outpost. ⑤ *Average main: $18* ⊠ *140 Reverend Blackman Rd., West Bay, Grand Cayman* ☎ *345/949–3226.*

$$$ ✕ **Morgan's Harbour.** *Eclectic.* Energetic, effervescent Janie Schweiger patrols the front while husband Richard rules the kitchen at this simpatico seaside spot with smashing North Sound views. Locals (and fishermen) literally cruise into the adjacent dock for refueling of all sorts. You can sit in one of the cozy buildings decorated with Depression-era chandeliers and vivid aquatic artworks ("It's the House of Doors," Janie quips. "Twenty-five ways in but of course we don't want you to leave") or admire the dexterous marine maneuverings from the interlocking decks. Richard's menu dances just as deftly from Asia to his Austrian home. Nifty, nimbly prepared nibbles include the wildly popular 10-ounce Brie-topped jerk burger and ceviche, but everything from chicken schnitzel to seafood risotto is expertly cooked to order, often with a creative twist. Lunch offers several of the restaurant's greatest hits at even more palatable prices. ⑤ *Average main: $28* ⊠ *Morgan's Harbour, West Bay, Grand Cayman* ☎ *345/946–7049* ⊕ *www.morgansharbour.net.*

$$$$ ✕ **Osetra Bay.** *Eclectic.* Whether by day (when fishing boats as brightly colored as a child's finger painting trawl the tourmaline North Sound) or by night (when Cayman Kai's lights twinkle as the moon dapples the water with a thousand gold doubloons), the view alone guarantees a memorable meal. The design is almost as appetizing, from glowing columns strategically placed to flatter diners to the intimate, billowingly draped dining cabanas to the stark Starck-ish white-on-white ultralounges. Every element infuses the casual Caribbean underpinnings with a chic South Beach sensibility, literally bringing caviar to Cayman. The ever-changing, sophisticated, seasonal menu emphasizes seafood:

yellowfin tuna tartare with foie gras, yuzu, jalapeño, and spring onion; turtle agnolotti with red wine–veal sauce and truffle oil; wahoo kissed by citrus essence and cilantro in sunchoke cream with cucumber, coconut, fennel, Shanghai cabbage, and beetroot—though vegetarians delight in the pastas, and carnivores can stake out dishes like the dry-aged rib eye. ⑤ *Average main: $42 ✉ Morgan's Harbour, West Bay, Grand Cayman* ☎ *345/325–5000, 345/623–5100* ⊕ *www.osetrabay.com* ⚭ *Reservations essential* ⊙ *No lunch. Closed Sun.*

$$$$ ✕ **Pappagallo.** *Italian.* Pappagallo, Italian for "parrot," hauntingly perches on the edge of a lagoon in a 14-acre bird sanctuary. Inside, riotously colored macaws, cockatoos, and parrots perch on swings behind plate glass, primping, preening, and practically commenting on the billing and cooing clientele. You feel like hacking through the luxuriant vegetation inside and out; the lost-in-the-jungle exoticism is enhanced by locally hewn stones, bamboo, homemade rope, and thatched palapas for outdoor seating. Yet the sleek deco-inspired black marble–and–polished brass accents bespeak the underlying seriousness. Chef Steve Wagner's food is definitely not for the birds. Chunky yet silken sweet potato chowder is enlivened by clams and jalapeño-cured bacon. The kick of a jerk Niman Ranch pork chop flamed with Jack Daniels and accompanied by mango-lime salsa is softened by downy sour cream–scallion mashed potatoes and griddle corn cakes, each element providing sterling textural counterpoints. Be sure to thank Bogie, the African gray parrot, who really rules the roost. ⑤ *Average main: $37 ✉ Barkers, 444B Conch Point Rd., West Bay, Grand Cayman* ☎ *345/949–1119* ⊕ *www.pappagallo.ky* ⚭ *Reservations essential* ⊙ *No lunch.*

EAST END

While it can be at least a half-hour drive out here, some of the restaurants in East End are worth the trip from George Town.

$$$$ ✕ **The Lighthouse.** *Seafood.* The nonworking, conical, white-stucco lighthouse surrounded by fluttering flags serves as a beacon for hungry East End explorers. The interior replicates a yacht: polished hardwood floors, ship's lanterns, mosaic hurricane lamps, steering wheels, marine artworks, portholes, and waiters in crew's garb with chevrons. Most tables afford sweeping sea vistas, but prize romantic seating is on the little deck. Shipshape starters include Miss Nell's

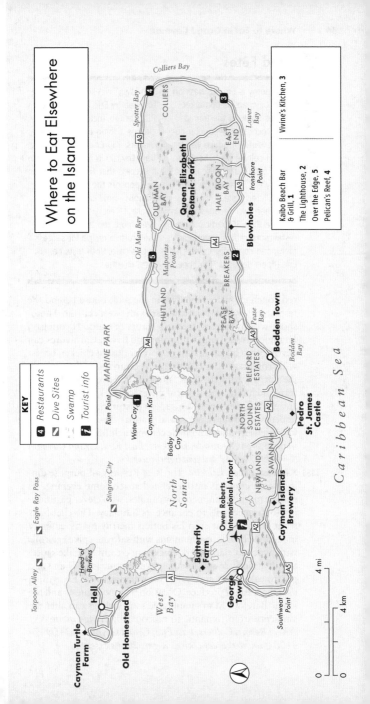

Food Fêtes

Gastronomy is big business on Grand Cayman, as upmarket eateries bank on the tourist dollar. Increasingly popular culinary events introduce visitors to local culture while beefing up biz, especially off-season. January's "A Taste of Cayman" has titillated taste buds for more than two decades, thanks to more than 30 participating restaurants, raffles, entertainment, and cook-offs. Celeb chef Eric Ripert debuted "Caribbean Rundown" weekend in 2007 at his Blue by Eric Ripert in the Ritz-Carlton, including cooking classes, fishing trips, and gala dinners, *Top Chef* competitor Dale Levitzki in tow. It was such a success that *Food & Wine* co-sponsors the subsequent editions—now called Cayman Cookout—every January, with even more top toques stirring the broth: a recipe for success in this case. Both fests benefit local charities.

red conch chowder (she lives in the pink house behind the restaurant) or flash-fried calamari with sweet chili dip. Photoshoot-worthy entrées (such as a platter of seafood floating on linguine alfredo) sing with color and flavor. Carnivores can devour osso bucco ravioli or porcini-dusted chicken breast with rosemary-Marsala sauce. Vegetarians will delight in the curries, tofu stir-fries, and pastas. Save room for desserts, including the tropical cheesecake. The comprehensive wine list extends to a superb postprandial selection of liqueurs, aged rums, ports, and grappas. The gift shop offers lovely jewelry and handmade ceramic lighthouses. ⑤ *Average main: $34* ⊠ *Oceanside, Breakers, East End, Grand Cayman* ☎ *345/947–2047* ⊕ *www.lighthouse.ky.*

$$$$ × **Pelican's Reef.** *Eclectic.* The Reef Resort's all-purpose dining room converts into a refined space come evening, its marine murals illuminated by candles, with clever partitioning by framed sails to enhance its intimacy. The chef hails from Jamaica, but even his buffets merrily marry culinary influences: he'll infuse hummus with saffron, spike egg rolls with avocado, flambé jerk chicken in creamy shiitake sauce. Standouts include conch sausage with caramelized onions and potato cakes, and crab cakes with mango salsa. Everything uses the freshest produce. Occasional limbo contests and the iconic Barefoot Man's inimitable song stylings can alter the ambience from romantic to raucous. ⑤ *Average main: $33* ⊠ *Reef Resort, Colliers, East End, Grand Cayman* ☎ *345/947–3100* ⊕ *www.thereef.com* ⚄ *Reservations essential.*

CLOSE UP

Eating at a Home Kitchen

Aspiring Anthony Bourdains on Grand Cayman should seek out roadside vans, huts, kiosks, and stalls dishing out unfamiliar grub that might unnerve wannabe *Survivor* contestants. These casual spots offer authentic fare at very fair prices, with main dishes and heaping helpings of sides costing under CI$10. If you thought Mickey D's special sauce or Coke was a secret formula, try prying prized recipes handed down for generations from these islanders.

Rankin's Jerk Centre. A faux cow and pig greet you at Rankin's Jerk Centre, where you can savor Miss Rankin's scrumptious turtle stew and jerk dishes in her alluring garden. ✉ *3032 Shamrock Rd., Bodden Town, Grand Cayman* ☎ *345/947-3155.*

Chester's Fish Fry. Chester's Fish Fry has a devoted following for his jerk pork, fried fish, and downy fritters. ✉ *563 Bodden Town Rd., Bodden Town, Grand Cayman* ☎ *345/939-3474.*

Two of these most casual eateries on the island are George Town institutions.

Tony's Jerk Foods. Even politicos stand in line at Tony's Jerk Foods, which serves everything from cow foot to conch stew (you can't miss the exterior's beach mural). ✉ *193 School Rd., George Town, Grand Cayman* ☎ *345/916-6860.*

Seymour's Jerk Centre. Seymour's Jerk Centre, in the parking lot of Roy's Boutique, is where island icon Seymour Silburn dishes out succulent slow-cooked smoky jerk (regulars have gotten their fix for more than two decades). ✉ *Shedden Rd., George Town, Grand Cayman* ☎ *345/916-8531, 345/916-5418.*

Heritage Kitchen. West Bay's popular family-run Heritage Kitchen serves up legendary raconteur Tunny Powell's fish tea, barbecue ribs, and fish fry—with a generous portion of local lore. It's only open sporadically, so look for it when you're in the area. ✉ *Just off Boggy Sand Rd., West Bay, Grand Cayman.*

$ ✕ **Vivine's Kitchen.** *Caribbean.* Cars practically block the road at this unprepossessing hot spot for classic Caymanian food. You're literally eating in Vivine and Ray Watler's home; the prime seating is in the waterfront courtyard, where you will be serenaded by rustling sea grape leaves, crashing surf, and screeching gulls dive-bombing for their lunch. Daily changing menu items, all sourced locally to guarantee freshness, are scrawled on a blackboard: perhaps stewed turtle, curried goat, barbecued chicken, and snapper made to order, with cassava and sweet-potato cake sides. Burgers, dogs, and chicken-and-chips make a concession to more timid taste buds. Alcohol isn't served, but fresh tamarind, mango, and sorrel juices pack a flavorful punch. Vivine's generally closes early (and occasionally on Monday night), but stays open if there's demand—and any food left. ⑤ *Average main: $11* ⊠ *Austin Dr., Gun Bay, East End, Grand Cayman* ☎ *345/947–7435* ⊟ *No credit cards.*

NORTH SIDE

The North Side has a few good places to eat.

$$$ ✕ **Kaibo Beach Bar and Grill.** *Caribbean.* Spectacularly overlooking the North Sound, this quintessential beach hangout rocks days (fantastic lunches that cost half the price of dinner, festive atmosphere including impromptu volleyball tourneys, and free Wi-Fi), but serves murderous margaritas and mudslides well into the evening to a boisterous bevy of yachties, locals, sports buffs, and expats. There's also a terrific selection of rums. Enjoy New England–style conch chowder with a hint of heat, spinach-artichoke dip, smoked mahimahi pâté, hefty burgers, and wondrous wraps (seared tuna in wasabi mayo, grilled, spice-marinated chicken with jerk mayo), either on the multitiered deck garlanded with ships' rope and Christmas lights or in hammocks and thatched cabanas amid the palms. The handsome, nautically themed second-floor dining room, open weekend nights, serves more creative fare (specialties include baked grouper with Kaffir lime–leaf crust in lemongrass velouté) at higher prices, but the ultimate in romance is the catered "Luna del Mar" evening hosted every Friday closest to the full moon. Tuesday beach barbecues are highly popular (including limbo dancing, live music, half-price drinks, and discounted water taxi service to the "mainland"). ⑤ *Average main: $30* ⊠ *585 Water Cay Rd., Cayman Kai, North Side, Grand Cayman* ☎ *345/947–9975* ⊕ *www.kaibo.ky.*

$$ ✕ **Over the Edge.** *Caribbean.* This fun, funky seaside spot brims with character and characters. (A soused regular might welcome you by reciting "the daily lunch special: chilled barley soup . . . That's beer.") The nutty nautical decor (brass ship's lanterns dangle from the ceiling, and steering wheels, lacquered turtle shells, and fishing photos adorn the walls) contrasts with cool mirrored ads for Gitanes and Mumm Cordon Rouge and the trendily semi-open kitchen with fresh fish prominently displayed. The

CLOSE UP

Culinary Quality Control

In more than a decade at the helm of New York's Le Bernardin, sometime *Top Chef* panelist Eric Ripert has garnered every gastronomic accolade. Born in Antibes on the French Riviera, Ripert apprenticed at Parisian institution La Tour d'Argent and Joël Robuchon's Jamin, then worked stateside with Jean-Louis Palladin and David Bouley before Le Bernardin reeled him in. He opened his first "name" restaurant, Blue by Eric Ripert, at the Ritz-Carlton Grand Cayman in 2005. Others have since followed.

The Caribbean wasn't on Ripert's radar, as he has told us, but "the resort owner, Michael Ryan, was in New York for dinner at Le Bernardin. He wanted to discuss the Ritz and me opening its signature restaurant. When I came down, he picked me up, put me on a boat to swim at Stingray City, loaded me with champagne, then came straight here to discuss business.... I loved it, felt confident because of his commitment to quality and service."

The greatest challenge was "the quality of the seafood, which sounds illogical, but most fish here comes frozen from the United States. We visited fishermen, created a network, to get fresh catch regularly. It's the only item the hotel allows cash for, so [executive chef Luis Lujan] carries a big wad! We fought passionately for the quality of the seafood, since that's one of my trademarks. And with so few farmers and growers on island...produce was even more challenging, but we found squash, salad greens, herbs."

"Trying to use what's already here inspires me," says Lujan. "It's cooking in the landscape.... I can now get lemongrass, thyme, mint, basil, papaya, mango, callaloo, sweet potatoes, good stew tomatoes, Scotch bonnet, and other peppers. I'm a big advocate of the locally produced Cayman sea salt." He encourages local purveyors, but paramount was persuading management to commit the funds for specialty products worth the price. "We work with a couple of commercial fishing boats that bring huge wahoo, ocean yellowtail, deep-water snapper from as far afield as Mexico.... So fresh and so beautiful, a pleasure to work with."

Ripert draws parallels to his Mediterranean upbringing. "It's a different feel and look, of course, as are the cooking ingredients and preparations. But both cultures place great emphasis on food as a key part of their lives and borrow from many heritages. And both cultures know how to relax and enjoy themselves!"

jukebox jumps (country music rules the roost), and the tiki-lighted terrace offers stunning views and fresh breezes. Expertly prepared local fare (curried chicken to conch steak to Cayman rock lobster escoveitch, served with rice and beans, plantains, and fried festival bread) is a bargain, especially at lunch, though the chef also surprises with such gussied-up fare as shrimp in Pernod sauce and turtle steak in port. Ⓢ *Average main: $19* ✉ *Old Man Bay, North Side, Grand Cayman* ☎ *345/947–9568* ⊕ *www.over-theedge.com.*

Where to Stay in Grand Cayman

WORD OF MOUTH

"The nicest beach in Cayman is where the Westin
is. Have stayed there and enjoyed it. . . . You may
want to stay in a condo to cut food costs, which are
very high in Cayman."

—summer04

By Jordan Simon

DESPITE ITS SMALL SIZE, GRAND Cayman offers a surprising range of accommodations: large luxury resorts, medium-size chain hotels, cozy condo enclaves, locally owned guesthouses—from boutique-y to budget, not to mention private villas.

The massive Ritz-Carlton resort on Seven Mile Beach was the first of several larger developments constructed under new laws allowing seven-story buildings. It was followed by the classy Caribbean Club Condominiums and the recently rebuilt upscale Beachcomber. Now high-rises sprout like fungi along Seven Mile Beach, each vowing and vying to be better—or at least grander—than the last.

Some of the acceptance of ever-grander development can be attributed to the lingering devastation of 2004's Hurricane Ivan, which totaled the island. The 230-room Hyatt Regency hotel, long the island standard-bearer, never recovered from the damage; Hyatt eventually withdrew from its last management responsibilities. For good or bad, Ivan provided many complexes with an excuse to renovate, even rebuild from the ground up and go ever higher. While the tacky, dilapidated condo enclaves were swept away, now practically every sizable lot of Seven Mile Beach is in various stages of development.

Brace yourself for resort prices—there are few accommodations in the lower-cost ranges in Grand Cayman. You'll also find no big all-inclusive resorts on Grand Cayman, and very few offer a meal plan of any kind. Happily, parking, at least, is always free at island hotels and resorts.

WHERE TO STAY

Seven Mile Beach is Boardwalk and Park Place for most vacationers. In a quirk of development, however, most of the hotels sit across the street from the beach (though they usually have beach clubs, bars, water-sports concessions, and other facilities directly on the sand). Most of Grand Cayman's condo resorts offer direct access to Grand Cayman's prime sandy real estate. Snorkelers should note that only the northern and southern ends of SMB feature spectacular reef development; the northern end is much quieter, so if you're looking for action, stay anywhere from the Westin Casuarina south, where all manner of restaurants and bars are walkable.

BEST BETS

Fodor's Choice ★
Caribbean Club, Lighthouse
Point, Reef Resort, Ritz-Carlton
Grand Cayman

BEST BEACHFRONT
Coral Stone Club, Lacovia
Condominiums, Reef Resort,
Westin Casuarina

**BEST FOR AN
ECO-FRIENDLY TRIP**
Cobalt Coast, Compass Point,
Lighthouse Point

BEST FOR FAMILIES
Ritz-Carlton Grand Cayman

BEST SERVICE
Reef Resort, Ritz-Carlton
Grand Cayman

BEST FOR ROMANCE
Caribbean Club, Cotton Tree,
Shangri-La B&B, Turtle Nest Inn

Tranquil **West Bay** retains the feel of an old-time fishing village; diving is magnificent in this area, but lodging options are limited, especially now that the long-promised Mandarin Oriental remains on indefinite hold.

Those who want to get away from it all should head to the bucolic **East End** and **North Side**, dotted with condo resorts and villas. The dive sites here are particularly pristine.

The **Cayman Kai/Rum Point,** starting at West Bay across the North Sound, offers the single largest concentration of villas and condo resorts, stressing barefoot elegance.

PRICES

Prices in the hotel reviews are the lowest cost of a standard double room in high season, excluding taxes, service charges, and meal plans (except at all-inclusives). Prices for rentals are the lowest per-night cost for a one-bedroom unit in high season.

HOTELS AND RESORTS

Grand Cayman offers something for every traveler, with well-known chain properties in every price range and style. Accommodations run the gamut from outrageously deluxe to all-suites to glorified motor lodges. Add to that locally run hostelries that often offer better bang for the buck. Still, in a Caymanian quirk, condo resorts take up most of the prime beach real estate. And, with a couple of exceptions, hotels along Seven Mile Beach actually sit across the road from the beach.

B&BS, INNS, AND GUESTHOUSES

They may be some distance from the beach and short on style and facilities—or they may be surprisingly elegant, but all these lodgings offer a friendly atmosphere, equally friendly prices, and your best shot at getting to know the locals. Rooms are clean and simple at the very least, and most have private baths.

CONDOMINIUMS AND PRIVATE VILLAS

On Grand Cayman the number of available condos and villas greatly outnumbers hotel rooms. Most condos are very similar, with telephones, satellite TV, air-conditioning, living and dining areas, patios, and parking. Differences are the quality of in-condo amenities, facilities within their individual complexes (though pools, hot tubs, and barbecue grills are usually standard), proximity to town and the beach, and views. Some condos are privately owned and rented out directly by the owners; other complexes are made up solely of short-term rentals.

Grand Cayman's private villa rentals range from cozy one-bedroom bungalows to grand five-bedroom manses. Some stand completely independent; others may be located in a larger complex or enclave. While at first glance rental fees for villas may seem high, larger units can offer significant savings over hotels for families or couples traveling together. For example, if the cost of a three-bedroom villa is divided among three couples, the seemingly high nightly rental cost of $900 per night would only be $150 per person ($300 per couple); few hotels on Grand Cayman are so moderately priced. And as in a condo, a full kitchen helps reduce the stratospheric price of dining out; a laundry room helps with cleanup, especially for families. Unless otherwise noted, all villas have landline phones, and local calls are usually free; phones are generally locked for international calls, though Internet phone service could be included. Villa agents can usually help you rent a cell phone.

Rates are highest during the winter season from mid-December through mid-April. Most condo and villa rentals require a minimum stay, often five to seven nights in high season (during the Christmas holiday season the minimum will be at least one week and is sometimes two weeks, plus there are exorbitant fees). Off-season minimums are usually three to five nights.

Several of the condo- and villa-rental companies have websites where you can see pictures of the privately owned units and villas they represent; many properties are represented exclusively, others handled by several agents. In general, the farther north you go on Seven Mile Beach, the older and more affordable the property. Note also that many offices close on Sunday; if that's your date of arrival, they'll usually make arrangements for your arrival. There's often no maid service on Sunday either, as the island practically shuts down.

We no longer recommend individual private villas, especially since they frequently change agents. However, among the properties we've inspected worth looking for are Coral Reef, Venezia, Villa Habana, Great Escapes, Fishbones, and Pease Bay House.

VILLA AND CONDO RENTAL AGENTS

The **Cayman Islands Department of Tourism** (⊕ *www. caymanislands.ky*) provides a list of condominiums and small rental apartments. There are several condo and villa enclaves available on the beach, especially on the North Side near Cayman Kai, away from bustling Seven Mile Beach.

Quoted prices for villa and private condo rentals usually include government tax and often service fees (be sure to verify this). As a general rule of thumb, Seven Mile Beach properties receive daily maid service except on Sunday, but at villas and condos elsewhere on the island, extra services such as cleaning must be prearranged for an extra charge.

Blue Escapes. Blue Escapes is an up-and-coming international broker that also works with top-notch on-island realtors. ☎ *512/892–3301* ⊕ *www.blueescapes.com.*

Cayman Island Vacations. Cayman Island Vacations was started by the affable couple Don and Linda Martin in 1989. Longtime Cayman homeowners, they represent more than 50 villas and condos (including their own). Extremely helpful with island suggestions, they can make arrangements for a rental car and extras. They arrange diving discounts, and Linda is one of Cayman's leading wedding coordinators. ☎ *813/854–1201, 888/208–8935* ⊕ *www. caymanvacation.com.*

Cayman Villas. Cayman Villas represents villas and condos on Grand Cayman and Little Cayman; from studios to six-bedrooms with private pool. They'll gladly facilitate connections with potential staff from chefs to chauffeurs, recommend restaurants and tour operators, and even put you in touch with wedding coordinators. A great selling

Buildings in George Town

point: Every property has a manager, available 24/7 via cell phone, who lives on-site or nearby. They work with industry leader WIMCO. ☎ *800/235–5888, 345/945–4144* ⊕ *www.caymanvillas.com.*

Grand Cayman Villas. Grand Cayman Villas was started by Virginia resident Jim Leavitt, who carries listings for dozens of fine properties island-wide. ✉ *Grand Cayman* ☎ *866/358–8455* ⊕ *www.grandcaymanvillas.net.*

Island Hideaways. Island Hideaways rents villas all over the Caribbean, including some in the Cayman Islands. ☎ *800/832–2302* ⊕ *www.islandhideaways.com.*

WIMCO. WIMCO, or the West Indies Management Company, is synonymous with quality throughout the world, especially the Caribbean. ☎ *800/449–1553* ⊕ *www.wimco.com.*

GEORGE TOWN AND ENVIRONS

If you are looking for a cheaper option and are willing to forego a beachfront location, there are a couple of guest-houses and simple hotels around George Town.

For expanded reviews, facilities, and current deals, visit Fodors.com.

$ 🏠 **Eldemire's Tropical Island Inn.** *B&B/Inn.* You're about 15 minutes from Seven Mile Beach at this guesthouse south of George Town, but less than 1 mile (1½ km) north of Smith

CLOSE UP

Market Watch

Most condo and villa rentals start on Saturday. Since all the island's major supermarkets (and most other stores) close on Sunday, condo and villa renters may want to stop off for essentials right after they pick up their rental car. There are several American-style supermarkets near the airport, along West Bay Road parallel to Seven Mile Beach, and elsewhere in the island; *for specific listings, see* ⇨ *Foodstuffs in Exploring Grand Cayman (with Shopping).* All stock fresh produce, poultry, and seafood; meats; baked goods; cold cuts and cheeses; hot and cold ready-made dishes at deli counters; and anything canned, frozen, and boxed. Just don't get sticker shock: Prices average 25%–30% more than at home. If you expect to arrive on a Sunday or holiday when the supermarkets are closed, ask the condo resort or rental agent to arrange a starter kit.

Cayman Vacation Shoppers. Cayman Vacation Shoppers is a godsend for advance provisioning; it's also the only outfit on the island permitted to deliver wine and spirits on Sunday. ☎ *345/916–2978* 🌐 *www.caymanshoppers.com.*

Cove Beach. **Pros:** authentic Cayman hospitality and feel; inexpensive (with constant deals and discounts for paying cash); great dive packages arranged. **Cons:** hard to find; slightly run-down; not on the beach. $ *Rooms from: $119* ✉ *18 Pebbles Way, off S. Church St., Box 482, George Town, Grand Cayman* ☎ *345/916–2022, 345/916–8369, 704/469–2635 toll-free 9 am to 9 pm from US and Canada* 🌐 *www.eldemire.com* *4 rooms, 2 studios, 2 apartments* 🍽 *No meals.*

$ **Sunset House.** *Hotel.* This amiable seaside dive-oriented resort is on the ironshore south of George Town, close enough for a short trip to stores and restaurants yet far enough to feel secluded. **Pros:** great shore diving and dive shop; lively bar scene; fun international clientele; great package rates. **Cons:** often indifferent service; somewhat run-down; no real swimming beach; spotty Wi-Fi signal. $ *Rooms from: $251* ✉ *390 S. Church St., George Town, Grand Cayman* ☎ *345/949–7111, 800/854–4767* 🌐 *www.sunsethouse.com* *58 rooms, 2 suites* 🍽 *No meals.*

4

Caribbean Club

SEVEN MILE BEACH

Most travelers to Grand Cayman choose to stay on one of the resorts or condo complexes along beautiful Seven Mile Beach. While not all properties have a beachfront location, they are mostly in close proximity to the action and nearby restaurants, nightlife, and shops.

For expanded reviews, facilities, and current deals, visit Fodors.com.

$$$ ☒ **The Anchorage.** *Rental.* Don't be deceived by the slightly dilapidated facade: this intimate resort's interiors were completely gutted and upgraded post-Ivan, and they're still a fine value. **Pros:** incredible vistas from George Town to West Bay from higher units; nice beach and snorkeling; great pool at the edge of the Caribbean. **Cons:** a bit isolated from action; boxy apartments. ⑤ *Rooms from: $310* ☒ *1989 West Bay Rd., Box 30986, Seven Mile Beach, Grand Cayman* ☎ *345/945–4088* ⊕ *www.theanchoragecayman.com* ⇆ *15 2-bedroom condos* ⦿ *No meals.*

$$$ ☒ **Aqua Bay Club.** *Rental.* One of the older condo complexes, ABC is scrupulously maintained, quiet, and affordable. **Pros:** great snorkeling very close to Cemetery Reef; friendly staff; free local calls. **Cons:** beach can be rocky; no elevator in complex. ⑤ *Rooms from: $425* ☒ *West Bay Rd., Seven Mile Beach, Grand Cayman* ☎ *345/945–4728, 800/825–8703* ⊕ *www.aquabayclub.com* ⇆ *21 units* ⦿ *No meals.*

★ Fodor'sChoice ☷ **Caribbean Club.** *Rental.* Sleek but not slick,
$$$$ this gleaming boutique facility includes a striking lobby
filled with aquariums, a stunning infinity pool, and the
aggressively contemporary trattoria, Luca. **Pros:** luxurious,
high-tech facilities beyond the typical apartment complex;
trendy Italian restaurant on-site; service on the beach.
Cons: stratospheric prices; though families are welcome,
they may find it rather imposing; smaller balconies on
top floor (albeit amazing views). ⑤ *Rooms from: $1256*
✉ *871 West Bay Rd., Seven Mile Beach, Grand Cayman*
☎ *345/623–4500, 800/941–1126* ⊕ *www.caribclub.com*
⬏ *37 3-bedroom condos* ⊙ *No meals.*

$$ ☷ **Christopher Columbus.** *Rental.* This enduring favorite is quite
☾ a discovery for families, sitting on the peaceful northern end
of Seven Mile Beach. **Pros:** excellent snorkeling from a fine
stretch of beach; great value; free Wi-Fi. **Cons:** car really
needed; often overrun by families during holiday seasons
and summer; top floors feature splendid vistas but diffi-
cult access for physically challenged. ⑤ *Rooms from: $365*
✉ *2013 West Bay Rd., Seven Mile Beach, Grand Cayman*
☎ *345/945–4354, 866/311–5231* ⊕ *www.christophercolum-
buscondos.com* ⬏ *30 2- and 3-bedroom condos* ⊙ *No meals.*

$ ☷ **Comfort Suites Grand Cayman.** *Hotel.* This no-frills, all-
suites hotel has an ideal location on West Bay Road, next
door to the Marriott and near numerous shops, restaurants,
and bars. **Pros:** affordable; nice complimentary extras like
Continental breakfast and Wi-Fi; fun, youngish crowd.
Cons: rooms nearly a block from the beach; new condo-
minium blocks sea views; no balconies; bar closes early.
⑤ *Rooms from: $208* ✉ *West Bay Rd., George Town,
Grand Cayman* ☎ *345/945–7300, 800/517–4000* ⊕ *www.
caymancomfort.com* ⬏ *108 suites* ⊙ *Breakfast.*

$$$$ ☷ **Coral Stone Club.** *Rental.* This exclusive enclave shines in
★ the shadow of the Ritz-Carlton by offering understated
barefoot luxury and huge three-bedroom condos. **Pros:**
largest ratio of beach and pool space to guests; walking
distance to several restaurants and shops; stellar service;
excellent off-season deals. **Cons:** expensive in high sea-
son; Ritz-Carlton guests sometimes wander over from
their packed section of sand trying to poach beach space.
⑤ *Rooms from: $775* ✉ *West Bay Rd., Seven Mile Beach,
Grand Cayman* ☎ *345/945–5820, 888/927–2322* ⊕ *www.
coralstoneclub.com* ⬏ *30 3-bedroom condos* ⊙ *No meals.*

$ ☷ **Discovery Point Club.** *Rental.* This older but upgraded
☾ complex of all oceanfront suites sits at the north end of
Seven Mile Beach, 6 miles (9½ km) from George Town,

Seven Mile Beach

with fabulous snorkeling in the protected waters of nearby Cemetery Reef. **Pros:** sensational snorkeling; caring staff; family-friendly; free Internet. **Cons:** car necessary to dine out and explore; beach entry is rocky in spots; studios are nothing but overpriced, glorified hotel rooms; no elevator. ⑤ *Rooms from: $250 ☒ West Bay Rd., Seven Mile Beach, Grand Cayman* ☎ *345/945–4724, 866/384–9980* ⊕ *www. discoverypointclub.com* ⤴ *37 1- and 2-bedroom condos* ⧉ *No meals.*

$$$$ ⧫ **Grand Cayman Beach Suites.** *Resort.* The former Hyatt all-suites section, now locally run, offers a terrific beachfront location and trendy eateries. **Pros:** fine beach; superior dining and water-sports facilities; free use of gym (unusual on Grand Cayman); supermarkets and restaurants within walking distance. **Cons:** most entrances face the street, making it noisy on weekends; several units need refurbishment; music often blaring around the pool. ⑤ *Rooms from: $695 ☒ West Bay Rd., Seven Mile Beach, Grand Cayman* ☎ *345/949–1234* ⊕ *www.grand-cayman-beach-suites.com and www.gcbs.ky* ⤴ *53 suites* ⧉ *No meals.*

$$ ⧫ **Grand Cayman Marriott Beach Resort.** *Resort.* The soaring,
★ stylish, if impersonal marble lobby (with exquisite art glass, spectacular blown-up underwater photos, and fun elements such as red British-style telephone boxes) sets the tone for this bustling beachfront property. **Pros:** lively bars and restaurants; good snorkeling and water sports; convenient to both George Town and Seven Mile Beach; airport con-

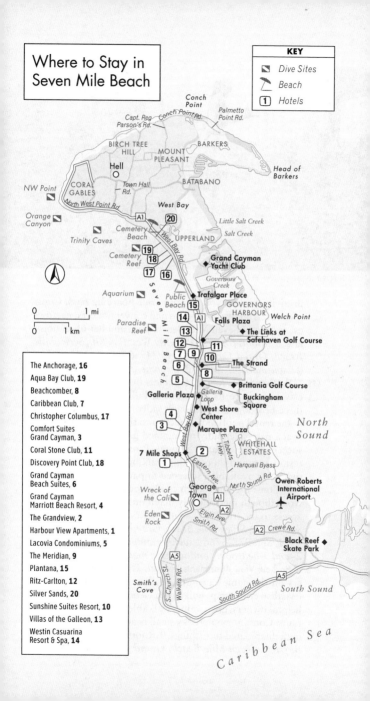

Covered chaise longues at the Ritz-Carlton Grand Cayman

nectivity enables you to print your boarding pass. **Cons:** often overrun by tour groups and conventioneers; narrowest section of Seven Mile Beach; pool and bar often noisy late. ⑤ *Rooms from: $349* ⌧ *389 West Bay Rd., Seven Mile Beach, Grand Cayman* ☎ *345/949–0088, 800/223–6388* ⊕ *www.marriott.com* ⮥ *273 rooms, 22 suites* ⑩ *No meals.*

$$$ ⌑ **The Grandview.** *Rental.* This older but well-groomed property lives up to its ostentatious billing: all 69 two- and three-bedroom units (though sadly only 15 are generally in the rental pool) look smack onto the Caribbean and the beach past splendidly maintained gardens (families play soccer on the expansive lawn). **Pros:** terrific snorkeling; restaurants and shops within walking distance; free Wi-Fi (when it's available); screened-in patios keep mosquitoes out. **Cons:** the long beach can be rocky; some units a tad worn though meticulously maintained; not all units have access to the free Wi-Fi signal. ⑤ *Rooms from: $475* ⌧ *95 Snooze La., Seven Mile Beach, Grand Cayman* ☎ *345/945–4511, 866/977–6766* ⊕ *www.grandviewcondos.com* ⮥ *69 2- and 3-bedroom condos* ⑩ *No meals.*

$ ⌑ **Harbour View Apartments.** *Rental.* This little enclave delivers on the name's promise, with smashing views of the leviathan cruise ships hulking off George Town. **Pros:** sweet, helpful owners; great value; walkable to shops and restaurants. **Cons:** no pool; rocky small beach (but great snorkeling); dilapidated furnishings. ⑤ *Rooms from: $115* ⌧ *West Bay Rd., Seven Mile Beach, Grand Cayman* ☎ *345/949–*

5681 ⊕ *www.harbourviewapartments.com* ⇔ *12 studio and 1-bedroom apartments* ⊙ *No meals.*

$$$ ☐ **Lacovia Condominiums.** *Rental.* The carefully manicured ★ courtyard of this handsome arcaded Mediterranean Revival property could easily be mistaken for a peaceful park. **Pros:** central location; exquisite gardens; extensive beach. **Cons:** rear courtyard rooms can be noisy from traffic and partying from West Bay Road; pool fairly small (though most people prefer the beach). ⑤ *Rooms from: $415* ⊠ *697 West Bay Rd., Seven Mile Beach, Grand Cayman* ☎ *345/949–7599* ⊕ *www.lacovia.com* ⇔ *35 1-, 2-, and 3-bedroom condos* ⊙ *No meals.*

$$$$ ☐ **The Meridian.** *Rental.* The lavish landscaping and neo-Edwardian architecture with gables, Palladian windows, and grillwork balconies sets the understated opulent tone. **Pros:** restaurants and supermarket right across the street; meticulously maintained; gorgeous beachfront; free calls to U.S., Canada, and U.K. **Cons:** some find it a little too popular with families; undeniably elegant but extremely pricey. ⑤ *Rooms from: $775* ⊠ *West Bay Rd., Box 30476, Seven Mile Beach, Grand Cayman* ☎ *345/945–4002* ⊕ *www. meridian.ky* ⇔ *32 2- and 3-bedroom condos* ⊙ *No meals.*

★ Fodor's Choice ☐ **Ritz-Carlton Grand Cayman.** *Resort.* Posh and
$$$$ pampering without pretension, the Ritz-Carlton offers
☾ unparalleled luxury and service infused with a welcome sense of place, including works by top local artists and craftspeople. **Pros:** exemplary service; exceptional facilities with many complimentary extras; marvelous local artworks including a corridor-length gallery with rotating exhibits. **Cons:** annoyingly high per-night resort fee; somewhat sprawling with a confusing layout; long walk to beach (over an interior bridge) from most rooms. ⑤ *Rooms from: $495* ⊠ *West Bay Rd., Seven Mile Beach, Grand Cayman* ☎ *345/943–9000* ⊕ *www.ritzcarlton.com* ⇔ *329 rooms, 12 suites, 24 condos* ⊙ *Breakfast.*

$ ☐ **Sunshine Suites Resort.** *Hotel.* This friendly, all-suites hotel is an impeccably clean money saver. **Pros:** good value and deals; cheerful staff; rocking little restaurant; thoughtful free extras. **Cons:** poor views; not on the beach. ⑤ *Rooms from: $202* ⊠ *1465 Esterley Tibbetts Hwy., off West Bay Rd., Seven Mile Beach, Grand Cayman* ☎ *345/949–3000, 877/786–1110* ⊕ *www.sunshinesuites.com* ⇔ *130 suites* ⊙ *Breakfast.*

$$$ ☐ **Villas of the Galleon.** *Rental.* People often overlook this
☾ gem because of the lack of pool and its ersatz Greek-isle look (white stucco with turquoise roofs). **Pros:** affable

management; central location; glorious beach. **Cons:** no pool; slightly boxy room configuration; one-bedroom units do not have a washer/dryer. Ⓢ *Rooms from: $420* ✉ *West Bay Rd., Box 1797, Seven Mile Beach, Grand Cayman* ☎ *345/945–4433, 866/665–4696* ⊕ *www.villasofthegalleon. com* ➳ *74 1-, 2-, and 3-bedroom condos* ⑩ *No meals.*

$$ ⑪ **Westin Casuarina Resort and Spa.** *Resort.* The Westin has
☾ something to offer everyone, from conventioneers to honeymooners to families, not to mention an excellent location. **Pros:** terrific children's programs; superb beach (the largest resort stretch at 800 feet). **Cons:** occasionally bustling and impersonal when large groups book. Ⓢ *Rooms from: $369* ✉ *West Bay Rd., Box 30620, Seven Mile Beach, Grand Cayman* ☎ *345/945–3800, 800/937–8461* ⊕ *www. westincasuarina.net* ➳ *339 rooms, 8 suites* ⑩ *No meals.*

WEST BAY

For those who are willing to be out of the thick of things yet who still want fairly close proximity to Seven Mile Beach, there are a handful of resorts and condo rentals available in West Bay. Some of these even have waterfront locations, though they are fronted by ironshore rather than a sandy white beach.

For expanded reviews, facilities, and current deals, visit Fodors.com.

$$ ⑪ **Cobalt Coast Resort and Suites.** *Resort.* This small eco-
★ friendly hotel is perfect for divers who want a sparkling, spacious room or suite right on the ironshore far, far from the madding crowds and who don't want to pay high prices. **Pros:** superb dive outfit; friendly service and clientele; free Wi-Fi; environmentally aware. **Cons:** poky golden-sand beach; unattractive concrete pool area; remote location, so a car (included in some packages) is necessary. Ⓢ *Rooms from: $290* ✉ *18-A Sea Fan Dr., West Bay, Grand Cayman* ☎ *345/946–5656, 888/946–5656* ⊕ *www.cobaltcoast.com* ➳ *7 rooms, 14 suites* ⑩ *Multiple meal plans.*

$$$$ ⑪ **Cotton Tree.** *Rental.* The motto of this exclusive villa
★ enclave in tranquil West Bay could easily be "If luxe could kill." **Pros:** peaceful and quiet setting; beautifully designed and outfitted accommodations; complimentary airport transfers; wonderful immersion in local culture. **Cons:** luxury comes with a price tag; remote location means a car is required; beach narrow and tangled with sea grape trees. Ⓢ *Rooms from: $890* ✉ *375 Conch Point Rd., West Bay,*

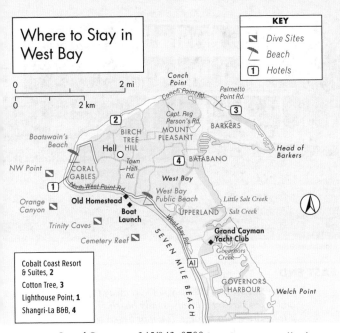

Where to Stay in West Bay

KEY	
🤿	Dive Sites
⚓	Beach
①	Hotels

0   2 mi
0   2 km

Conch Point

Palmetto Point Rd.

Conch Point Rd.

Capt. Reg Parson's Rd.

BARKERS

③

Boatswain's Beach

BIRCH TREE HILL

MOUNT PLEASANT

Head of Barkers

Hell

②

Town Hall Rd.

④ BATABANO

NW Point

CORAL GABLES

North West Point Rd.

West Bay

①

Old Homestead

West Bay Public Beach

Little Salt Creek

Salt Creek

Orange Canyon

Boat Launch

UPPERLAND

Trinity Caves

Grand Cayman Yacht Club

Cemetery Reef

SEVEN MILE BEACH

Governors Creek

West Bay Rd.

GOVERNORS HARBOUR

Welch Point

A1

Cobalt Coast Resort & Suites, 2

Cotton Tree, 3

Lighthouse Point, 1

Shangri-La B&B, 4

Grand Cayman ☎ 345/943–0700 ⊕ *www.caymancottontree. com* ⇨ *4 2-bedroom cottages* ⊘ *Closed Sept.* ⦿ *No meals.*

★ **Fodor's Choice** 🏨 **Lighthouse Point.** *Resort.* For travelers who
$$$ want to "live lightly on the planet," leading scuba operator DiveTech's stunning new development takes the lead, from sustainable wood interiors and recycled concrete to an eco-sensitive gray-water system, energy-saving appliances and lights, and Cayman's first wind turbine generator. **Pros:** eco-friendly; fantastic shore diving (and state-of-the-art dive shop); creative and often recycled upscale look. **Cons:** no real beach; car necessary; bit difficult for physically challenged to navigate. ⑤ *Rooms from: $450* ⊠ *571 N.W. Point Rd., West Bay, Grand Cayman* ☎ 345/949–1700 ⊕ *www.lighthouse-point-cayman.com* ⇨ *9 2-bedroom apartments* ⦿ *No meals.*

$ 🏨 **Shangri-La B&B.** *B&B/Inn.* Accomplished pianist George
★ Davidson and wife Eileen built this lavish lakeside retreat and truly make guests feel at home, along with dogs Roxie and Stella. **Pros:** use of kitchen; elegant decor. **Cons:** rental car necessary; not on the beach. ⑤ *Rooms from: $149* ⊠ *1 Sticky Toffee Lane, West Bay, Grand Cayman* ☎ 345/526–1170 ⊕ *www.shangrilabandb.com* ⇨ *6 rooms, 1 apartment* ⦿ *Breakfast.*

Lighthouse Point

EAST END

A stay in East End allows you to get away from the crowds and often stay on a lovely, sandy beach. The downside is a long drive into George Town or Seven Mile Beach of at least a half hour or 40 minutes.

For expanded reviews, facilities, and current deals, visit Fodors.com.

$$ ⊤ **Compass Point Dive Resort.** *Resort.* This tranquil, congenial
★ little getaway run by the admirable Ocean Frontiers scuba operation would steer even nondivers in the right direction. **Pros:** top-notch dive operation; good value especially with packages; affable international staff and clientele. **Cons:** no restaurant or bar; isolated location requires a car. ⑤ *Rooms from: $295* ⊠ *Austin Conolly Dr., East End, Grand Cayman* ☎ *345/947–7500, 800/348–6096, 345/947–0000* ⊕ *www. compasspoint.ky* ⮡ *17 1-bedroom, 9 2-bedroom, and 3 3-bedroom condos* ⊺⊙⊺ *No meals.*

★ **Fodor's** Choice ⊤ **Reef Resort.** *All-Inclusive.* This exceedingly
$$ well-run time-share property (don't worry: no aggressive hawking!) seductively straddles a 600-foot beach on the less hectic East End. **Pros:** romantically remote; glorious beach; enthusiastic staff (including a crackerjack wedding coordinator); great packages. **Cons:** remote; few dining options within easy driving distance; sprawling layout. ⑤ *Rooms from: $351* ⊠ *Queen's Hwy., East End, Grand Cayman*

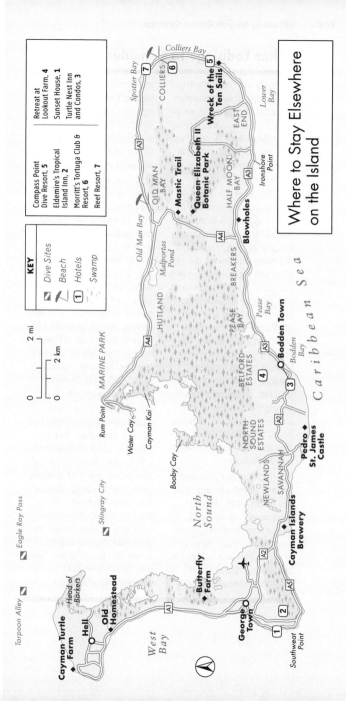

Where to Stay Elsewhere on the Island

KEY

- Dive Sites
- Beach
- **1** Hotels
- Swamp

Compass Point Dive Resort, **5**
Eldemire's Tropical Island Inn, **2**
Morritt's Tortuga Club & Resort, **6**
Reef Resort, **7**

Retreat at Lookout Farm, **4**
Sunset House, **1**
Turtle Nest Inn and Condos, **3**

Other Lodgings to Consider

Obviously, we can't include every property deserving mention without creating an encyclopedia. Our favorites receive full reviews, but you might consider the following accommodations, many of them equally meritorious.

Beachcomber. Beachcomber rose phoenixlike post-Ivan as a glam high-rise with 40 spacious 2- to 4-bedroom condos (roughly 24 in the rental pool). The decor is high-end, the amenities and appliances high-tech, and there's free underground parking, long distance calls to North America, and Wi-Fi; HDTV with DVD, a washer/dryer, and a dishwasher. The beach is gorgeous, and the location is ideal (walking distance to groceries and restaurants). It compares favorably to neighbors Caribbean Club and Meridian. ⊠ West Bay Rd., Seven Mile Beach, Grand Cayman ☎ 345/943–6500 ⊕ www.beachcomber.ky.

Morritt's Tortuga Club and Resort. Morritt's Tortuga Club and Resort offers 146 well-maintained, fully equipped, mostly time-share units, albeit many lacking beach views and/or access (the best and priciest are branded "Grand Resort"). The more than adequate activities and amenities include the respected Tortuga Divers outfit. It's right next door to the Reef Resort. ⊠ East End, Grand Cayman ☎ 345/947–7449, 800/447–0309 ⊕ www.morritts.com.

Plantana. Plantana is exceedingly lush, set on a stunning stretch of sand with smashing views of the leviathan ships lumbering into George Town and permeated with the sounds of surf and birdsong. The 49 individually decorated 1- to 3-bedroom units are fully outfitted (including washer/dryers and Wi-Fi) and handsomely appointed, with designs running from contemporary to colonial, even Asian-inspired. ⊠ 1293 West Bay Rd., Seven Mile Beach, Grand Cayman ☎ 345/945–4430 ⊕ www.plantanacayman.com.

Silver Sands. Silver Sands is an older compound that anchors the quieter northernmost end of Seven Mile Beach, with terrific snorkeling off the spectacular sweep of glittering sand. Most of the 42 cramped units have balconies with fabulous views; second-floor units with vaulted ceilings are preferable. ⊠ West Bay Rd., Seven Mile Beach, Grand Cayman ☎ 345/949–3343 ⊕ www.silversandscondos.com.

The Reef Resort

☎ 345/947–3100, 888/232–0541 ⊕ www.thereef.com.ky and www.thereef.com ⇨ 152 suites ⊙ Multiple meal plans.

$ ⊡ **Retreat at Lookout Farm.** *B&B/Inn.* *Peaceful* is an overused word, yet it sums up the appeal of this difficult-to-find, back-to-nature hideaway swallowed up in 20 acres of foliage off the main road. **Pros:** utter peace and quiet; genuine Caymanian ambience and warmth; wonderful breakfasts. **Cons:** car needed; no cooking facilities; hard to find and comparatively far from most tourist attractions and top beaches. ⑤ *Rooms from: $149* ⊠ *521 Lookout Rd., Bodden Town, Grand Cayman* ☎ *345/947–2386, 705/719–9144* ⊕ *www.retreatatlookout.com* ⇨ *8* ⊙ *Breakfast.*

$$ ⊡ **Turtle Nest Inn and Condos.** *Rental.* This affordable, inti-
★ mate, Mediterranean-style seaside inn has roomy one-bedroom apartments and a pool overlooking a narrow beach with good snorkeling. **Pros:** wonderful snorkeling; thoughtful extras; caring staff; free Wi-Fi. **Cons:** car necessary; occasional rocks and debris on beach; ground-floor room views slightly obscured by palms; road noise in back rooms. ⑤ *Rooms from: $149* ⊠ *166 Bodden Town Rd., Bodden Town, Grand Cayman* ☎ *345/947–8665* ⊕ *www.turtlenestinn.net* ⇨ *8 apartments, 10 2-bedroom condos* ⊙ *No meals.*

Grand Cayman Nightlife and the Arts

WORD OF MOUTH

"[I]f you plan on hitting the Ritz on Friday night . . . take something hip and stylish. A sexy sequin top, nice pants, and hot shoes, with an evening bag for women. Hip collared shirt, linen or black pants, nice shoes for men."

—lukesaunt

By Jordan
Simon

DESPITE GRAND CAYMAN'S CONSERVATISM AND small size, the nightlife scene looms surprisingly large, especially on weekends. Choices include boisterous beach-and-brew hangouts, swanky wine bars, pool halls, sports bars, jammed and jamming dance clubs, live entertainment, and cultural events. A smoking ban was instituted in 2010 for nightspots and restaurants (one preexisting cigar bar and a hookah lounge received special dispensation).

Most major resorts, clubs, and bars offer some kind of performance, including lavish rum-and-reggae limbo/fire-eating/stilt-walking extravaganzas. Local bands with a fan(atic) following include soft-rock duo Hi-Tide; the Pandemonium Steelband; reggae-influenced trio Swanky; hard rockers Ratskyn (who've opened for REO Speedwagon, Mötley Crüe, and Bon Jovi); blues/funk purveyors Madamspeaker; and neo-punk rockers the Blow Holes. Other names to look for are Musical Crew, Sucker Box, Ka, Noel's Band, Wild Knights, Island Vibes, Exit, 45 C.I., Lammie, Heat, Gone Country, and Coco Red.

Consult the "Get Out" section in the Friday edition of the *Caymanian Compass* for listings of live music, movies, theater, and other entertainment. Local magazines such as *Key to Cayman, What's Hot,* and *Destination Cayman* can be picked up free of charge around the island, sometimes providing coupons for discounts and/or freebies. Bars remain open until 1 AM, and clubs are generally open from 10 PM until 3 AM, but they can't serve liquor after midnight on Saturday or permit dancing on Sundays. While shorts and sarongs are usually acceptable attire at beachside bars, smart casual defines the dress code for clubbing.

TIPSY TIPS. Don't drive and drink! Local police set sobriety checkpoints in heavily trafficked areas. The law is strict, the punishment (fine and/or prison) harsh. Revel away: The watering holes will happily pour you into a taxi. Or stick to the walkable cluster of bars in George Town and along Seven Mile Beach. Staggering isn't illegal, just embarrassing.

BEST BETS

■ **A Smokin' Time.** Even if you're not into stogies, Grand Cayman's cigar and wine bars are civilized hangouts where you might see stars or over-hear insider trading tips.

■ **Local Rhythms.** Cayman's musicians have fanatic followings; it's worth a trip to The Reef for the hilarious Barefoot Man. Lammie, Coco Red, Karen Edie, Gary Ebanks & Intransit, and Hi-Tide are other memorable musicians.

■ **Fish Feedings.** It's touristy, but watching tarpons pirouet-

ting for bait at sunset reels even locals into waterfront watering holes.

■ **Culture Vultures.** If you want a real feel for Cayman life, take in an original play, particularly such annual special performances and festivals as Rundown and Gimistory.

■ **Full Moon Parties.** Various beach bars host celebrations with almost pagan abandon, and these parties are over-flowing with cocktails and camaraderie.

5

GEORGE TOWN

BARS AND MUSIC CLUBS

Hammerheads Brew Pub and Grill. The popular restaurant and bar, adorned with fab old-timer photos and surfboards doubling as signs, offers a classic Cayman sight: fishers anchor their boats right offshore and display their catch right outside (condo and villa renters, head here if you're in the market for fresh fish!). This is also a prime pyrotechnic sunset- and cruise-ship-watching spot, where locals laze in locally carved chairs, slowly getting hammered from the house microbrews, on the vast thatch-shaded, tiered deck. Stop by the Swanky Shack by the entrance for cool T-shirts and island gossip. ⊠ *N. Church St., George Town, Grand Cayman* ☎ *345/949–3080.*

Hard Rock Café. Grand Cayman's Hard Rock replicates its 137-odd brethren around the world, only with more spe-cialty drinks (try the Orangelicious margarita with Monin pomegranate and blood-orange juices) to complement its extensive burger selection (the Red White and Blue—crum-bled blue cheese, Cajun seasoning, and Buffalo sauce—is surprisingly tasty). The usual T-shirts, plasma-screen TVs streaming videos, and rotating memorabilia (including gold records, glasses, costumes, and autographed photos from the likes of Elton John, John Lennon, Madonna, U2, and *NSYNC before Justin broke out and Lance came out) are the decor. In truth, it only rocks hard on weekends, when the bar can be a prime Grade-A meet market. ✉ *43 S. Church St., George Town, Grand Cayman* ☎ *345/945–2020.*

Margaritaville. Grand Cayman's Margaritaville is a vast upstairs space that usually bustles with life (especially down its Green Monster waterslide); the Friday-evening happy hour is especially popular, with an overgrown frat-party ambience, and though drinks may be a bit pricier than at other waterfront locations, the jollity definitely compensates. It closes early except on Friday nights. ✉ *Island Village, Cardinal Ave., George Town, Grand Cayman* ☎ *345/949–6274.*

★ **My Bar.** This bar is optimally perched on the water's edge, looking almost due west with a perfect vantage point for watching the sunset. The leviathan open-sided cabana is drenched in vivid Rasta colors and crowned by an intricate South Seas–style thatched roof (containing approximately 36,000 palm fronds). Christmas lights and the occasional customer dangle from the rafters year-round. Great grub and a mischievous mix of locals, expats, and tourists from all walks of life prove that ecocentric Cayman offers wild life alongside the wildlife. ✉ *Sunset House, S. Church St., George Town, Grand Cayman* ☎ *345/949–7111* ⊕ *www.sunsethouse.com.*

Rackam's Waterfront Pub and Restaurant. A Cayman mosaic of fishermen to Who's-the-Hugo-Boss financiers savors sensational sunsets followed by exuberantly pirouetting tarpon feeding at the open-air, marine-theme happenin' bar built on a jetty jutting into the harbor (boaters, even snorkelers cruise right up the ladder for drinks while anglers leave their catch on ice) that has complimentary snacks on Friday and serves pub fare at fair prices until midnight. ✉ *93 N. Church St., George Town, Grand Cayman* ☎ *345/945–3860* ⊕ *www.rackamswaterfront.ky.*

Royal Palms. The Royal Palms is where notable local bands like Coco Red and Footloose gig weekend nights and DJs make waves on Wednesday's Industry Chill evenings; it's an outdoor beach bar with plenty of room for dancing under the stars and a great Sunday-afternoon hangout to socialize, sit in the sun (or at the swim-up bar), and listen to music. ✉ *West Bay Rd., George Town, Grand Cayman* ☎ *345/945–6358.*

The Wharf. You can dance near the water to mellow music on Saturday evenings; when there's a wedding reception in the pavilion, the crashing surf and candles twinkling as if competing with the stars bathe the proceedings in an almost Gatsby-esque glow. For something less sedate, Roger and Sarah conduct sizzling salsa dancing and lessons on Tuesdays after dinner, while most Fridays morph into a wild 1970s disco night. The stunning seaside setting on tiered decks compensates for often-undistinguished food and service. The Ports of Call bar is a splendid place for sunset fanciers, and tarpon feeding off the deck is a nightly 9 pm spectacle. ⊠ *West Bay Rd., George Town, Grand Cayman* ☎ *345/949–2231.*

SEVEN MILE BEACH

BARS AND MUSIC CLUBS

★ **Aqua Beach Bar.** This place feels like a country bar gone (coco)nuts: palm trees burst through thatching; art naïf portraits of musicians explode in neon reds, yellows, blues, and greens; private tiki huts provide intimacy; and neon beer signs illuminate the wood paneling. Fairly good Tex-Mex fare is dished out late. There's a variety of live bands, open-mike nights, and theme nights, such as Thursday acoustic jams. Also, there are plenty of daily drink-and-eat specials such as Sunday's NASCAR Bud buckets. ⊠ *426 West Bay Rd., Seven Mile Beach, Grand Cayman* ☎ *345/949–8498.*

★ **The Attic.** The Attic is a chic sports bar with three billiard tables, classic arcade games (Space Invaders, Donkey Kong), air hockey, and large-screen TVs (you can nab a private booth with its own flat-panel job). Events encompass daily happy hours, trivia nights, and the Caribbean's reputedly largest Bloody Mary bar on Sunday. Along with downstairs sister hot spot "O" Bar, it's ground zero for the Wednesday Night Drinking Club. For a $25 initiation fee (you get a T-shirt and personalized leather wristband, toga optional) and $10 weekly activity fee, you'll be shuttled by bus to several different bars, with free shots and drinks specials all night. ⊠ *Queen's Court, 2nd fl., West Bay Rd., Seven Mile Beach, Grand Cayman* ☎ *345/949–7665* ⊕ *www.attic.ky.*

★ **Calico Jack's.** For a casual drink, visit this friendly outdoor beach bar at the north end of the public beach with a DJ on Saturday and open-mike night on Tuesday, bands many Friday nights, and riotous parties during the full moon when even Ritz-Carlton guests let their hair and inhibitions down. ⊠ *West Bay Rd., Seven Mile Beach, Grand Cayman* ☎ *345/945–7850.*

Caymans Captivating Carnival

CLOSE UP

Held annually during the first week of May (or the week after Easter), the four-day **Batabano Cayman Carnival** (⊕ *www.caymancarnival.com*) is the island's boisterous answer to Mardi Gras, not to mention Carnival in Rio and Trinidad. Though not as hedonistic, the pyrotechnic pageantry, electricity, and enthralled throngs are unrivaled (except for during Pirates Week). Events include a carnival ball, soca and calypso song competitions, massive Mas (masquerade) parade with ornate floats, street dance, and a beach fete. The festivities are enhanced by tasty concession stands offering Caymanian and other Caribbean cuisine and delicacies.

The word *batabano* refers to the tracks that turtles leave as they heave onto beaches to nest. Locating those tracks was reason to celebrate in the olden times, when turtling was a major part of the economy, so it seemed an appropriate tribute to the islands' heritage, alongside the traditional Caribbean celebration of the region's African roots. Indeed, many of the increasingly elaborate costumes are inspired by Cayman's majestic marine life and maritime history from parrots to pirates, though some offer provocative social commentary. Thousands of revelers line the streets each year cheering their favorite masqueraders and boogying to the Mas steel pan and soca bands. The organizers also hold a stand-alone street parade for Cayman's youth called Junior Carnival Batabano the weekend before the adult parade. Equally exciting, it stresses the importance of teaching students the art of costume making and Mas, ensuring Carnival won't become another dying Caymanian custom.

Coconut Joe's. You can sit at the bar or swing under a century-old poinciana tree and watch the traffic go by. There are murals of apes everywhere, from gorillas doing shots to a baboon in basketball uniform (in keeping with management's facetious suggestion that you attract your server's attention by pounding your chest while screeching and scratching yourself). It's particularly popular with the younger tourism- and hospitality-industry crowds (ply them with beers for some hair- and eyebrow-raising backstage stories). Friday really swings with DJs and free happy-hour munchies. ✉ *Across from Comfort Suites, West Bay Rd., Seven Mile Beach, Grand Cayman* ☎ *345/943–5637.*

Calico Jack's Bar and Grill

Deckers. Always bustling and bubbly, Deckers takes its name from the red English double-decker bus that forms the focal point of the main outdoor bar. You can luxuriate indoors on cushy sofas over a chess game and signature blood-orange mojito; hack your way through the 18-hole safari miniature-golf course; find a secluded nook in the garden terrace framed by towering palms, old-fashioned ornate streetlamps, and colonial columns; or groove to the easy-listening potpourri of pop, reggae, blues, and country courtesy of the Hi-Tide duo. Worthy Carib-Mediterranean fusion cuisine is a bonus (try the Caribbean lobster mac 'n' cheese or the Portabello vodka-lime risotto). ⊠ *West Bay Rd., Seven Mile Beach, Grand Cayman* ☎ *345/945–6600* ⊕ *www.deckers.ky.*

Fidel Murphy's Irish Pub. This pub has an unusual logo, a stogie-smoking Castro surrounded by shamrocks. Indeed, the congenial Irish wit and whimsy are so thick that you half expect to find Fidel and Gerry Adams harping on U.S. and U.K. policy over a Harp. The pub's Edwardian decor of etched glass, hardwood, and brass may be prefabricated (it was constructed in Ireland, disassembled, and shipped), but everything else is genuine, from the warm welcome to the ales and cider on tap to the proper Irish stew (though the kitchen also turns out conch fritters and chicken tandoori wraps). Sunday and Monday host all-you-can-eat extravaganzas (fish-and-chips, carvery) at rock-bottom prices. Weekends welcome live televised Gaelic soccer, rugby, and hurling, followed by karaoke and *craic* (if you go, you'll learn the definition soon enough). ✉ *Queen's Court, West Bay Rd., Seven Mile Beach, Grand Cayman* ☎ *345/949–5189.*

Legendz. A sports bar with a clubby, retro feel (Marilyn Monroe and Frank Sinatra photos channel the glamour days), it's the usual testosterone test drive with plentiful scoring of both types. Good luck wrestling a spot at the bar for Pay-Per-View and major live sporting events (though 10 TVs, including two 6-by-8 foot, high-resolution screens broadcast to every corner). It doubles as an entertainment venue, booking local bands, stand-up comics, and leading island DJs. ✉ *Falls Centre, West Bay Rd., Seven Mile Beach, Grand Cayman.*

Lone Star Bar and Grill. The bar and restaurant proudly calls itself Cayman's top dive (and indeed, locals from dive masters to dentists get down and occasionally dirty over kick-ass margaritas). The noisy bar glorifies sports, Texas, T&A, and the boob tube, from murals of Cowboys cheerleaders to an amazing sports memorabilia collection (including items signed by both Bushes), and 14 big-screen TVs tuned to different events. ✉ *686 West Bay Rd., Seven Mile Beach, Grand Cayman* ☎ *345/945–5175* ⊕ *www. lonestarcayman.com.*

Stingers Resort and Pool Bar. Stingers Resort and Pool Bar offers tasty food in an appealing setting (check out the stupendous "stinger" mosaic), with cover-free live music and dancing Thursday and Friday. Wednesday and Saturday nights, there's a very affordable all-you-can-eat Caribbean luau. The band Heat, a local institution, sizzles with energetic, emotionally delivered calypso, reggae, soca, salsa, and oldies; then the limbo dancers and fire-eaters keep the temperature rising. If you recoil from audience participation, stay far away. More exhibitionistic "spring break" sorts might find their photo adorning the "Wall of Shame," but the worst blackmail is persuading you to buy another blue-green Stingers punch. ✉ *Comfort Suites, West Bay Rd., Seven Mile Beach, Grand Cayman* ☎ *345/945–3000.*

CIGAR AND WINE LOUNGES

★ **Bamboo Lounge.** Come here for the quiet, refined, but theatrically designed bar with sublime sushi (and other Asian standbys) and luscious libations (with suggestive names like Foreplay and Love Potion #69) abetted by an extensive wine and sake list. You can roll what you eat during

A wall mural at the Havana Club Restaurant and Cigar Lounge

Master Sushi Chef Wonhee's cooking demonstrations at 5:30 Fridays. The musical menu runs from jazz (luring couples conducting affairs both personal and professional) to DJ nights, when younger soigné singles sweat elegantly on the minuscule dance floor. ✉ *Grand Cayman Beach Suites, West Bay Rd., Seven Mile Beach, Grand Cayman* ☎ *345/947–8744* ⊕ *www.grand-cayman-beach-suites.com.*

★ **Havana Club Restaurant and Cigar Lounge.** The latest venture from Cubano-phile Raglan Roper, who sailed his boat from Florida to Grand Cayman 20 years ago, stopping off along the way, serves authentic Cuban cuisine (scrumptious steak in garlic sauce and near-definitive black-bean soup). Ironically, it's smoke-free, though you can purchase not just Cuban cigars but cigarettes (there's a small adjacent hut for fuming). The back lounge is intimate, with back-to-the-future touches like curved bars and chartreuse walls amid the handsome mahogany furnishings. Live jazz and blues animate the evenings from Thursday through Saturday. A state-of-the-art ventilation system ensures the air remains clean. Best of all is meeting and admiring the dexterity of septuagenarian Jesus Lara Perez, the in-house *torcedor,* or cigar roller, who started working in Cuban factories when he was 14 and has since traveled from the Bahamas to Belgium demonstrating his craft. ✉ *Regency Court, 672 West Bay Rd., Seven Mile Beach, Grand Cayman* ☎ *345/945–5391* ⊕ *www.havanaclub-cigars.com.*

Calling All Corsairs

For 11 days in November, Grand Cayman is transformed into a nonstop, fun-filled festivity every bit as flamboyant as Johnny Depp's Jack Sparrow performances. The annual **Pirates Week Festival** (⊕ www.piratesweekfestival.com) is the country's largest celebration, encompassing more than 30 different events, including street dances, five heritage days (where various districts showcase their unique craft and culinary traditions), a float parade, landing pageant, fireworks, song contests, costume competitions, cardboard-boat regattas, golf tournaments, swim meets, autocross, races, kids' fun day, teen music nights, underwater treasure hunt, and more.

Everyone gets involved in the high-spirited high jinks (for example, dive boats stage mock battles and play practical jokes like filling the decks of "rivals" with cornflakes or jam, while swashbucklers "capture" hotel employees and guests). The opening night is an explosion of sights and sounds, from fireworks to rocking, rollicking bands that keep thousands shaking booty in the George Town streets into the wee hours of the morning. Later in the week, another highlight is the mock pirate invasion of Hog Sty Bay and the spirited defense of the capital, culminating in the buccaneers' trial and extravagantly costumed street parades with ornate floats.

Most of the major events are free. The music sizzles, and the evening functions feature heaping helpings of yummy, affordable local fare (turtle stew, conch, jerk chicken). Given the enormous popularity of the festival, travelers should make reservations for hotel rooms and rental cars well in advance. Even taxis are in short supply for those wanting to attend the farther-flung heritage days. Hotels, shops, and the festival's administrative office do a brisk biz in corsair couture (though you can bring your own stuffed parrot and patch; just leave the sword at home).

Nectar. Don't let the location of Nectar, which is in the back of a plain strip mall, fool you. This is a chic New York–style martini lounge and sushi bar with a tapestry of tapas on tap and more than 30 different drinks—including many 'tinis with 'tude. Choose from bar, tall tables, or sofas in the sleek, slick, mostly black-and-white space with chrome accents and blue lighting. There's new art on the walls every month, DJs spinning Thursday and Friday, and special shisha (hookah) evenings. ⊠ *Seven Mile Shops,*

Seven Mile Beach, Grand Cayman ☎ *345/946–3496* ⊕ *www. nectarcayman.com.*

★ **Silver Palm Lounge.** The Silver Palm drips with cash and cachet. One section faithfully replicates a classic English country library (perfect for civilized, proper afternoon tea or a pre- or postdinner Champagne or single malt). Then there's the sexy, überhip, black-clad Taikun lounge, with hardwood wainscoting, carved bamboo, marble floors, lacquer tables, and model (in both senses) waitstaff. Also on tap: fab cocktails, including specialty martinis (the Silver Palm cosmopolitan is a winner—Ketel One citron, triple sec, a squeeze of fresh lime juice, and a splash of cranberry topped off with Moët Champagne); pages of wines by the glass; an impressive list of cigars, cognacs, and aged rums; and marvelous sushi and creative tapas. Everyone's chic-by-jowl after 10 pm, especially on funked-out DJ Fridays, when Arab sheiks mingle with American CEOs, and tonsorially challenged agent-types wear trophy wives (and mistresses) on their arms like Rolexes: it puts the sin in scintillating. ⊠ *Ritz-Carlton, West Bay Rd., Seven Mile Beach, Grand Cayman* ☎ *345/943–9000.*

DANCE CLUBS

JET. For a rowdy time, zoom into this late-night, yup-scaled, slim-hipper-than-thou version of previous tenant Next Level that delivers a dancing high, spinning everything from retro remixes to hip-hop for Jessica Alba wannabes poured into spandex and Gap poster-boy slackers (potential hell for anyone over 30 years old or 20% body fat). ⊠ *West Bay Rd., opposite Marriott, Seven Mile Beach, Grand Cayman* ☎ *345/324–0221* ⊕ *www.jet.ky.*

★ **"O" Bar.** "O" Bar is a trendy black-and-crimson, industrial-style dance club with mixed music and juggling, flame-throwing bartenders—practically local celebs—flipping cocktails with cojones every night. It's as close to a stand-and-pose milieu as you'll find on Cayman, with the occasional fashion fascist parading in Prada. An upper-level private loft is available by reservation. ⊠ *Queen's Court, West Bay Rd., Seven Mile Beach, Grand Cayman* ☎ *345/943–6227* ⊕ *www.obar.ky.*

WEST BAY

BARS AND MUSIC CLUBS

★ **Macabuca Oceanside Tiki Bar.** A classic hip-hopping happening beach bar, Macabuca has a huge deck over the water, thatched roof, amazing Asian-inspired mosaic murals of waves, spectacular sunsets (and sunset-colored libations), and tiki torches illuminating the reef fish come evening. Macabuca means "What does it matter?" in the indigenous Antillean Taíno language, perfectly encapsulating the mellow vibe. Big-screen TVs, live bands on weekends, excellent pub grub, and daily specials (CI$7 jerk dishes weekends; Monday all-night happy hour, DJ, and CI$15 all-you-can-eat barbecue) lure everyone from well-heeled loafers to barefoot bodysurfers animatedly discussing current events and dive currents in a Babel of tongues. ⊠ *Northwest Point Rd., West Bay, Grand Cayman* ☎ *345/945–5217* ⊕ *www.crackedconch.com.ky.*

Rusty Pelican. This spot draws an eclectic group of dive masters, expats, honeymooners, and mingling singles. The knockout, colorful cocktails pack quite a punch, making the sunset last for hours. The bar dialogue is entertainment enough, but don't miss local legend, country-calypsonian Barefoot Man, when he plays "upstairs" at Pelican's Reef—he's to Cayman what Jimmy Buffett is to Key West. ⊠ *Reef Resort, Colliers, East End, Grand Cayman* ☎ *345/947–3100* ⊕ *www.thereef.com.ky.*

★ **South Coast Bar and Grill.** South Coast Bar and Grill is a delightful seaside slice of old Cayman (grizzled regulars slamming down dominoes, fabulous sea views, old model cars, karaoke nights, Friday-night dances to local legend Lammie's beats, local Elvis impersonator Errol Dunbar, and reasonably priced local eats like barbecued ribs and fried crabs). It's also a big politico hangout ("that big shark mural ain't just about nature," one bartender cackled), attested to by the fascinating photos, some historical, of local scenes and personalities. The juke jives, from Creedence Clearwater Revival to Mighty Sparrow. ⊠ *Breakers, East End, Grand Cayman* ☎ *345/947–2517.*

Barefoot Man

H. George Nowak, aka "Barefoot Man," is hardly your ordinary Calypsonian. The blond-haired German-born, self-described "Nashville musical reject" moved from Munich to North Carolina after his mother remarried an Air Force officer. But "the inveterate map lover" dreamed of island life.

He started his island-hopping career in the U.S. Virgin Islands, then Hawaii, then the Bahamas ("the smaller, less populated, the better"), finally settling in the Cayman Islands in 1971. "'But there's nothing there,' people said. I replied, 'That's the point!'" Needless to say, Barefoot prefers the casual lifestyle.

He quickly realized that the audience "didn't want 'Folsom Prison Blues,' they wanted 'Banana Boat Song.'" He was dubbed Barefoot Boy ("since the nicest pair of footwear I owned were my Voit diving flippers") in 1971. While he'll still throw in a country or blues tune, Barefoot came to love the calypso tradition, especially its double entendres and political commentary. His witty ditties say it all: "Thong Gone Wrong," "Ship Faced," "The Gay Cruise Ship Song," and "Save the Lap Dance for Me."

One of the most passionate, outspoken, articulate expats on the subject of sustainable tourism, he wittily rants in song and print (including his own self-published *Fun News*, the überglossy coffee-table *Grand Cayman* magazine, and hilarious tomes like *Which Way to the Islands?*). "I've seen the island go from three taxi drivers to, I think, 380 in the taxi association... saw how the first high-rise, the former Holiday Inn, changed Cayman irrevocably in the '70s.... I compare tourism to aspirin—a couple are okay, but take the whole bottle, you die," he jokes (mostly).

He'll regale you between sets or over beers with colorful (expletive deleted) anecdotes of island life, recounting adventures from a bogus murder charge in the Bahamas to the necessity of scheduling spliff breaks when recording in Jamaica to being mistaken for a DEA agent.

Barefoot sums up his philosophy simply and eloquently in one of his most popular lyrics (add gentle reggae-ish lilt), "I wish I were a captain, Sailin' on the sea. I'd sail out to an island, Take you there with me. I'd throw away the compass, Oh what a dirty scheme.... Someday I might wake up, realize where I am, dreamin' like some 10-year-old, out in Disneyland, There is no tomorrow when you're living in a dream."

Preserving Caymans Cultural Heritage

Several worthy organizations are dedicated to keeping Caymanian traditions alive, including the National Trust of the Cayman Islands, which restores historic buildings and offers craft demonstrations and talks. The Cayman National Cultural Foundation mounts storytelling, musical, dance, and theatrical presentations, as well as readings and art exhibits that respect the "old ways" while seeking new forms of expression. The National Gallery also seeks to ensure vibrant vital world-class artistic development.

Respected local artist Chris Christian (who curates the Ritz-Carlton Gallery exhibits), co-founded **Cayman Traditional Arts** (*CTA ⊠ 60 W. Church St., West Bay* ☎ *345/946–0117* ⊕ *artcayman.blogspot.com*),

which offers interactive classes for children and adults interested in learning authentic Caymanian arts, crafts, and recipes: Thatch weaving, kite making, gig making and spinning, rope making, and an old-style cook-out on the wood-burning oven called a caboose are just some of the topics. The network of freelance artisans has practiced these traditional crafts and customs their entire lives, often handed down over several generations, and represent the best in their disciplines. You really get hands-on in CTA's "living museum" headquarters, a 1917 mauve-and-mint wattle-and-daub cottage with ironwood posts that also doubles as a studio for Chris and Carly Jackson. It's a unique interactive immersion in local culture.

THE ARTS

Grand Cayman mounts special events throughout the year. The Cayman National Orchestra performs in disparate venues from the Cracked Conch restaurant to First Baptist Church. There's a burgeoning theater scene. Many new works use religious themes as a launching pad for meditations on issues relevant to current events, such as the Cayman Drama Society (⊕ *www.caymandrama.org.ky*), which put on a provocative offering, *The Judith Code*, updating the biblical heroine's story to a present-day London of TV talk-show hosts and terrorist coalitions; the company also produces stimulating children's fare (*Mort*, based on Terry Pratchett's *Discworld* novels about a young boy apprenticed to Death), as well as escapist crowd-pleasing revivals like *Hairspray* and *Godspell*.

TELLING TALES. **The Cayman National Cultural Foundation started "Gimistory" as a means of preserving the rich but vanishing oral-culture tradition once passed from generation to generation. Held annually the last week of November, it features storytellers, often in elaborate garb, from Cayman and the Caribbean "spinnin' yarn" about old-time legends (duppies, spirits who return as bogeymen; or Pierrot Grande, the clown dressed in a colorful patchwork quilt of rags) as well as their travels and experiences. Free admission includes Caymanian delicacies like conch fritters and swanky (lemonade), part of a culinary competition.**

VENUES

Harquail Theatre. This state-of-the-art facility seats 330 for theatrical performances, concerts, dance recitals, fashion shows, beauty pageants, art exhibits, and poetry readings sponsored by the Cayman National Cultural Foundation. ⊠ *17 Harquail Dr., George Town, Grand Cayman* ☎ *345/949–5477.*

Lions Centre. The center hosts events throughout the year: "Battle of the Bands" competitions, concerts by top names on the Caribbean and international music scene such as Maxi Priest, stage productions, pageants, and sporting events. ⊠ *Harquail Dr., Red Bay, Grand Cayman* ☎ *345/945–4667, 345/949–7211.*

Prospect Playhouse. A thrust proscenium stage allows the Cayman Drama Society and its partner arts organizations to mount comedies, musicals, and dramas (original and revival) year-round. ⊠ *223B Shamrock Rd., Prospect, Grand Cayman* ☎ *345/947–1998, 345/949–5054.*

The Lowdown on Rundown

Rundown is a steamy Caymanian fish stew combining a potpourri of ingredients. A rundown is also a quick summary, and this enduringly popular show performed annually in October since 1991 puns on both definitions. The format is a series of skits, music, stand-up comedy, monologues, cabaret, dance, and impersonations—written from scratch each year by playwright-actor Dave Martins: a light-hearted, topical, satirical lampoon of daily Caymanian life, current events, politics, personalities, and nationalities. Caymanians call it their answer to The Daily Show and Colbert Report.

Martins started Rundown because he'd "seen topical shows in other Caribbean countries... and felt something similar would work here, but Cayman is very conservative and people said that would get me in hot water." After seeing caricatures of prominent people hanging in their offices, "I concluded that Caymanians were ready to laugh at themselves and wrote the first show. Some of the cast were very apprehensive in rehearsals, but it was a hit from day one." Every year provides fodder and inspiration aplenty,

but the show is more gently mocking than controversial, and the targets of its barbs usually laugh along with everyone else.

The audience's nonstop guffawing may bemuse tourists. Martins explains, "A lot of the stuff I write... is very contextual and almost always local, so the lyrics generally make little sense to someone outside that frame." Recent skits spoofed the red tape involved in putting up a little backyard shed to play dominoes; interplay among a crowd of people lining up to get Caymanian Immigration Status (the rollover policy); a Jamaican trying to teach a Londoner to speak the J dialect; and a lost tourist trying to get directions from a group that includes a Cuban, a Barbadian, a Pakistani, a Jamaican, a Chinaman, and, of course, a Caymanian... "all of whom are incomprehensible to the visitor.... To understand it fully, you'd need to have lived here 10, 15 years." He doesn't Americanize or clean up the dialect, but that augments the honest authenticity. And much of the material, from frustrating daily interactions to bureaucratic blundering, transcends any cultural divide.

6

Grand Cayman Sports and Outdoor Activities

WITH BEACHES

WORD OF MOUTH

"I definitely recommend buying snorkel gear before you go and bringing it with you. We kept it in our rental car and were able to just pull over and snorkel anywhere we found a great beach."

—MMN

By Jordan Simon

WATER, WATER, AND STILL MORE water rippling from turquoise to tourmaline; and underneath lies nature's even more kaleidoscopically colorful answer to Disney World for scuba divers and snorkelers. The Cayman Islands' early aggressive efforts on behalf of marine conservation paid off by protecting some of the most spectacular reefs in the Western Hemisphere. There are innumerable ways to experience their pyrotechnics without getting your feet or hair wet, from submarines to remote-controlled robots, not to mention a bevy of other water sports from windsurfing to wrangling big-game fish, parasailing to paddling kayaks through mangrove swamps.

While most activities on Grand Cayman are aquatic in nature, landlubbers can do more than just loll on the lovely beaches. There are nature hikes, bird-watching treks, and horseback rides through the island's wilder, more remote areas. The golf scene is well above par for so small an island, with courses designed by Jack "The Golden Bear" Nicklaus and, fittingly, "The White Shark" Greg Norman. Even the most seasoned sea salts might enjoy terra firma, at least for half a day.

BEACHES

Grand Cayman is blessed with many fine beaches, ranging from cramped, untrammeled coves to long stretches basking like a cat in the sun, lined with bustling bars and water-sports concessions. All beaches are public, though access can be restricted by resorts. Remember that the Cayman Islands are a conservative place: Nudity is strictly forbidden and punishable by a hefty fine and/or prison time.

GEORGE TOWN AND ENVIRONS

★ **Smith's Cove.** South of the Grand Old House, this tiny but popular protected swimming and snorkeling spot makes a wonderful beach wedding location. The bottom drops off quickly enough to allow you to swim and play close to shore. Although slightly rocky (its pitted limestone boulders resemble Moore sculptures), there's little debris and few coral heads, plenty of shade, picnic tables, restrooms, and parking. Surfers will find some decent swells just to the south. Note the curious obelisk cenotaph "In memory of James Samuel Webster and his wife Arabella Antoinette (née Eden)," with assorted quotes from Confucius to John Donne. Local scuttlebutt calls it a place for dalliances dur-

BEST BETS

■ **A Ray-diant Experience.** Feeding and stroking the silky denizens of Stingray City and Stingray Sandbar are highlights of any Cayman trip.

■ **Snorkeling or Diving from Shore.** Whether you make it to Stingray City or even scuba dive, you're all wet if you don't check out the pyrotechnic reef life glittering just offshore.

■ **Hiking the Mastic Trail.** The eco-centric should hike (and sometimes hack their way) through this mix of ecosystems, including ancient dry forest that embraces 716 plant species as well as (harmless) wildlife.

■ **ROV-ing the Ocean's Depths.** Deep See Cayman's ROV robot explores 2,000 feet under the sea while you watch in comfort on a yacht; the kids can steer if they're handy with joysticks.

■ **Putting on the Night-lights.** Kayak when the moon is waning to a bioluminescent bay; millions of microorganisms glow like fireflies when disturbed.

ing work hours; it's also a romantic sunset spot. ⊠ *Off S. Church St., George Town, Grand Cayman.*

South Sound Cemetery Beach. A narrow, sandy driveway takes you past the small cemetery to a perfect beach. The dock here is primarily used by dive boats during winter storms. You can walk in either direction; the sand is talcum-soft and clean, the water calm and clear (though local surfers take advantage of occasional small reef breaks; if wading, wear reef shoes, since the bottom is somewhat rocky and dotted with sea urchins). You'll definitely find fewer crowds. ⊠ *S. Sound Rd., Prospect, Grand Cayman.*

SEVEN MILE BEACH

★ **Fodor's Choice** **Seven Mile Beach.** Grand Cayman's west coast is dominated by the famous Seven Mile Beach—actually a 6½-mile-long (10-km-long) expanse of powdery white sand overseeing lapis water stippled with a rainbow of parasails and kayaks. The width of the beach varies with the season; toward the south end it narrows and disappears altogether south of the Marriott, leaving only rock and ironshore. It starts to broaden into its normal silky softness anywhere between Tarquyn Manor and the Reef Grill at Royal Palms. Free of litter and pesky peddlers, it's an unspoiled (though often crowded) environment. Most of the island's resorts, restaurants, and shopping centers

sit along this strip. At the public beach toward the north end you can find chairs for rent ($10 for the day, including a beverage), a playground, water toys aplenty, two beach bars, restrooms, and showers. The best snorkeling is at either end, by the Marriott and Treasure Island or off the northern section called Cemetery Reef Beach. ☒ *West Bay Rd., Seven Mile Beach, Grand Cayman.*

WEST BAY

★ **Barkers.** A series of secluded, spectacular beaches are accessed via a dirt road just past Papagallo restaurant. There are no facilities (that's the point!), but some palms offer shade. Unfortunately, the shallow water and rocky bottom discourage swimming, and it can be cluttered at times with seaweed and debris. ☒ *Conch Point Rd., Barkers, West Bay, Grand Cayman.*

NORTH SIDE

Old Man Bay. The North Side features plenty of hidden coves and pristine stretches of perfect sand, where you'll be disturbed only by seabirds dive-bombing for lunch and the occasional lone fishers casting nets for sprats, then dumping them into buckets. This area is easily accessed off Frank Sound Road. Off the Edge restaurant is less than 1 mile (1½ km) west. Otherwise, it's fairly undeveloped for miles, save for the occasional private home. Snorkeling is spectacular when waters are calm. ☒ *Queen's Hwy., just off Frank Sound Rd., North Side, Grand Cayman.*

★ **Rum Point.** This North Sound beach has hammocks slung in towering casuarina trees, picnic tables, the thatched Wreck Bar and Grill, a "fancier" dining option, a well-stocked shop for seaworthy sundries, and Red Sail Sports, which offers various water sports and boats to explore Stingray City. The barrier reef ensures safe snorkeling and soft sand. The bottom remains shallow for a long way from shore, but it's littered with small coral heads, so kids shouldn't wrestle in the water here. The Wreck is ablaze with color—yellow with navy-blue trim and lime-and-mango picnic tables—as if trying to upstage the snorkeling just offshore; an ultracasual hangout turns out outstanding pub grub from fish-and-chips to wings, as well as lethal mudslide cocktails. Showers are available. Just around the bend, another quintessential beach hangout, Kaibo, rocks during the day. ☒ *Rum Point, North Side, Grand Cayman.*

Water Cay. If you want an isolated, unspoiled beach, bear left at Rum Point on the North Side and follow the road to the end. When you pass a porte cochere for an abandoned condo development and see a soft, sandy beach, stop your car. Wade out knee deep and look for the large, flame-hued starfish. (Don't touch—just look.) Locals also call it Starfish or Ivory Point. ☒ *North Side, Grand Cayman.*

EAST END

East End Beaches. Just drive along and look for any sandy beach, park your car, and enjoy a stroll. The vanilla-hue stretch at Colliers Bay, by the Reef and Morritt's resorts, is a good, clean one with superior snorkeling. ☒ *Queen's Hwy., East End, Grand Cayman.*

Spotts Beach. Families often barbecue weekends at this idyllic spot caught between ironshore cliffs and a barrier reef. A jungle gym and swing set keep the kids occupied when they're not chowing down at the picnic tables and cabanas. During the week it's usually deserted. Follow South Church Street through South Sound past Red Bay; you'll see yet another little cemetery with a turnoff to the beach. ☒ *Queen's Hwy., Spotts Newlands, East End, Grand Cayman.*

SPORTS AND ACTIVITIES

BIRD-WATCHING

The Cayman Islands are an ornithologist's dream, providing perches for a wide range of resident and migratory birds— 219 species at last count, many of them endangered, such as the Cayman parrot. The National Trust organizes regular bird-watching field trips conducted by local ornithologists through the Governor Michael Gore Bird Sanctuary, Queen Elizabeth II Botanic Park, Mastic Reserve, Salina Reserve, Central Mangrove Wetland, Meagre Bay Pond Reserve in Pease Bay, Colliers Pond in East End, and Palmetto Pond at Barkers in West Bay. Prime time for bird-watching is either early in the morning or late in the afternoon; take strong binoculars and a field guide to identify the birds.

Silver Thatch Tours. Silver Thatch Tours is run by Geddes Hislop, who knows his birds and his island (though he's Trinidadian by birth). He specializes in customizable five-hour natural and historic heritage tours that culminate at the Queen Elizabeth II Botanic Park's nature trail and lake or other prime birding spots. The cost is $50 per hour for one to four people. Serious birders leave at the crack of dawn, but you can choose the time and leave at the crack of noon instead. The cost includes guide service, pickup and return transport, and refreshments such as local drinks (a great excuse for discourse on herbal medicinal folklore); tours must be arranged in advance. ⊠ *Grand Cayman* ☏ *345/925–7401* ✍ silvert@hotmail.com.

DIVING

One of the world's leading dive destinations, Grand Cayman has dramatic underwater topography that features plunging walls, soaring skyscraper pinnacles, grottoes, arches, swim-throughs adorned with vibrant sponges, coral-encrusted caverns, and canyons patrolled by lilliputian grunts to gargantuan groupers, darting jacks to jewfish, moray eels to eagle rays. Gorgonians and sea fans wave like come-hither courtesans. Pyrotechnic reefs provide homes for all manner of marine life, ecosystems encased within each other like an intricate series of Chinese boxes.

REEF WATCH. This progressive program, a partnership between the Department of the Environment and Cayman Islands Tourism Association, debuted in 1997 during Earth Day activities. The DOE designed a field survey to involve diving and snorkeling tourists in counting and cataloging marine life. To date, more than 1,000 surveys have been completed, helping to estimate species' populations and travel patterns based on sightings and their distance from buoys and other markers, as well as gauging how often equipment touches the fragile reefs. Though not scientifically sound, it does enhance awareness through interaction.

DIVE SITES

There are more than 200 pristine dive sites, many less than a half mile from the island and easily accessible, including wreck, wall, and shore options. Add exceptional visibility from 80 to 150 feet (no rivers deposit silt) and calm, current-free water at a constant bathlike 80°F. Cayman is serious about conservation, with stringently enforced laws to protect the fragile, endangered marine environment (fines up to $500,000 and a year in prison for damaging living coral, which can take years to regrow), protected by the creation of Marine Park, Replenishment, and Environmental

Learn to Dive

Diving is an exciting experience that does not have to be strenuous or stressful. Almost anyone can enjoy scuba, and it's easy to test the waters via a three-hour resort course costing $120–$150, including one or two dives. After a quick rundown of dos and don'ts, you stand in the shallow end of a pool, learning how to use the mask and fins and breathe underwater with a regulator. The instructor then explains some basic safety skills, and before you know it you're in the drink. The instructor hovers as you float above the reef, watching fish react to you. Don't worry—there are no dangerous fish in Cayman, and they don't bite (as long as you're not "chumming," or handling fish food). You can see corals and sponges, maybe even a turtle or ray. It's an amazing world that you can enter with very little effort.

The resort course only permits shallow, instructor-guided dives in Cayman's calm, clear waters. The next step is full Open Water certification (generally three to four days, including several dives, for around $500, less as part of a hotel package). This earns you a C-card, your passport to the underwater world anywhere you travel. From there, addicts will discover dozens of specialty courses. The leading teaching organizations, both with their adherents, are PADI (Professional Association of Dive Instructors) and NAUI (National Association of Underwater Instructors), affectionately nicknamed "Pay and Dive Immediately" and "Not Another Underwater Idiot" (those are the polite versions in scuba's colorful slang). Worry not: Cayman's instructors are among the world's best. And the water conditions just might spoil you.

Park Zones. Local water-sports operators enthusiastically cooperate: Most boats use biodegradable cleansers and environmentally friendly drinking cups. Moorings at all popular dive sites prevent coral and sponge damage due to continual anchoring; in addition, diving with gloves is prohibited to reduce the temptation to touch.

Pristine water, breathtaking coral formations, and plentiful marine life including hammerheads and hawksbill turtles mark the **North Wall**—a world-renowned dive area along the North Side of Grand Cayman.

Trinity Caves, in West Bay, is a deep dive with numerous canyons starting at about 60 feet and sloping to the wall at 130 feet. The South Side is the deepest, with the top of

Dive Tips

CLOSE UP

Here are a few helpful hints to maximize your enjoyment:

■ If you're not strong, ask someone to carry your tank and don't go in rough water from shore.

■ Always orient yourself on the sandy bottom near the boat: Check gauges and camera/video equipment, fine-tune your buoyancy, and ensure that your buddy is also secure.

■ Use a flashlight to explore crevices and illuminate the true dazzling colors of soft corals, sponges, and tunicates.

■ Check overhangs and outcroppings where grouper, tarpon, minnows, and other fish hang out in the shade.

■ Never touch black coral, usually found near 100-foot depths under outcroppings or inside tunnels. It's quite fragile, growing a mere inch every two to three years.

■ Fire coral is prevalent in the tropics and assumes many forms. Skin contact is painful (explaining the name). Vinegar or isopropyl alcohol helps alleviate pain; hydrocortisone cream or gel ameliorates the itch.

■ When shore diving off George Town, always use a surface float marker to indicate your position to the snorkeler/boater traffic.

■ If you become fatigued, float on your back; the seawater buoys you.

its wall starting 80 feet deep before plummeting, though its shallows offer a lovely labyrinth of caverns and tunnels in such sites as **Japanese Gardens** and **Della's Delight.**

The less-visited, virgin East End is less varied geographically beyond the magnificent **Ironshore Caves** and **Babylon Hanging Gardens** (trees of black coral plunging 100 feet), but it teems with "Swiss-cheese" swim-throughs and exotic life in such renowned gathering spots as **The Maze** (a hangout for reef, burse, and occasional hammerhead sharks), **Snapper Hole,** and **Grouper Grotto.**

The Cayman Islands government acquired the 251-foot, decommissioned **USS _Kittiwake_** (⊕ *www.kittiwakecayman. com).* Sunk in January 2011, it has already become an exciting new dive attraction, while providing necessary relief for some of the most frequently visited dive sites. The top of the bridge is just 15 feet down, making it accessible to snorkelers. There's a single-use entry fee of $10 ($5 for snorkelers).

A stingray at Stingray City, widely considered the best 12-foot dive in the world

★ **Fodor's Choice Stingray City.** Most dive operators offer scuba trips to Stingray City in the North Sound. Widely considered the best 12-foot dive in the world, it's a must-see for adventurous souls. Here dozens of stingrays congregate—tame enough to suction squid from your outstretched palm. You can stand in 3 feet of water at **Stingray Sandbar** as the gentle stingrays glide around your legs looking for a handout. Don't worry—these stingrays are so acclimated to tourist encounters that they pose no danger; the experience is often a highlight of a Grand Cayman trip.

SHORE DIVING

Shore diving around the island provides easy access to kaleidoscopic reefs, fanciful rock formations, and enthralling shipwrecks. The areas are well marked by buoys to facilitate navigation. If the water looks rough where you are, there's usually a side of the island that's wonderfully calm.

★ **Eden Rock.** If someone tells you that the silverside minnows are in at Eden Rock, drop everything and dive here (on South Church Street in George Town across from Harbour Place Mall by Paradise Restaurant). The schools swarm around you as you glide through the grottoes, forming quivering curtains of liquid silver as shafts of sunlight pierce the sandy bottom. The grottoes themselves are safe—not complex caves—and the entries and exits are clearly visible at all times. Snorkelers can enjoy the outside of the grottoes as the reef rises and falls from 10 to 30 feet deep.

Avoid carrying fish food unless you know how not to get bitten by eager yellowtail snappers.

★ **Devil's Grotto.** Its neighbor, Devil's Grotto, resembles an abstract painting of anemones, tangs, parrotfish, and bright purple Pederson cleaner shrimp (nicknamed the dentists of the reef, as they gorge on whatever they scrape off fish teeth and gills). Extensive coral heads and fingers teem with blue wrasse, horse-eyed jacks, butterfly fish, Indigo hamlets, and more. The cathedral-like caves are phenomenal, but tunnel entries here aren't clearly marked, so you're best off with a dive master.

Turtle Reef. Turtle Reef, at the Cracked Conch restaurant in West Bay, begins 20 feet out and gradually descends to a 60-foot miniwall pulsing with sea life and corals of every variety. From there it's just another 15 feet to the dramatic main wall. Ladders provide easy entrance to a shallow cover perfect for predive checks, and since the area isn't buoyed for boats, it's quite pristine.

DIVE OPERATORS

As one of the Caribbean's top diving destinations, Grand Cayman is blessed with many top-notch dive operations offering diving, instruction, and equipment for sale and rent. A single-tank boat dive averages $75, a two-tank dive about $100. Snorkel-equipment rental is about $15 a day. Divers are required to be certified and possess a "C" card. If you're getting certified, to save time during your limited holiday you can start the book and pool work at home and finish the open-water portion in warm, clear Cayman waters. Certifying agencies offer this referral service all around the world.

When choosing a dive operator, here are a few things to ask: Do they require that you stay with the group? Do they include towels? camera rinse water? protection from inclement weather? tank-change service? beach or resort pickup? snacks between dives? Ask what dive options they have during a winter storm (called a nor'wester here). What kind of boat do they have? (Don't assume that a small, less crowded boat is better. Some large boats are more comfortable, even when full, than a tiny, uncovered boat without a marine toilet. Small boats, however, offer more personal service and less-crowded dives.)

Strict marine protection laws prohibit you from taking any marine life from many areas around the island. Always check with the **Department of Environment** (☎ 345/949–8469) before diving, snorkeling, and fishing. To report violations, call **Marine Enforcement** (☎ 345/948–6002).

Ambassador Divers. Ambassador Divers is an on-call, guided scuba-diving operation offering dive trips to parties of two to eight persons. Co-owner Jason Washington's favorite spots include the excellent dive sites on the West Side and South and North Wall. Ambassador offers three boats, a 28-foot custom Parker (maximum six divers), another 28-foot completely custom overhauled boat, and a 26-footer primarily for snorkeling. They are available around the clock, and interested divers can be picked up from their hotels or condos. The price for a two-tank boat dive is $105 ($90 for two or more days). ✉ *Comfort Suites, West Bay Rd., Seven Mile Beach, Grand Cayman* ☎ *345/743–5513, 345/949–4530* ⊕ *www.ambassadordivers.com.*

Cayman Aggressor IV. Cayman Aggressor IV, a 110-foot live-aboard dive boat refitted in 2007, offers one-week cruises for divers who want to get serious bottom time, as many as five dives daily. Nine staterooms with en suite bathrooms sleep 18. The fresh food is basic but bountiful (three meals, two in-between snacks), and the crew offers a great mix of diving, especially when weather allows the crossing to Little Cayman. Digital photography and video courses are also offered (there's an E-6 film-processing lab aboard) as well as Nitrox certification. The price is $2,495 to $2,895 double occupancy for the week. ✉ *Grand Cayman* ☎ *345/949–5551, 800/348–2628* ⊕ *www.aggressor.com.*

🗘 **Deep Blue Divers.** Deep Blue Divers has two custom-designed 27-foot outward driven Dusky boats, which ensure a smooth, speedy ride and can access sites that much larger boats can't. They accept a maximum of eight guests, under the watchful eyes of Patrick Weir and Nick Buckley, who joke that diving is "relaxing under pressure." Personalized valet attention and flexibility have ensured a high repeat clientele; Nick's particularly good with kids and has taught three generations of families. He's often asked by happy customers to join them on dive trips around the world. He and his crew delight in telling stories about Cayman culture and history, including pirate tales and often-hilarious anecdotes about life in the Cayman Islands. He offers underwater photo–video services and a range of PADI-certified courses; beach pickup is included. ✉ *245 N. Church St., George*

Town, Grand Cayman ☎345/916–1293, 345/946–8685 ⊕*www.deepbluediverscayman.com.*

★ **Fodor's**Choice **DiveTech.** DiveTech has opportunities for shore
☾ diving at its two north-coast locations, which provide loads
of interesting creatures, a miniwall, and the North Wall.
With quick access to West Bay, the boats are quite comfortable. Technical training (a specialty of owner Nancy
Easterbrook) is unparalleled, and the company offers good,
personable service as well as the latest gadgetry such as
underwater DPV scooters. They even mix their own gases,
and there are multiple dive instructors for different specialties, with everything from extended cross-training Ranger
packages to Dive and Art workshop weeks, popular photography–video seminars with Courtney Platt, deep diving, less
disruptive free diving, search and recovery, stingray interaction, reef awareness, and underwater naturalist. Snorkel
and diving programs are available year-round for children
ages eight and up, SASY (supplied-air snorkeling, which
keeps the unit on a personal flotation device) for five and up.
Excellent multiday discounts are a bonus. ⊠ *Cobalt Coast
Resort & Suites, 18-A Sea Fan Dr., West Bay, Grand Cayman* ☎345/946–5658, 888/946–5656 ⊕*www.divetech.com*
⊠ *Lighthouse Point, near Boatswain's Beach, 571 N.W.
Point Rd., West Bay, Grand Cayman* ☎345/949–1700.

Don Foster's Dive Cayman Islands. Don Foster's Dive Cayman
Islands has a pool with a shower as well as snorkeling
along the ironshore at Casuarina Point, easily accessed
starting at 20 feet, extending to depths of 55 feet. There's
an underwater photo center, and there are night dives
and Stingray City trips with divers and snorkelers in the
same boat (perfect for families). Specialties include Nitrox
courses and Underwater Naturalist guided dives. Rates are
competitive, and there's free shuttle pickup–drop-off along
Seven Mile Beach. If you go out with Don, he might recount
stories of his wild times as a drummer in the islands, but
all the crews are personable and efficient. The drawback
is larger boats and groups. ⊠ *218 S. Church St., George
Town, Grand Cayman* ☎345/949–5679, 345/945–5132
⊕*www.donfosters.com.*

Eden Rock Diving Center. Eden Rock Diving Center, south
of George Town, provides easy access to Eden Rock and
Devil's Grotto. It features full equipment rental, lockers,
shower facilities, and a full range of PADI courses from
a helpful, cheerful staff on its Pro 42 jet boat. ⊠ *124 S.*

Divers exploring one of Grand Cayman's famous reefs

Church St., George Town, Grand Cayman ☎ *345/949–7243* ⊕ *www.edenrockdive.com.*

★ **Indigo Divers.** Indigo Divers is a full-service PADI teaching facility specializing in exclusive guided dives from its 28-foot Sea Ray Bow Rider or 32-foot Donzi Express Cruiser. Comfort and safety are paramount, and the attention to detail is superior. Luxury transfers in a Chevy Avalanche are included, and the boat is stocked with goodies like fresh fruit and homemade cookies. Captain Chris Alpers has impeccable credentials: a licensed U.S. Coast Guard captain, PADI master scuba diver trainer, and Cayman Islands Marine Park officer. Katie Alpers specializes in wreck, DPV, dry suit, boat, and deep diving, but her primary role is resident videographer, and she edits superlative DVDs of your adventures, complete with music and titles. They guarantee a maximum of six divers. The individual attention is a bit pricier, but the larger your group, the more you save. ⊠ *Seven Mile Beach, Grand Cayman* ☎ *345/946–7279, 345/525–3932* ⊕ *www.indigodivers.com.*

Neptune's Divers. Neptune's Divers offers competitive package rates, in addition to free shuttle service along Seven Mile Beach. It's also one of the best companies for physically challenged divers. Captain Keith Keller and his staff try to customize trips as best they can, taking no more than eight divers out on their 30-foot custom Island Hopper and 36-foot Crusader. A wide range of PADI courses are available; the instructors are patient and knowledgeable about reef life. The operation is computer-friendly to permit longer bottom time. ⊠ *West Bay Rd., Seven Mile Beach, Grand Cayman* ☎ *345/945–3990* ⊕ *www.neptunesdivers.com.*

★ **Fodor's Choice Ocean Frontiers.** Ocean Frontiers is an excellent eco-centric operation, offering friendly small-group diving and a technical training facility, exploring the less trammeled, trafficked East End. The company provides valet service, personalized attention, a complimentary courtesy shuttle, and an emphasis on green initiatives and specialized diving, including unguided computer, Technical, Nitrox Instructor, and cave diving for advanced participants. But even beginners and rusty divers (there's a wonderful Skills Review and Tune-Up course) won't feel over their heads. Special touches include hot chocolate and homemade muffins on night dives; the owner, Steve, is an ordained minister and will conduct weddings in full-face masks. ⊠ *Compass Point, 346 Austin Connelly Dr., East End, Grand Cayman* ☎ *345/947–7500, 800/348–6096, 345/947–0000* ⊕ *www.oceanfrontiers.com.*

↻ **Red Sail Sports.** Red Sail Sports offers daily trips from most of the major hotels. Dives are often run as guided tours, a perfect option for beginners. If you're experienced and your air lasts a long time, consult the boat captain to see if he requires that you come up with the group (determined by the first person who runs low on air). There is a full range of kids' dive options for ages 5 to 15, including SASY and Bubblemakers. The company also operates Stingray City tours, dinner and sunset sails, and just about every major water sport from Wave Runners to windsurfing. ⊠ *Grand Cayman* ☎ *345/949–8745, 345/623–5965, 877/506–6368* ⊕ *www.redsailcayman.com.*

Sundivers. Sundivers, owned by Ollen Miller, one of Cayman's first dive masters, has the on-site dive shop at the Cracked Conch restaurant next to Boatswain's Beach, offering competitive rates for air, lessons, and rentals; shore access to Turtle Reef; and such amenities as showers, rinse tanks, and storage. ⊠ *The Cracked Conch, N.W. Point Rd., West Bay, Grand Cayman* ☎ *345/916–1064, 345/949–6606.*

Sunset Divers. Sunset Divers, a full-service PADI teaching facility at the George Town hostelry catering to the scuba set, has great shore diving and six dive boats to hit all sides of the island. Divers can be independent on their boats as long as they abide by the maximum time and depth

CLOSE UP

Learning In-Depth

A common kitschy T-shirt reads "DIVERS DO IT DEEPER AND LONGER," but that's certainly the goal of any scuba enthusiast. That's where new specialized equipment and courses come in. Technical diving refers to advanced dives conducted beyond the 130-foot depth limit, requiring a decompression stop, or into an overhead environment. DiveTech's Nancy Easterbrook compares it to "skiing a really steep mogul-ly double black diamond, or scaling a sheer cliff face. It takes practice and determination." The courses and equipment are also much more expensive.

Terms you'll soon hear are Nitrox, Advanced Nitrox, Normoxic, Trimix, and Advanced Trimix. These all enable divers to explore deeper depths safely at greater length. Nitrox, for example, is highly oxygenated nitrogen (32% as opposed to "normal" air, with 21%), which enables you to dive for a longer time before reaching decompression limits. And just like the oxygen-bar craze of the last decade, Nitrox invigorates you, reducing fatigue after dives.

Rebreather diving (Closed Circuit Rebreathers, or CCR) is another popular way to extend dive time, up to three hours 100 feet down. You breathe warmer, moister air (reducing the chance of chills at lower depths). As a bonus, denizens of the deep are less wary, as there are no bubbles.

6

standards. Instruction and packages are comparatively inexpensive. Though the company is not directly affiliated with acclaimed underwater shutterbug Cathy Church (whose shop is also at the hotel), she'll often work with the instructors on special courses. ⊠ *Sunset House, 390 S. Church St., George Town, Grand Cayman* ☎ *345/949–7111, 800/854–4767* ⊕ *www.sunsethouse.com.*

FISHING

The Cayman Islands are widely hailed as a prime action-packed destination for all types of sportfishing, from casting in the flats for the wily, surprisingly strong "gray ghost" bonefish to trolling for giant, equally combative blue marlin. Conditions are ideal for big game fish: The water temperature varies only eight to 10 degrees annually, so the bait and their pelagic predators hang out all year. The big lure for anglers is the big game-fish run near the coast, as close as a quarter-mile offshore.

Experienced, knowledgeable local captains charter boats with top-of-the-line equipment, bait, ice, and often lunch included in the price (usually $550–$750 per half-day, $900–$1,500 for a full day). Options include deep-sea, reef, bone, tarpon, light-tackle, and fly-fishing. June and July are particularly good all-around months for reeling in blue marlin, yellow- and blackfin tuna, dolphinfish (dorado), and bonefish. Bonefish have a second season in the winter months, along with wahoo and skipjack tuna. Marine Park laws prohibit fishing or taking any type of marine life in protected areas. Local captains promote conservation and sportsmanship through catch-and-release of both reef and pelagic fish not intended for eating and all billfish, unless they are local records or potential tournament winners.

★ **Bayside Watersports.** Longtime fisherman Captain Eugene Ebanks established Bayside Watersports in 1974. The family-run West Bay–based company operates two first-class fishing boats, the "Hooker" fleet, ranging from 31 feet (*Lil Hooker*) to 53 feet (the *Happy Hooker,* which sleeps six for overnight charters farther afield). The tradition began with the original *Hooker,* named after the Moldcraft Hooker lure, whose team led by son Al Ebanks caught a 189.4-pound yellowfin tuna in 1989 that still stands as the island record. They do reef-, tarpon-, and bonefishing trips as well, but their real specialty is deep-water fishing, such as at 12-Mile Bank, a 3-mile (5-km) strip just 90 minutes west of Grand Cayman, where leviathan fighters congregate around the submerged peak of an underwater mountain. ✉ *Grand Cayman* ☎ *345/949-3200* ⊕ *www.baysidewatersports.com.*

Black Princess Charters. Black Princess Charters, owned by Captain Chuckie Ebanks, is fully equipped for deep-sea and reef fishing as well as snorkel trips on his fully equipped and supplied eponymous 40-foot Sea Ray. His rates are comparatively reasonable, and he can arrange clean, inexpensive local accommodations. ✉ *Grand Cayman* ☎ *345/916-6319, 345/949-0400* ⊕ *www.fishgrandcayman.com.*

Captain Asley's Watersports. Captain Asley's Watersports prides itself on personable, flexible, and customized charter services for deep-sea, light-tackle, and bonefishing. The cost for a privately chartered fishing vessel can run from $500 (small boat, half day) to $1,200 (big boat, full day). The owner of this family-run operation, Captain Asley has plied these waters since the 1960s; now his affable, patient kids and extended family (usually Darrin, Dwight, and Kevin) captain the five boats. They're all expert coaches, coaxing a confident approach even from first-timers, though they'll take experts to troll all the lesser-known depths; ESPN's Bass Pros selected them as a "preferred outfitter guide." Like many other operators, they also run snorkeling, diving, and sunset and dinner cruises. ⊠ *Grand Cayman* ☎ *345/949–3054* ✆ cayfish@candw.ky.

Ocean Frontiers. The excellent, environmentally conscious dive outfit Ocean Frontiers also offers fishing on a 26-foot, diesel-powered MerPanga with depth sounder, GPS, six lines, and all safety gear including life jackets and emergency radio beacons. Captain Joey Welcome plies his secret spots along the East End, where marlin, wahoo, and tuna congregate within a mile offshore, and at Coxain Bank, which teems with snapper. The inner reef is ideal for shore and night fishing, providing a sheltered site for tarpon, snapper, and barracuda. ⊠ *Compass Point, Austin Connelly Dr., East End, Grand Cayman* ☎ *345/947–7500, 800/348–6096, 345/947–0000* ⊕ *www.oceanfrontiers.com.*

Oh Boy Charters. Oh Boy Charters charters a 60-foot yacht with complete amenities for day (and overnight) trips, as well as sunset and dinner cruises, plus a 34-foot Crusader. Alvin Ebanks—son of Caymanian marine royalty, the indomitable Captain Marvin Ebanks (still going strong in his 90s)—jokingly claims he's been playing in and plying the waters for a century and tells tales (tall and otherwise) of his father reeling him in for fishing expeditions. No more than eight passengers on the deep-sea boats ensures the personal touch (snorkeling on the 60-footer accommodates more people). Guests always receive a good selection of their catch; if you prefer others to do the cooking, go night fishing (including catch-and-release shark safaris), which includes dinner. All trips include a free Seven Mile Beach shuttle. ⊠ *Grand Cayman* ☎ *345/949–6341, 345/926–0898* ⊕ *www.ohboycharters.com.*

★ **R&M Fly Shop and Charters.** Captain Ronald Ebanks of R&M Fly Shop and Charters is arguably the island's most knowledgeable fly-fishing guide, with more than 10 years' experience in Cayman and Scotland. He also runs light-tackle trips on a 24-foot Robalo. Everyone from beginners—even children—to experienced casters will enjoy and learn from the trip (whether wading or poling from a boat); free transfers are included. Captain Ronald even ties his own flies

6

(he'll show you how). ✉ *Grand Cayman* ☎ *345/947–3146, 345/946–0214* ⊕ *www.flyfishgrandcayman.com.*

★ **Sea Star Charters.** Sea Star Charters, aka Clinton's Watersports, is run by Clinton Ebanks, a fine and very friendly Caymanian who will do whatever it takes to make sure that you have a wonderful time on his two 27- and 28-foot cabin cruisers (and from the 35-foot trimaran used primarily for snorkeling cruises), enjoying light-tackle, bone-, and bottom-fishing. He's a good choice for beginners and offers a nice cultural experience as well as sailing charters and snorkeling with complimentary transportation and equipment. Only cash and traveler's checks are accepted. ✉ *Grand Cayman* ☎ *345/949–1016, 345/916–5234.*

GOLF

Blue Tip. The 9-hole, 3,515-yard, par-36 Blue Tip was designed by Greg Norman and built near mangroves. Five of the holes are par-4s, and two are par-5s, including a 600-yarder. The course is open only to guests of the Ritz-Carlton and to owners of the Residences (luxury condominiums). No jeans are allowed, and you must wear collared golf shirts. Club rentals are available at the golf shop. Greens fees are $150 for 9 holes, $215 for 18 holes. ✉ *Ritz-Carlton Grand Cayman, West Bay Rd., Seven Mile Beach, Grand Cayman* ☎ *345/943–9000, 345/815–6500* ⊕ *www.ritzcarlton.com.*

Britannia. The Britannia golf course, next to the Grand Cayman Beach Suites, was designed by Jack Nicklaus. The course is really three in one—a 9-hole, par-70 regulation course; an 18-hole, par-57 executive course; and a Cayman course played with a Cayman ball that travels about half the distance of a regulation ball. Signature tough holes include 3 and 10; beware tricky winds on 7 through 11. Greens fees are $100 for 9 holes, $150 for 18 ($75/$100 during the off-season), including the cart. Amenities include a full pro shop and the Britannia Golf Grille (with particularly good breakfasts and local fare). ✉ *West Bay Rd., Seven Mile Beach, Grand Cayman* ☎ *345/745–4653* ⊕ *www. britannia-golf.com.*

North Sound Club. Formerly the Links at Safehaven, the par-71, 6,605-yard, 18-hole North Sound Club is infamous among duffers for its strong gusts, giving the ball unexpected loft or backspin. Roy Case factored the wind into his design, which incorporates lots of looming water and sand traps; the handsome setting features many mature mahogany and silver thatch trees where iguana skulk. Wear shorts at least 14 inches long (15 inches for women); no T-shirts are allowed, only collared shirts. Green fees change seasonally; in winter they're $175 ($105 for 9 holes) including cart. There are twilight and walking discounts (though carts are recommended), fine pro shop, and open-air bar with large-screen TVs. ⊠ *Off West Bay Rd., Seven Mile Beach, Grand Cayman* ☎ *345/947–4653* ⊕ *www.northsoundclub.com.*

GUIDED TOURS

Taxi drivers will give you a personalized tour of Grand Cayman for about $25 per hour for up to three people. Or you can choose a fascinating helicopter ride, a horseback or mountain-bike journey, a 4x4 safari expedition, or a full-day bus excursion. Ask your hotel to help you make arrangements.

Costs and itineraries for island tours are about the same regardless of the tour operator. Half-day tours average $40–$50 a person and generally include a visit to Hell and the Turtle Farm at Boatswain's Beach aquatic park in West Bay, as well as shopping downtown. Full-day tours ($60–$90 per person) add lunch, a visit to Bodden Town (the first settlement), and the East End, where you stop at the Queen Elizabeth II Botanic Park, blowholes (if the waves are high) on the ironshore, and the site of the wreck of the *Ten Sails* (not the wreck itself—just the site). The pirate graves in Bodden Town were destroyed during Hurricane Ivan in 2008, and the blowholes were partially filled. As you can tell, land tours here are low-key. Children under 12 often receive discounts.

A.A. Transportation Services. A.A. Transportation Services offers taxis and tour buses—ask for Burton Ebanks. ⊠ *Grand Cayman* ☎ *345/949–6598, 345/926–8294, 345/ 949–7222.*

Cayman Safari. Cayman Safari hits the usual sights but emphasizes interaction with locals, so you learn about craft traditions, folklore, and herbal medicines; careening along in Land Rovers is incidental fun. ⊠ *Grand Cayman* ☎ *345/925–3001, 866/211–4677* ⊕ *www.caymansafari.com.*

Majestic Tours. Majestic Tours caters mostly to cruise-ship and incentive groups but also offers similar options to indi-

Turtles and Cats

Blessed with arguably the world's largest turtle nesting grounds, Cayman developed into the center of the Caribbean turtle industry for nearly two centuries. English settlers on Jamaica became particularly proficient turtlers. Once they hunted the population into near-extinction by the early 1800s, Caymanians went to sea for months, trapping and supplying turtles from Cuba and Nicaragua well into the 20th century. Even today roughly 20 locals are licensed to catch four turtles annually, and the Cayman Turtle Farm (an environmentally sensitive "working" part of the Boatswain's Beach marine theme park) supplies the local market with farm-raised meat.

Turtling led indirectly to one of the proud Caymanian contributions to shipbuilding, the catboat. The design of this basic sailboat (not a catamaran) is usually credited to Cayman Brac's Daniel Jervis circa 1904, though Cape Cod and Chesapeake Bay boaters debate the origin. He decided to bring the stern to a sharp point, similar to New England/Canadian whalers and peapods, placing the mast in the bow. Supposedly, the shape permitted quicker course reversal and less drag, while the lack of keel depth facilitated beaching the boat. Ballast provided stability, and only a yoke was used to steer the rudder.

The Cayman Catboat Club holds several annual regattas as well as free rides during special events, including Pirates Week.

---

viduals and can customize tours; it's particularly good for West Bay, including Boatswain's Beach and Hell. ⊠ *Grand Cayman* ☎ *345/949–7773* ⊕ *www.majestic-tours.com.*

McCurley Tours. McCurley Tours is owned by B. A. McCurley, a free-spirited, freewheeling midwesterner who's lived in Cayman since the mid-1980s and knows everything and everyone on the East End. Not only is she encyclopedic and flexible, but she also offers car rentals and transfers for travelers staying on the North Side or East End; don't be surprised if she tells you what to order at lunch, especially if it's off the menu. ⊠ *Grand Cayman* ☎ *345/947–9626, 345/916–0925.*

Tropicana Tours. Tropicana Tours offers several excellent Cayman highlights itineraries on its larger buses, including Stingray City stops, as well as reef runner adventures across the North Sound through the mangrove swamps. ✉ *Grand Cayman* ☎ *345/949–0944* ⊕ *www.tropicana-tours.com.*

HIKING

★ **Mastic Trail.** The National Trust's internationally significant Mastic Trail, used in the 1800s as the only direct path to and from the North Side, is a rugged 2-mile (3-km) slash through 776 dense acres of woodlands, black mangrove swamps, savannah, agricultural remnants, and ancient rock formations. It embraces more than 700 species, including Cayman's largest remaining contiguous ancient forest (one of the heavily deforested Caribbean's last examples). A comfortable walk depends on weather—winter is better because it's drier, though flowering plants such as the banana orchid set the trail ablaze in summer. Call the National Trust to determine suitability and to book a guide for $30; tours are run daily from 9 to 5 by appointment only, regularly on Wednesday at 9 am (sometimes earlier in summer). Or walk on the wild side with a $5 guidebook that provides information on the ecosystems you traverse, the endemic wildlife you might encounter, seasonal changes, poisonous plants to avoid, and folkloric uses of various flora. The trip takes about three hours. ✉ *Frank Sound Rd., entrance by fire station at botanic park, Breakers, East End, Grand Cayman* ☎ *345/749–1121, 345/749–1124 for guide reservations* ⊕ *www.nationaltrust.org.ky.*

HORSEBACK RIDING

Coral Stone Stables. Coral Stone Stables offers 90-minute leisurely horseback rides along the white-sand beaches at Bodden Town and inland trails at Savannah; complimentary photos are included. Your guide is Nolan Stewart, whose ranch contains 20 horses, chickens, and "randy" roosters. Nolan offers a nonstop narrative on flora, fauna, and history. He's an entertaining, endless font of local information, some of it unprintable. Rides are $80; swim rides cost $120. ✉ *Grand Cayman* ☎ *345/916–4799* ⊕ *www.csstables.com.*

Horseback in Paradise. Horseback in Paradise is the domain of gregarious Nicki Eldemire, who loves telling stories about horse training and life on Cayman. She leads guided tours through Barkers National Park on the West End: a pristine peninsular area filled with enthralling plant and animal life along the beaches and wetlands. The steep price of $100 includes transportation, but it's a private, exclu-

Horseback riding in Barkers National Park

sive experience with no more than four riders per group.
✉ *Grand Cayman* ☎ *345/945–5839, 345/916–3530* ⊕ *www. caymanhorseriding.com.*

Mary's Stables and Equestrian Center. Mary's Stables and Equestrian Center, the top-notch training facility for the Cayman national equestrian team, offers classic English riding lessons (dressage is also an option) and allows you to help groom the exotic horses. ✉ *Grand Cayman* ☎ *345/949–7360, 345/516–1751.*

🕃 **Pampered Ponies.** Pampered Ponies offers what is called "the ultimate tanning machine": horses walking, trotting, and cantering along the beaches. You can do either private tours or a variety of guided trips, including sunset, moonlight, and swim rides along the uninhabited beach from Conch Point to Morgan's Harbour on the north tip beyond West Bay. ✉ *Grand Cayman* ☎ *345/945–2262, 345/916–2540* ⊕ *www.ponies.ky.*

KAYAKING

★ **Cayman Kayaks.** Cayman Kayaks explores Grand Cayman's
🕃 protected mangrove wetlands, providing an absorbing discussion of the indigenous animals (including a mesmerizing stop at a gently pulsing, nonstinging Cassiopeia jellyfish pond) and plants, the effects of hurricanes, and conservation efforts. Even beginners will find the tours

easy (the guides dub it low-impact aerobics), and the sit-on-top tandem kayaks are quite stable and comfortable. The Bio Bay tour involves more strenuous paddling, but the underwater light show is magical as millions of bioluminescent microorganisms called dinoflagellates glow like fireflies when disturbed. It runs only on moonless nights for full effect and books well in advance. All tours depart from Kaibo Beach Bar in Cayman Kai; costs run from $39 to $59 (some tours offer kids' and group discounts). ⊠ *Grand Cayman* ☎ *345/746–3249, 345/926–4467* ⊕ *www. caymankayaks.com.*

SAILING

Though Cayman has a large sailing community, it isn't a big charter-yacht destination. Still, you can skipper your own craft (albeit sometimes under the watchful eye of the boat's captain). The protected waters of the North Sound are especially delightful, but chartering a sailboat is also a wonderful way to discover lesser-known snorkeling, diving, and fishing spots around the island.

Cayman Island Sailing Club. Cayman Island Sailing Club is a private club that sometimes offers lessons to nonmembers but always has boats, including J-22s, for hourly or half- and full-day rental (CI$30–CI$300). The club's a great hangout, and chatting up the friendly members provides invaluable insights into all subjects Caymanian. ⊠ *Spinnaker Rd., Selkirk Dr., Red Bay, Grand Cayman* ☎ *345/947–7913* ⊕ *www.sailing.ky.*

Sail Cayman. Neil Galway, an experienced RYA Yacht Master, runs Sail Cayman, offering 30-foot Gemini RIB ecotours and a plush 45-foot Gibsea, the *NautiGal*, for full-day or half-day private sailing or snorkeling. Though not bareboating, it is hands-on: you can crew and even captain if you enjoy sailing. Neil personalizes the cruise to suit any family or group, accommodating a maximum of 12–15 passengers. A half day runs $600–$700, a full day $1,000–$1,200: if you have a large group, it's little more than the total price for crowded excursions with twice as many strangers. ⊠ *Grand Cayman* ☎ *345/916–4333* ⊕ *www.sailcayman.com.*

Getting SASY

A few years ago, Wayne Hasson, a Cayman resident and owner of the live-aboard dive boat *Cayman Aggressor,* faced a dilemma. He and his wife, Anne, were both ardent, accomplished scuba divers and marine environmentalists. His children, then five and seven, understandably longed to share the diving experience, but their mother insisted that they simply snorkel atop the surface until they reached the age minimum of 12. They hated breathing in water and sputtering. So Hasson developed an ingenious compromise device that has already profoundly impacted the scuba industry and ocean education.

Hasson rigged a life vest with a pony bottle and regulator and let his kids try breathing from an air tank while positively buoyant at the surface. They remained face down without inhaling water, mimicking the feel of actual diving. The family worked on R&D for nearly a year with Custom Buoyancy, inventing and refining SASY (Supplied Air Snorkeling for Youth). The units resemble the real thing with life vest, small scuba tank (13 cubic feet as opposed to 19) in an adjust-able holder, and regulator (all integrating crucial safety features like child-proof attachments and stabilizing straps); any kid five or older could now enjoy "diving" with Mom and Dad safely and comfortably. Recognizing adults might also feel awkward with snorkeling gear, Hasson created SASA (Supplied Air Snorkeling for Adults), which differs in the tank size (19 to 30 cubic feet). Although "snuba" allows you to go underwater, the hose can prove cumbersome and restrict the scope of your movement; kids as young as four can enjoy the feel of dive equipment with SASY, but the snuba minimum age is eight.

The device promotes interest in diving from a younger age, but equally important, the patent, trademarks, and income from sales and licensing agreements belong to Oceans for Youth, a nonprofit organization the Hassons subsequently founded to educate youth about the marine environment and the vital connection between sea and land life. As Hasson states, "...the health of the world's oceans will soon become the responsibility of today's children."

SEA EXCURSIONS

The most impressive sights in the Cayman Islands are on and under water, and several submarines, semisubmersibles, glass-bottom boats, and Jules Verne–like contraptions allow you to see these underwater wonders without getting your feet wet. Sunset sails, dinner cruises, and other theme (dance, booze, pirate) cruises are available from $30–$70 per person.

★ **Atlantis Submarines.** This submarine takes 48 passengers safely and comfortably along the Cayman Wall down to 100 feet. You peep through panoramic portholes as good-natured guides keep up a humorous but informative patter. A guide dons scuba gear to feed fish, who form a whirling frenzy of color rivaling anything by Picasso. At night, the 10,000-watt lights show the kaleidoscopic underwater colors and nocturnal stealth predators more brilliantly than during the day. Try to sit toward the front so you can watch the pilot's nimble maneuverings and the depth gauge. If that literally in-depth tour seems daunting, get up close and personal on the *Seaworld Observatory* semisubmersible (glorified glass-bottom boat), which just cruises the harbor (including glimpses of the *Cali* and *Balboa* shipwrecks). The cost is $89–$99 (children $49–$59) for the submarine, $39 for the semisubmersible. There are frequent online booking discounts. ⊠ *30 S. Church St., George Town, Grand Cayman* ☎ *345/949–7700, 800/887–8571* ⊕ *www. caymanislandssubmarines.com.*

★ **Fodor's**Choice **Deep See Cayman.** Scientists often call our oceans just as mysterious as deep space, and Deep See Cayman provides spellbinding proof. Its personable owner was pilot for Paul Allen's *Octopus,* one of the world's largest yachts; helped film David Attenborough's compelling *The Blue Planet;* and currently works with Scripps on underwater research with his little toy, an ROV underwater robot that plumbs the Cayman Trench's depths down to 2,400 feet while you comfortably watch the real-time high-definition images it transmits aboard a luxury yacht, the *Deep Seeker.* Some wrecks have gradually sunk to those depths, but the real prize is otherworldly oddly shaped creatures straight out of sci-fi. The two-hour excursions depart from the West Bay dock several times daily (including a night tour), with an eight-person maximum, costing a reasonable $74 ($5 discount for advance online booking). Gary will even let kids particularly adept with joysticks from video game mastery navigate the Little Tyche (an appropriate name, given the eager would-be pilots). ☎ *345/926–3343* ⊕ *www. deepseecayman.com.*

☻ *Jolly Roger.* The *Jolly Roger* is a two-thirds-size replica of Christopher Columbus's 17th-century Spanish galleon *Niña*; the company also owns the *Anne Bonny,* a wooden Norwegian brig built in 1934 that holds more than 100 passengers. On the afternoon snorkel cruise, play Captain Jack Sparrow while experiencing swashbuckling pirate antics, including a trial, sword fight, and walking the plank; the kids can fire the cannon, help hoist the main sail, and scrub the decks (it's guaranteed that they will love it even if they loathe doing chores at home). The evening options (sunset and dinner sails) are more standard booze cruises, less appropriate for the kiddies. Food is more appropriate to the brig, and it's more yo-ho-hokum than remotely authentic, but it's fun. Prices range from $40 to $60. ⊠ *Grand Cayman* ☎ *345/945–7245* ⊕ *www.jollyrogercayman.com.*

Nautilus. On the semisubmersible *Nautilus* you can sit above deck or venture below, where you can view the reefs and marine life through a sturdy glass hull. A one-hour undersea tour is $50. Watch divers feed the fish, or take the Captain Nemo's Tour that includes snorkeling; a catamaran cruise to Stingray City and land-sea tours are also offered. As on the *Atlantis* semisubmersible, you get a close-up look at the Cheeseburger Reef and two of Cayman's mysterious shipwrecks (*Cali* and *Balboa*), with a bit of entertaining educational narrative. ⊠ *Grand Cayman* ☎ *345/945–1355* ⊕ *www.nautilus.ky.*

☻ **Sea Trek.** Sea Trek offers helmet diving, permitting you to walk and breathe 26 feet underwater—without getting your hair wet—for an hour. No training or even swimming ability is required, and you can wear glasses. Guides give a thorough safety briefing, and a sophisticated system of compressors and cylinders provides triple the amount of air necessary for normal breathing while a safety diver program ensures four distinct levels of backup. The result at near-zero gravity resembles an exhilarating moonwalk. The minimum age is eight. The cost is $89 to $99 per person (the latter for an "Ultimate Stingray City" excursion). ⊠ *Grand Cayman* ☎ *345/949–0008* ⊕ *www.seatrekcayman.com.*

SKATING AND SKATEBOARDING

★ **Fodor'sChoice Black Pearl Skate and Surf Park.** Black Pearl Skate
☻ and Surf Park, a great skating park (skateboards, in-line skates), is the size of a football field (at 52,000 square feet the world's second-largest such facility) with stairs, half

pipe, rails, 20-foot vert ramp, and flow course offering innumerable lies. International professional skaters such as Tony Hawk, Ryan Sheckler, and Mark Appleyard have practiced their kickflips, tailslides, wheelies, and grinds. The park also has one of only three Waveloch standing wave–surf machines in the world, which generates adjustable 11-foot swells. You can arrange lessons or rent anything you need at the adjacent skate–surf shop. The outdoor patio of the surprisingly elegant Brick House restaurant (terrific pizzas and playground) is the perfect vantage point for the rad performances local daredevils mount Friday and Saturday nights. ⊠ *Red Bay Rd., Grand Harbour, Grand Cayman* ☎ *345/947–4161, 345/925–8576* ⊕ *www.blackpearl.ky*.

SNORKELING

The proximity of healthy, Technicolor reef to the Grand Cayman shore means endless possibilities for snorkelers. Some sites require you to simply wade or swim into the surf; others are only accessible via boat. Nearly every snorkeling outfit follows the same route, beginning with the scintillating Stingray City and Sandbar. They usually continue to the adjacent Coral Gardens and often farther out along the Barrier Reef. Equipment is included, sometimes drinks, snacks, and lunch. Half-day tours run $35–$40, full-day $60–$70, and there are often extras such as kids' discounts and a complimentary shuttle to and from Seven Mile Beach resorts. Other popular trips combine Eden Rock, Cheeseburger Reef, and the wreck of the *Cali* off George Town. Most decent-size boats offer cover, but bring sunscreen and a hat.

SNORKELING SITES

Barrier Reef. A Barrier Reef separates the North Sound and Cayman's celebrated wall drop-off (part of a 6,000-foot underwater mountain). You can snorkel along the shallow side, which is crawling with critters of all shapes, sizes, and colors. ⊠ *Grand Cayman.*

★ **Cemetery Reef.** Cemetery Reef sits 50 yards out from the north end of Seven Mile Beach, within walking distance of several condo resorts. Fish here are also accustomed to being fed, so blue tangs to blue-headed wrasse and bat jacks to black durgeon could swarm around you. ⊠ *Grand Cayman.*

Cheeseburger Reef. Cheeseburger Reef earned its unusual moniker thanks to its location straight out from the downtown Burger King. It's also known as Soto's Reef after

Stingray City

Hundreds of gray and khaki Atlantic Southern stingrays, resembling inquisitive alien life forms, enact an acrobatic aqua-ballet as they circle this North Sound site seeking handouts from divers and snorkelers. The area actually encompasses two separate locations: Stingray City, called by many the world's greatest 12-foot dive, and the nearby sandbar, where people can wade in waist-deep water.

Steve Irwin's tragic demise rekindled humankind's age-old fear of these beautiful, mysterious "devil" creatures with their barbed tails. The Atlantic southern stingrays are a different, smaller species than the stingray that killed Irwin and as close to tame as possible. Shy and unaggressive by nature, they use their tails only in defense; nonetheless, don't pick rays up unless you follow your guide's careful instructions.

Stingray City's origins can be traced to local fishermen who would moor inside the fringe reef, then clean their catch, tossing the scraps overboard. Captain Marvin Ebanks, who still runs trips in his 90s, recalls feeding them as a child. The rays, who hunt via keen smell (and sensitive electro-receptors stippling their underside, near the mouth), realized they'd discovered their own restaurant and began hanging around. They slowly became inured to human interaction, rarely displaying the species' typical timidity. They glide like graceful giants (up to 4 feet in diameter), practically nuzzling you with their silken bellies, begging pet-like for food. Indeed, crews recognize them (and vice versa), fondly giving the rays nicknames (Hoo-Ray, X-Ray, Gamma Ray), insisting they have distinct personalities.

Instead of teeth, their mouths contain vise-like sucking grips. Keep your palms face-up and as flat as possible so they don't unintentionally "swallow" your fingers (their eyes are located atop their bodies, so they hover over and practically hoover your hand in excitement).

More formal visitation guidelines have now been established because five to 20 boats visit twice daily, and the population is growing at an alarming rate. Feeding is restricted to appointed tour operators; only natural bait fish like ballyhoo and squid are permitted; the food amount is limited; and any remains and litter must be removed. Many Caymanians and divers oppose altered feeding because it changes the ecosystem's natural food chain. But some concede the good outweighs the bad: The interaction is magical, not to mention fostering greater appreciation and environmental awareness.

legendary diver Bob Soto, one of the islands' original dive operators. The eye-popping, 12,000-year-old coral formations begin 20 yards offshore, with larger heads a mere 10 feet down, though it reaches depths of 40 feet. You can swim through numerous tunnels where turtles and tarpon hang out; people have long fed fish in the area, and they're not shy, wanting it their way, but beware of snapping snappers if you bring food. ⊠ *Grand Cayman.*

Coral Gardens. Coral Gardens, which is very near Stingray Sandbar, attracts nurse sharks, moray eels, queen conch, lobster, and not just schools but universities of jacks, tangs, sergeant majors, parrot fish, yellowtails, and others playing hide-and-seek with riotously colored soft and hard corals. It really is like swimming in an aquarium. ⊠ *Grand Cayman.*

Eden Rock. Eden Rock, in George Town next to Paradise Bar & Grill, is even more spectacular for divers, who can explore its caves and tunnels, then proceed to Devil's Grotto. Still, from the surface you can see schools of sergeant majors, yellowtail snappers, parrot fish, tarpon, Bermuda chubs, even the occasional stingray and turtle. ⊠ *Grand Cayman.*

★ **Fodor's Choice** **Stingray Sandbar.** Stingray Sandbar (as opposed to Stingray City, the popular 12-foot dive) is the stellar snorkeling attraction on Grand Cayman and simply not to be missed; dozens of boats head here several times daily. The area is always less crowded if you can go on a day when there are fewer cruise ships in port. ⊠ *Grand Cayman.*

Wreck of the *Cali*. The Wreck of the *Cali* sits offshore in George Town harbor roughly 50 yards out from Rackam's and Hammerheads pubs. You can still identify parts such as engines and winches of this old sailing freighter, which settled about 20 feet down. The sponges are particularly vivid, and tropical fish, shrimp, and lobster abound. Many operators based in George Town and Seven Mile Beach come here, as well as Eden Rock. ⊠ *Grand Cayman.*

SNORKELING OPERATORS

Bayside Watersports. Bayside Watersports offers half-day snorkeling trips, North Sound beach lunch excursions, Stingray City and dinner cruises, and full-day deep-sea fishing. The company operates several popular boats out of West Bay's Morgan's Harbour. Full-day trips include lunch and conch diving in season (November–April). ⊠ *Grand Cayman* ☎ *345/949–3200* ⊕ *www.baysidewatersports.com.*

🕓 **Captain Crosby's Watersports.** Captain Crosby's Watersports offers favorably priced snorkeling (and dive) excursions on a well-equipped 47-foot trimaran; $30 includes lunch. Captain Crosby is one of the more colorful captains among a group of genuine characters (he maintains a friendly rivalry with his fellow sailors regarding who really jump-started Stingray City tours). He's actively involved in preserving Cayman's maritime heritage as a founder of the Catboat Association. As a bonus, the trips are usually a little longer in duration; expect a sing-along with the captain on his guitar at some point. You can also arrange deep-sea fishing charters. ⊠ *Grand Cayman* ☎ *345/945–4049, 345/916–1725* ⊕ *www.captaincrosbyswatersports.com.*

Captain Marvin's. Multistop North Sound snorkeling trips, as well as fishing charters and land tours, are offered here. The indomitable, irrepressible Captain Marvin, one of the first regular Stingray City operators (in business since 1951), is still going strong in his 90s. Full-day trips include lunch and conch dives in season (November–April), when the crew prepares marinated conch as the appetizer. The half-day (three hours) is a better deal than the quickie trips; the only drawback is the relatively large groups. Reservations can be made only from 10 am to 3 pm on weekdays or via the website. Cash payments usually receive a discount. ⊠ *Grand Cayman* ☎ *345/945–4590, 345/945–6975, 345/945–7306, 866/978–6364* ⊕ *www.captainmarvins.com.*

🕓 **Ebanks Watersports.** Ebanks Watersports is run by a large family long known for its aquatic activities. Shawn Ebanks offers a range of water-sports activities, including various snorkeling tours, private charters, fishing, and his popular Yamaha wave-runner snorkel tours (the last are costlier, $125 for single riders, $175 for two). The crew is both friendly and experienced; they're particularly adept at holding the stingrays for the ultimate photo op; they'll even teach you how to pick one up yourself. His two custom-fitted boats (a 45-foot Garcia and 34-foot Wellcraft Scarab) include GPS navigation, VHS radio, freshwater shower, and other necessities. ⊠ *Grand Cayman* ☎ *345/925–5273* ⊕ *www.ebankswatersports.com.*

🕓 **Fantasea Tours.** Captain Dexter Ebanks runs Fantasea Tours on his 38-foot trimaran, *Don't Even Ask.* He doesn't pack you in like sardines (20 people max) and is particularly helpful with first-timers. Like many of the captains, he has his own pet names for the rays (ask him to find Lucy, whom he "adopted") and rattles off fascinating factoids during an entertaining, nonstop narration. It's a laid-back trip, with Bob Marley and Norah Jones on the sound system, and fresh fruit and rum punch on tap. ☎345/916–0754 ⊕ www.dexters-fantaseatours.com.

Kirk Sea Tours. Kirk Sea Tours caters to cruise-ship passengers on 60- to 65-foot boats, as well as the 28-passenger glass-bottom *Reef Roamer,* snorkeling along the West Wall including Cheeseburger Reef. Sometimes it seems the snorkelers outnumber the fish, but the price is right and it's less frenzied when fewer cruise ships are in port. Kirk also rents kayaks for $20 (and can arrange guided tours), Jet Skis ($65 single, $90 double per half hour), paddleboats ($20), and Snuba gear (with instruction). ⊠ *Grand Cayman* ☎345/949–7278, 345/949–6986.

♻ **Red Sail Sports.** Red Sail Sports offers Stingray City, sunset, and evening sails (including dinner in winter) on its luxurious 65-foot catamarans, the *Spirits of Cayman, Poseidon, Calypso,* and *Ppalu.* It often carries large groups; although the service may not be personal, it will be efficient. In addition to the large cats, a glass-bottom boat takes passengers to Stingray City/Sandbar and nearby coral reefs. The cost ranges from $40 to $80. ⊠ *Grand Cayman* ☎345/949–8745, 345/623–5965, 877/506–6368 ⊕ *www. redsailcayman.com.*

SQUASH AND TENNIS

Most resorts and condominium complexes have their own courts, often lit for night play, but guests have top priority. When empty, you can book a court, which normally costs around $25 per hour.

The Courts. The Courts is a collaboration between Ritz-Carlton Grand Cayman and tennis coach Nick Bollettieri (former mentor of Andre Agassi, Monica Seles, Jim Courier, and the Williams sisters at his legendary Florida academy). The club offers three French-style red clay courts and a Wimbledon-worthy grass court. Bollettieri personally trained the director, who gives private lessons ($125); Bollettieri himself occasionally drops by for tournaments and clinics. Court rental is $40 per hour. ⊠ *West Bay Rd., Seven Mile Beach, Grand Cayman* ☎345/943–9000.

South Sound Squash Club. This club has seven international courts, a changing room, a bar and lounge, and coaches.

It's a private club, but temporary memberships can be arranged. ⊠ *25 Anne Bonny Crescent, South Sound, George Town, Grand Cayman* ☏ *345/949–9469* ⊕ *www.squash.ky.*

WINDSURFING AND KITEBOARDING

The East End's reef-protected shallows extend for miles, offering ideal blustery conditions (15 to 35 mph in winter, 6- to 10-knot southerlies in summer) for windsurfing and kiteboarding. Boarders claim only rank amateurs will "tea-bag" (kite-speak for skidding in and out of the water) in those "nuking" winds. They also rarely "Hindenburg" (stall due to lack of breeze) off West Bay's Palmetto Point and Conch Point.

Cayman Windsurfing with Red Sail Sports at Morritt's. Cayman Windsurfing with Red Sail Sports at Morritt's offers a full range of top-flight equipment as well as lessons. Rentals start at $40 per hour; lessons are $65 per hour. ⊠ *Morritt's Tortuga Resort, Colliers, East End, Grand Cayman* ☏ *345/947–2097* ⊕ *www.tortugadivers.com.*

Kitesurf Cayman. Here you can take full advantage of the gusty conditions at Barkers Beach. Head instructor Jhon Mora is a member of the Columbian National Kitesurfing Team; lessons, including tricks such as loops and rolls, are geared toward experienced boarders. Group rates are $150 for two hours (private introductory courses are $225). ⊠ *Barkers, near Papagallo's Restaurant, West Bay, Grand Cayman* ☏ *345/916–5483* ⊕ *www.kitesurfcayman.com.*

Ocean Frontiers. Ocean Frontiers offers kiteboarding rentals and instruction, working with the respected Kitehouse team, with locations from Costa Rica to Key West. Private two-hour lessons are $250; half-day rental is $75. They'll help you achieve 60 feet of big air to practice your triple loops. ⊠ *Compass Point, Austin Connelly Dr., East End, Grand Cayman* ☏ *345/947–7500, 800/348–6096, 345/947–0000* ⊕ *www.oceanfrontiers.com.*

7

Cayman Brac

WORD OF MOUTH

"Cayman Brac is VERY laid-back. Hardly anyone there. Most tourists are divers. The diving at Brac was the best dive vacation we have done."

—Kima

By Jordan Simon **CAYMAN BRAC IS NAMED FOR** its most distinctive feature, a moody, craggy limestone bluff (*brac* in the Gaelic of the Scottish highlands fishermen who settled the islands in the 18th century) that runs up the spine of the 12-mile (19-km) island, culminating in a sheer 140-foot cliff at its eastern end, the country's highest and easternmost point. The Bluff holds the angry Atlantic at bay, gradually tapering like a coil losing its spring in the west. Nature's artistry—and awesome power—is also evident in the many caves and sinkholes that stipple the crag, long rumored to hold pirates' gold. The islandscape is by far the most dramatic in the Cayman Islands, though divers the world over come for the spectacular underwater topography and sponge-encrusted wrecks.

The Brac, as it's commonly called, sits 90 miles (143 km) northeast of Grand Cayman, accessible only via Cayman Airways (and private boat), but it's nothing like the cosmopolitan and Americanized Grand Cayman. With only 1,800 residents—they call themselves Brackers—the island has the feel and easy pace of a small town. Brackers are known for their friendly attitude toward visitors, so it's easy to strike up a conversation. You're never treated like a stranger; locals wave when they pass and might invite you home for a traditional rundown (a thick, sultry fish stew) and storytelling, usually about the sea, the turtle schooners, and the great hurricane of 1932 (when the caves offered shelter to islanders). Brackers are as calm and peaceful as their island is rugged, having been violently sculpted by sea and wind, most recently by Hurricane Paloma, which leveled the island in November 2008 (locals quip that all 18 churches sustained significant damage—but no bars).

Columbus first discovered the island by mistake during his final voyage in 1503; explorers and privateers made infrequent pit stops over the next three centuries, the Bluff serving as a vital navigational landmark. Though the Brac wasn't permanently settled until the 1830s, its short history seethes with dramatic incident, from marauding pirates to ravaging hurricanes. Today, despite its small size (roughly 12 miles by 1½ mile, or 14 square miles), the Brac is reinventing itself as an eco-centric, adventure destination. Aside from diving, bonefish in the shallows and game fish in the deeper offshore waters lure anglers. The island hosts numerous ecosystems from arid semidesert stubbled with cacti to ancient dry woodlands thick with exotic, fragrant flowers and trees. More than 200 bird species, both indigenous and migratory—including the endangered Cayman Brac parrot—flutter about. Nature trails filigree the interior, and several caves can be easily accessed. No surprise that the island is also considered one of the world's most exotic rock-climbing destinations, famous for its sheer vertical cliffs.

Hamlets with names like Watering Place, Cotton Tree Bay, Creek (Rock), and Spot Bay hold charming restored homes typical of seafaring architecture embroidered with carefully tended yards bursting with tropical blooms. Dozens of tiny churches line the road, bordered by sand graveyards. Despite the expats gradually boosting the year-round population, development remains as blissfully slow as the pace, though one longtime escapee from the stateside rat race grumbles about fancier cars and faster driving. There's still no stoplight, and traffic is defined by two locals stopping in the middle of the road to chat. It's as idyllic as a semideveloped island can be. Indeed, the Brac is the affectionate butt of jokes from other Caymanians: "Two 60-year-old Brackers were so bored they decided to put in a bomb threat," starts one; the punch line, depending on the teller, is that they fall asleep first—or that nothing results. Another, referring to the three or four families dominating the phone book, runs: "The most confusing day of the year on the Brac is Father's Day."

But Brackers take it all in stride, knowing their tranquil existence and abundant natural splendors give them the last laugh in the tourism sweepstakes.

ORIENTATION AND PLANNING

ORIENTATION

The island is quite easy to navigate for the most part. One main road hugs the north coast, another the south, while a paved rollercoaster bypass (Ashton Reid Drive) across the Bluff roughly bisects the island, linking the two sides. Numerous gravel and dirt roads crisscross the island, but these are best avoided. The main hotel development and nicest beaches lie near the airport in the West End (the island's lowest point, at sea level). The southern road climbs the Bluff, passing spectacular caves and cliffs, ending at the Parrot Reserve and Lighthouse, with their splendid panoramic trails. The north road accesses the tiny towns of Stake Bay and Spot Bay, where several historic attractions are located.

TOP EXPERIENCES

■ **Diving.** This is unquestionably one of the world's great scuba destinations, from walls and wrecks exploding with kaleidoscopic marine life to wondrous man-made creations like the "Lost City of Atlantis" underwater installation.

■ **Lighthouse Walk.** In addition to thrilling Caribbean vistas and an eerie, almost lonely lunar look, you experience nature's fierce elemental savagery, the crescendo of crashing surf and whipping wind.

■ **Local Crafts.** Several "old timer" artisans keep traditions alive. Visiting their shops (often in their homes) is a marvelous immersion in Bracker culture.

■ **Caving.** Several caves are accessible—most easily, some via a mildly strenuous hike; in addition to striking natural formations, they played a vital role in sheltering islanders during storms.

■ **Museum-hop.** The Cayman Brac Museum pays tribute to this remote island's maritime tradition; though small, it's jam-packed with odd, often poignant little artifacts.

PLANNING

WHEN TO GO

The Brac is sleepy year-round, and there's slightly less difference pricewise between low and high season than on other islands, since diving, climbing, and fishing excel throughout the year, as does bird-watching (though winter attracts the migrant fowl). Still, summer represents savings, though some properties might close for maintenance in September during hurricane season.

GETTING HERE AND AROUND

BY AIR

Cayman Airways Express provides Twin Otter service several times daily from Grand Cayman to Cayman Brac. Depending on the flight route, you may land on Little Cayman first. The flight is approximately 40 minutes nonstop. Cayman Brac has its own small airport, Gerrard Smith International Airport (CYB).

BY CAR

You need a car to really explore Cayman Brac, though hotels often provide complimentary bikes. Your own valid driver's license is necessary to obtain a temporary local driving permit ($7.50), which can be used on any of the Cayman Islands. Figure $35 to $50 per day, with compacts and midsize generally at the low end, Jeeps and full-size median, and SUVs high-end.

Driving is on the left, British-style. Gasoline is quite expensive; there are only two stations (one at each end of the island), whose hours can be erratic. The main road circumnavigating the island and the bypass over the Bluff connecting the north and south coasts are well maintained. Yellow lines on roads indicate no parking zones. Most locals park on the side of the road.

Four D's, which carries mostly Nissans, tends to have cheaper rates, though rarely offers discounts; pickup and drop-off are included. B&S Motor Ventures offers compacts, midsize vehicles, Jeeps, SUVs, and vans. The only on-site airport agency, CB Rent-A-Car, has Hondas and Toyotas from compact to minivan.

Contacts B&S Motor Ventures ☎ 345/948–1646 ⊕ www.bandsmv. com. **CB Rent-A-Car** ✉ Airport Dr., Gerrard Smith Airport, West End, Cayman Brac ☎ 345/948–2424, 345/948–2847 ⊕ www.cbrentacar. com. **Four D's Car Rental** ☎ 345/948–1599.

BY TAXI

Brackers often wear several hats, so your tour guide might also take you out fishing or serve you drinks; all of them are fonts of local lore and legend. An island day tour generally costs $24 per person, with a minimum of two people. Occasionally, you may have to wait to be picked up. Your hotel can arrange airport transfers. Rates are generally fixed: $8 to the closest hotels like Brac Reef Beach Resort, $15 to Cayman Breakers near the southeastern tip, $20 to the Bight and Spot Bay on the north side. Drivers will generally load up passengers from several properties, including individual villas.

The tourist office and the hotels have a list of preferred providers, including D&M Taxi and Tours, run by David Hurlston, who has a minivan as well as a 24-passenger bus for larger groups. He and his daughter Monica are courteous, knowledgeable guides, as is his father, O'Neil, who sometimes spells him and can regale you with soft-spoken stories of scaling the Bluff to collect water or herd cattle at 4 AM, as well as his adventures running bananas from Ecuador to Virginia.

Contacts D&M Taxi and Tours ☎ 345/939–0583, 345/916–7226.

VISITOR INFORMATION

From 8:30 to 5 weekdays, the affable staff at the Sister Islands office of the Cayman Islands Department of Tourism can supply brochures on accommodations, dive outfits, activities, and nature and heritage trails. This office also services Little Cayman.

Contacts Cayman Islands Department of Tourism ⊠ *209 West End Community Park, West End, Cayman Brac* ☎ *345/948–1649* ⊕ *www.caymanislands.ky.*

RESTAURANTS

Most resorts offer optional meal plans, but there are several independent restaurants on the island, some of which provide free transport from your hotel. Local restaurants serve island fare (local seafood, chicken, and curries, as well as addictive beef patties). On Friday and Saturday nights the spicy scent of jerk chicken fills the air; several roadside stands sell take-out dinners. Look for the local specialty, a sweetish, pillow-soft, round bread.

HOTELS

Lodgings are small and intimate, and guests are often treated like family, congregating in the lobby or bar to swap stories, tall or otherwise, of their exploits. There are only a few full-service resorts, two of them condo complexes. There are also a couple of cozy guesthouses and several private villas (usually second homes for snowbirds) for rent throughout the island. In November 2008, Hurricane Paloma wiped out most of the island's larger properties. All have been rebuilt, in some cases from the ground up.

HOTEL AND RESTAURANT PRICES

Prices in the restaurant reviews are the average cost of a main course at dinner or, if dinner is not served, at lunch; taxes and service charges are generally included. Prices in the hotel reviews are the lowest cost of a standard double room in high season, excluding taxes, service charges, and meal plans (except at all-inclusives). Prices for rentals are the lowest per-night cost for a one-bedroom unit in high season.

EXPLORING CAYMAN BRAC

The Brac abounds in both natural and historic attractions. Many of the former include botanic gardens and preserves set aside to protect threatened indigenous species. The latter revolve around the maritime heritage and hardscrabble lives of the earliest settlers and their descendants up until the island developed better communication with the outside world in the 1970s. *For more specific listings of caves and nature trails of particular significance, see ⇨ Sports and the Outdoors.*

If you're exploring on your own, be sure to pick up the *Cayman Brac Heritage Sites & Trails* brochure, available at the tourist office and most hotels; it lists all the major points of interest.

The **Sister Islands District Administration** *(☎345/948–2222 Ext. 4420, ask for organizer Chevala Burke ⊕www. naturecayman.com)* offers free government-sponsored guided nature and cultural tours with trained local guides Cantrell Scott and Keino Daley. Options include the Parrot Reserve, nature trails, wetlands, Lighthouse/Bluff View, caving, birding, and heritage sites. You just supply the wheels and spirit of adventure.

WHAT TO SEE

★ **Cayman Brac Museum.** Here you'll find a diverse, well-displayed collection of historic Bracker implements from scary dental pliers to pistols to pottery. A meticulously crafted scale model of the Caymanian catboat *Alsons* has pride of place. The front room faithfully reconstructs the Customs, Treasury, bank, and post office as they would have looked decades ago. Permanent exhibits include those on the 1932 hurricane, turtling, shipbuilding, and typical old-time home life, including a child's bedroom; the back room hosts rotating exhibits such as one on herbal folk medicine. ⊠ *Old Government Administration Bldg., Stake Bay, Cayman Brac* ☎*345/948–2622, 345/244–4446* ☞*Free* ⊙ *Weekdays 9–4, Sat. 9–noon.*

Heritage House. The acre of beautifully landscaped grounds dotted with thatched gazebos and fountains includes an old-fashioned well and tannery, as well as Cola Cave (used to shelter the former estate owners during hurricanes), with informational panels. The main building, though new, replicates a traditional house; the interior has a few displays and videos depicting Brac history, but the treat is watching local artists at work. It's a great resource for books on natural history and Caymanian crafts; daily slide shows, various cultural events, and talks by visiting naturalists are often scheduled. Call ahead before visiting to make sure that the house is open. ⊠ *Northeast Bay Rd., Spot Bay, Cayman Brac* ☎*345/948–0563* ☞*Free* ⊙ *Weekdays 9:30–1 and 2–5, Sat. 10–3.*

Cayman Brac

KEY

⚲	Beaches
⬧	Dive Sites
1	Restaurants
①	Hotels

Restaurants

Alexander Hotel
Restaurant, 3
Aunt Sha's Kitchen, 1
Captain's Table, 2
Coral Isle Club, 4
La Esperanza, 5

Hotels

Alexander Hotel, 3
Brac Caribbean and
Carib Sands, 2
Brac Reef
Beach Resort, 1
Cayman Breakers, 4
La Esperanza, 5
Walton's Mango
Manor, 6

★ **Parrot Preserve.** The likeliest place to spot the endangered Cayman Brac parrot—and other indigenous and migratory birds—is along this National Trust hiking trail off Major Donald Drive, aka Lighthouse Road. Prime time is early morning or late afternoon; most of the day they're camouflaged by trees, earning them the moniker "stealth parrot." The loop trail incorporates part of a path the Brackers used in olden days to cross the Bluff to reach their provision grounds on the south shore or to gather coconuts, once a major export crop. It passes through several types of terrain: old farmland under grass and native trees from mango to mahogany unusually mixed with orchids and cacti. Wear sturdy shoes, as the terrain is rocky, uneven, and occasionally rough. The 6-mile (10-km) gravel road continues to the lighthouse at the Bluff's eastern end, where there's an astonishing view from atop the cliff to the open ocean—the best place to watch the sunrise. ⊠ *Lighthouse Rd., ½ mile (1 km) south of town, Tibbetts Turn, Cayman Brac* ☎ *345/948–0319* ☞ *Free* ⊙ *Daily sunrise–sunset.*

★ **Spellman McLaughlin Home.** This green-trimmed, whitewashed clapboard house, built by Captain Spellman McLaughlin between 1926 and 1930, is one of the last surviving examples of classic Bracker architecture (most were blown away by the great 1932 hurricane). McLaughlin constructed the house from pine timber he ferried on his own schooner from Mobile and Pensacola. Eschewing the expedient custom of using precut lengths for prefabricated designs, he instead cut the planks to specification on-site. It's supported on 60 full-section log posts sunk into the ground. Wooden pegs (rather than rustable nails) join many sections. Three individually pitched gable ends tower above the verandah roof (fashioned from salvaged curved boat boards), forming the optical illusion of a second story. The eight exterior rooms surround the dining room, the focal point of Bracker life; each features a window and door to the wraparound verandah, ensuring that the house captures the light and the breezes. His youngest daughter, Mrs. Brunzil Rivers, still lives in her childhood home and proudly shows people around, almost apologizing for the modern modifications (the kitchen once occupied a separate building to minimize fire risk and reduce heat, and closets have replaced the wardrobes standard at the time). Especially exceptional are the dining room's diagonal wall patterning and the front north parlor's domed beaded ceiling. ⊠ *Northeast Bay Rd., Creek, Cayman Brac* ☎ *345/949–0121* ☞ *Free* ⊙ *Call for appointment.*

THE GREAT HURRICANE OF '32. Brackers were ill prepared for hurricanes, especially the deadly storm with 200 mph winds that blustered its way over the island in 1932, destroying virtually everything in its path. Most Brackers took shelter in the caves sculpted from the Bluff. Others flooded into the McLaughlin home, which miraculously stood fast, saving 130 people. A "tear of sea" (archaic argot for a tidal wave) crashed onto shore, sending a boulder hurtling through the front door. Other than some damage from flooding, the house withstood the brunt of the storm quite well, and even the windows remained unbroken. Even younger Brackers still discuss the storm with awe, though Paloma matched its fury.

WHERE TO EAT

$$$ ✕ **Alexander Hotel Restaurant.** *European.* This potentially fine eatery is all over the place, from cuisine to decor. The kitchen's one-from-column-A approach tries to accommodate all tastes, running from conch fritters in fruit chutney to Parmesan-crusted chicken in chardonnay sauce to salmon Oscar (hollandaise and crabmeat). Save for handsome portraits of Brackers in traditional island scenes, the space likewise lacks identity, resembling a sterile conference room gussied up with burgundy chairs, wainscoting, and potted plants. Service is smiling, however, and the chef Errol Buckner promises to infuse more individual (and local) flair into the menu. ⑤ *Average main: $28* ⊠ *West End, Cayman Brac* ☎ *345/948–8222* ⊕ *www.alexanderbrac.com* ⌕ *Reservations essential.*

$$ ✕ **Aunt Sha's Kitchen.** *Caribbean.* Sharon Connolly is the eponymous owner of this unassuming pretty-in-pink spot, which is usually packed with locals, from ladies in hairnets to fishers with buckets of catch flirting or gossiping (the island's best eavesdropping). Sea green and sky blue walls, ceramic fish, nature photos, and fringe lamps lend some decorative flair, but you come here for stellar Caymanian cuisine, from brown stew tuna to conch fritters, Cayman-style lobster (the most expensive item by far, also prepared curried or broiled in mushroom sauce), or even fried chicken, all served with heaping helpings of sides such as dumplings. You can add heat with homemade hot sauce (pickled peppers, cabbage, onions, and tomato) that will knock your socks (and shoes) off. Everyone swears by Aunt Sha's velvety key lime pie. ⑤ *Average main: $16* ⊠ *West End, Cayman Brac* ☎ *345/948–1581* ⊙ *No dinner Sun.*

$$ ✕ **Captain's Table.** *European.* This weathered, powder blue, wooden building wouldn't be out of place on some remote New England shore, except perhaps for the garish pirate at the entrance. The nautical yo-ho-hokum continues inside (painted oars, model sailboats, faux portholes, droll touches like a skeleton with a chef's toque), but fortunately the kitchen isn't lost at sea, despite voyaging from India to Italy. Teriyaki chicken and scampi Florentine are worthy house specialties. Lunch is cheaper, from standbys (wraps, burgers, nachos) to more creative options like "honey-stung" fried chicken. The outdoor poolside bar is a popular hangout for dive masters. Ⓢ *Average main: $20* ⊠ *Brac Caribbean, West End, Cayman Brac* ☎ *345/948–1418* ⚑ *Reservations essential.*

$$ ✕ **Coral Isle Club.** *Caribbean.* This seaside eatery daubed in a virtual rainbow of blues from turquoise to teal serves up fine local food, emphasizing fresh seafood and, on weekends, mouth- and eye-watering barbecue. The lusciously painted outdoor bar offers equally colorful sunsets, cocktails, and characters (one regular swears, "If I were any better, I'd be dangerous," before buying another round). At night, spotlights illuminate the reef sharks and lobsters lurking in the turtle grass below the patio. The congenial owner, Carlton Ebanks, offers regular entertainment from DJs to fashion shows to domino tournaments, whenever possible on weekends in season. Ⓢ *Average main: $15* ⊠ *Off South Side Rd., West End, Cayman Brac* ☎ *345/925–4848.*

$$ ✕ **La Esperanza.** *Caribbean.* Known island-wide as Bussy's— after the larger-than-life owner—this combination grocery store, restaurant, and club encompasses a wildly colored lounge, alfresco bar with elevated gazebo, and covered pier jutting into the Caribbean. Drink in the sunset views, and then dine on fresh-caught seafood (conch is particularly yummy, whether as fritters or prepared "Cayman style" in lemon-butter sauce with onions and bell peppers). Burgers, fish-and-chips, and chicken chop suey are evergreen favorites. The place really jumps Friday and Saturday nights, when Bussy cranks up his grills and "jerks" chicken (he'll give you impromptu "jerking" lessons). Wife Velma makes a luscious key lime pie that would give Aunt Sha's a run for the top prize if the Brac had county-fair-style bake-offs. Ⓢ *Average main: $17* ⊠ *The Creek, Stake Bay, Cayman Brac* ☎ *345/948–0531* ◷ *No dinner Sun.*

WHERE TO STAY

Cayman Brac has a handful of hotels and resorts, as well
as a decent B&B and several apartments. Several private
villas on Cayman Brac can also be rented, most of them
basic but well maintained, ranging from one to four bedrooms. The rental fees are quite reasonable, and normally
the price for extra couples in the larger units is only $200
per week (singles $100–$135, children often free), representing substantial savings for families or couples traveling
together, while the kitchen helps reduce the price of dining
out. In addition, government tax and often a service fee
are sometimes included in the quoted rate (be sure to verify
this), and most villa owners arrange a 10% discount with
car-rental agencies. As a general rule of thumb, properties
are thoroughly cleaned before your arrival; you must pay
extra if you want daily maid service, and a one-time cleaning fee of $50 to $75 is usually assessed for end-of-rental
cleaning. Owners can sometimes arrange to prestock the
fridge. Each villa has a manager who must meet you at the
airport (or car-rental agency), then escort you to your home;
you'll be provided with his or her contact information during the reservation process. Rates are sometimes discounted
in the off-season. Contact the tourist office for information.

Most villa owners mandate a three- to seven-night minimum stay in high season (assume at least one week's booking during the Christmas holiday unless otherwise noted),
though this is often negotiable. Some owners will leave a
kayak or snorkeling gear out for guests' use. If such amenities are included, they're mentioned. Unless otherwise
noted, properties have landline phones; local calls are usually free, but phones are generally locked for international
calls. If your GSM provider works in the Cayman Islands,
activate the international capability, but note that service
is poor or nonexistent at some villas on the South Side
beneath the Bluff.

$ ☷ **Alexander Hotel.** *Hotel.* This chic boutique business hotel
★ elevates Brac lodging to a new level, though with no on-
site activities to offer vacationers who make up the larger
proportion of Brac travelers, its ultimate target audience
is unclear.**Pros:** high-tech amenities; stylish yet affordable;
next door to small shopping mall for sundries and food;
delightful alfresco bar. **Cons:** two-minute walk to a peb-
bly beach; small pool; inadequate bedside and bathroom
lighting; no on-site activities; Wi-Fi spotty in some rooms.

⑤ *Rooms from: $156* ✉ *Cayman Brac* ☎ *345/948–8222, 800/381–5094* ⊕ *www.alexanderbrac.com* ↪ *29 rooms, 2 2-bedroom suites* ⑩ *No meals.*

$ ⊡ **Brac Caribbean and Carib Sands.** *Resort.* These neighboring, beachfront, sister complexes, almost completely rebuilt (and expanded) after Paloma, offer condos with one to four bedrooms, all individually owned and decorated beyond a "starter" design. **Pros:** lively restaurant-bar; excellent value for families, especially with weekly discounts. **Cons:** pretty but narrow, often unmaintained beach; limited staff; Wi-Fi dodgy. ⑤ *Rooms from: $148* ✉ *Bert Marson Dr., Cayman Brac* ☎ *345/948–2265, 866/843–2722* ⊕ *www.866thebrac.com* ↪ *65 condos* ⑩ *No meals.*

$ ⊡ **Brac Reef Beach Resort.** *All-Inclusive.* Popular with divers,
★ this well-run eco-friendly resort, entirely rebuilt from the ground up, features a beautiful sandy beach shaded by sea grape trees slung with hammocks. **Pros:** lovely beach; great dive outfit; friendly staff and clientele; free Wi-Fi; good online packages. **Cons:** noise from planes; view often obscured from ground-floor units; mandatory airport transfer of $20 per person. ⑤ *Rooms from: $157* ✉ *West End, Cayman Brac* ☎ *345/948–1323, 727/323–8727 for reservations in Florida, 800/594–0843* ⊕ *www.bracreef.com* ↪ *40 rooms* ⑩ *Multiple meal plans.*

$ ⊡ **Cayman Breakers.** *Rental.* This attractive, pink-brick, col-
★ onnaded condo development sitting between the Bluff and the southeast coastal ironshore caters to climbers, who scale the Bluff's sheer face, as well as divers, who appreciate the good shore diving right off the property. **Pros:** spectacular views; thoughtful extras like complimentary bikes, jigsaw puzzles, and climbing-route guides; very attentive managers who live on-site. **Cons:** nearest grocery is a 15-minute drive; gorgeous beach is rocky and has rough surf; some units slightly musty and faded. ⑤ *Rooms from: $150* ✉ *Cayman Brac* ☎☎ *345/948–1463* ⊕ *www.caybreakers.com* ↪ *26 2-bedroom condos* ⑩ *No meals.*

$ ⊡ **La Esperanza.** *Rental.* This fun, funky seaside cluster of mango-and-teal buildings with magenta accents is run by industrious, affable owners who also rent cars and offer free use of (and sometimes transportation to) their private beach 6 miles (10 km) away on the gentler south shore. **Pros:** fun ambience; good snorkeling; party time on weekends; grocery on-site. **Cons:** slightly threadbare; weekend parties get loud. ⑤ *Rooms from: $94* ✉ *Stake Bay, Cayman Brac* ☎ *345/948–0591* ⊕ *www.laesperanza.net* ↪ *4 2-bedroom apartments, 2 3-bedroom houses* ⑩ *No meals.*

$ ⊞ **Walton's Mango Manor.** *B&B/Inn.* This beautifully restored
★   traditional West Indian home has five rooms (all with bath),
accented with lovely antique furnishings, nautical gadgets,
maps, model catboats, and bric-a-brac from the Waltons'
world travels. **Pros:** true Caymanian hospitality; beautiful
grounds; excellent snorkeling; free Wi-Fi access. **Cons:** poky
beach across the street; car required. ⑤ *Rooms from: $120*
⊠ *Stake Bay, Cayman Brac* ☎ *345/948–0518, 321/226–0440
from U.S., 888/866–5809* ⊕ *www.waltonsmangomanor.
com* ↪ *5 rooms, 1 2-bedroom cottage* ⦿ *Breakfast.*

BEACHES

Much of the Brac's coastline is ironshore, though there
are several pretty sand beaches, mostly along the southwest coast (where swimmers will also find extensive beds
of turtle grass, which creates less than ideal conditions
for snorkeling). In addition to the hotel beaches, where
everyone is welcome, there is a public beach with good
access to the reef; it's well marked on tourist maps. The
north-coast beaches, predominantly rocky ironshore, offer
excellent snorkeling.

Buccaneer's Beach. Just north of the airport, the rocky stretch
is somewhat rough, but the snorkeling is sublime; you'll
recognize the area when you see the 1860 windlass (winch)
of the SS *Kersearge* in the ironshore. ⊠ *Georgiana Dr., just
before North Side Rd. E, West End, Cayman Brac.*

Pollard Bay. The beach by Cayman Breakers is fairly wide
for this eastern stretch of the island. You can start clamber-
ing east underneath the imposing Bluff, past the end of the
paved road, to find strikingly beautiful deserted stretches
accessible only on foot, but the water here starts churning
like a washing machine. It becomes progressively rockier,
littered with driftwood; you might stumble upon locals
searching for whelks here. There are also new steps by
the Breakers leading to shore dive sites. Flocks of seabirds
darken the sun for seconds at a time, while blowholes spout
as if answering migrant humpback whales. Don't go beyond
the gargantuan rock called First Cay—the sudden swells
can be hazardous—unless you're a serious rock climber.
⊠ *South Side Rd. E, East End, Cayman Brac.*

Public Beach. Roughly 2 miles (3 km) east of the Brac Reef
and Carib Sands/Brac Caribbean resorts, just past the wetlands (the unsightly gate is visible from the road; if you

House of Worship

The pale blue, circular Temple Beth Shalom nestles incongruously in the Waltons' serene garden, replete with the only consecrated Jewish cemetery in the Cayman Islands. A plaque by the imposing carved mahogany door reads "House of Welcome, May All Who Enter Here Find Peace." Brooklyn-born Lynne presides over services, though rabbis and cantors fly in for special occasions and holidays. George erected the synagogue as a gift to his wife but says, "I hope that any person from around the world will talk to God as they understand Him without intervention.... Protestants love the temple; they spend more time here than the Jews, even one of the most hard-core Baptist families we have." Indeed, visitors from Argentina to Austria to Australia have renewed their spirits here.

Swiss architect Fredy Schulteiss designed the building, but George and Lynne practically built it by themselves. It includes stained glass, Italian marble accents from Italy, and polished gray Minnesota granite floors they laid themselves. Lynne carved everything from the marble to the Honduran mahogany doors and inlaid scrolling fashioned from dead limbs of wild plum, cedar, mahogany, ironwood, and candlewood trees. Her father created a menorah in the shape of a shofar; another was a family heirloom brought by Lynne's grandmother from Odessa. The synagogue is actually one structure encased within another, "one for the Torah, the other to reach toward the heavens, in a small way making a statement to God that we're trying to get there." The 28-foot ceiling fittingly depicts a starry sky, with the 12 lights representing the 12 tribes of Israel. As a bonus, the space has splendid acoustics and a piano. Members of the Cayman National Orchestra, including flutists, pianists, and cellists, occasionally perform memorable classical concerts.

hit the Bat Cave you've passed it), lie a series of strands culminating in this relatively deserted beach (despite its name). The surf is calm and the crystalline water fairly protected for swimming. There are picnic tables and showers in uncertain condition. Snorkeling is quite good. ⊠ *South Side Rd. W, South Side, Cayman Brac.*

Sea Feather Bay. The central section of the south coast features several lengthy ribbons of soft ecru sand, with little shade aside from the occasional coconut palm, no facilities, and blissful privacy (aside from the occasional villa). ⊠ *South Side Rd. just west of Ashton Reid Dr., Sea Feather Bay, South Side, Cayman Brac.*

SPORTS AND THE OUTDOORS

BIRD-WATCHING

Bird-watching is sensational on the Sister Islands, with almost 200 species patrolling the island from migratory to endemic, including the endangered Cayman Brac parrot and brown booby. The best place to spy the feathered lovelies is on the north coast and in the protected woodland reserve *(see* ⇨ *Parrot Reserve in Exploring Cayman Brac)* on the Bluff. Other species to look out for include the indigenous vitelline warbler and red-legged thrush. The wetlands and ponds in the West End teem with herons and shorebirds, including splendid frigates, kestrels, ospreys, and rare West Indian whistling ducks. Most coastal areas offer sightings, but the best may be just inland at the **Westerly Ponds** (which connect during rainy season; otherwise boardwalks provide excellent viewing areas). A hundred species flap about, particularly around the easternmost pond off Bert Marson Drive by Mr. Billy's house: The old Bracker feeds them late afternoon and occasionally early morning, when the whistling ducks practically coat the entire surface of the water.

DIVING AND SNORKELING

Cayman Brac's waters are celebrated for their rich diversity of sea life, from hammerhead and reef sharks to stingrays to seahorses. Divers and snorkelers alike will find towering coral heads, impressive walls, and fascinating wrecks. The snorkeling and shore diving off the **north coast** are spectacular, particularly at West End, where nearby coral formations attract all kinds of critters. The walls feature remarkable topography with natural gullies, caves, and fissures blanketed with Technicolor sponges, black coral, gorgonians, and sea fans. Some of the famed sites are the West Chute, Cemetery Wall, Airport Wall, and Garden Eel Wall.

The **South Wall** is a wonderland of sheer drop-offs carved with a maze of vertical swim-throughs, tunnels, arches, and grottoes that divers nickname Cayman's Grand Canyon. Notable sites include Anchor Wall, Rock Monster Chimney, and the Wilderness.

Notable diving attractions around the island include the 330-foot MV *Capt. Keith Tibbetts,* a Russian frigate purchased from Cuba and deliberately scuttled in 1996 within swimming distance of the northwest shore, accessible to divers of all levels. Many fish have colonized the Russian frigate—now broken in two and encrusted with magnificent orange and yellow sponges. Other underwater wrecks include the *Cayman Mariner,* a steel tugboat, and the *Prince Frederick,* a wooden-hulled twin-masted schooner that allegedly sank in the 19th century.

Oceanic Voyagers, a 7-foot-tall bronze statue created by world-renowned marine sculptor Dale Evers, depicts spotted dolphins cavorting with southern stingrays and was sunk off the Brac's coast near Stake Bay in January 2003 as part of the Cayman Islands' yearlong quincentennial celebration. An artist named Foots has created an amazing underwater Atlantis off Radar Reef.

Other top snorkeling/shore diving spots include the south coast's **Pillar Coral Reef, Tarpon Reef,** and **Lighthouse Reef;** the north shore counters with **Greenhouse Reef, Snapper Reef,** and **Jan's Reef.**

★ **Reef Divers.** Pluses here include five boats, valet service, and enthusiastic, experienced staff. Certified divers can purchase à la carte dive packages even if they aren't guests of the hotel. ⊠ *Brac Reef Beach Resort, West End, Cayman Brac* ☎ *345/948–1642, 345/948–1323* ⊕ *www.bracreef.com.*

FISHING

Cayman Brac offers superior bonefishing along the shallows off the southwest coast and even finer light-tackle action. The offshore waters mostly compose a marine park, so fishers go out a few hundred feet from the dive buoys, themselves ranging ¼ to ½ mile (½ to 1 km) from shore. The pristine environment teems with wahoo, marlin, and sushi-grade tuna. Most charter-boat operators also run snorkeling trips; a memorable excursion is to Little Cayman Brac, passing several fanciful rock formations.

Robin Walton. This experienced guide has been fishing the waters commercially for years and knows the best times and secret spots where mahimahi, wahoo, marlin, grouper, and tuna hang out. His 21-foot Bayliner Trophy, *TLC,* is equipped with GPS tracking, he quips, "Because I'm lazy." He takes you to truly wonderful sites since he doesn't like

A diver swimming between coral formations

the dive-boat traffic. The maximum is four anglers, though he can fit up to eight comfortably for snorkeling. His rates are also fairly reasonable ($125 per hour) because you subsidize his income with your catch, though he generally allots 50% "or whatever you can manage" to his guests, most of whom cook at their rental condos or villas. ⊠ *Stake Bay, Cayman Brac* ☎ *345/948–2382.*

HIKING

Public footpaths and hiking trails filigree the island, with interpretive signs identifying a staggering variety of resident and nonresident bird species that call the Brac home. You'll also find reptile habitats, indigenous flora, and historically and geologically significant sites. Arguably the most scenic route traverses the eastern Bluff to the tip, where the remains of a lighthouse stand sentinel over the roaring Caribbean. This is one of the routes taken by early Brackers scaling the Bluff via the steep **Lighthouse Steps** up past Peter's Cave (*see* ⇨ *Spelunking*), then down the 2½-mile (4-km) **Lighthouse Footpath** adjacent to Major Donald Drive (aka Lighthouse Road). This was used to bring cattle to pasture, as well as to access plantations of cassava, peppers, beans, tomatoes, sweet potatoes, mangoes, bananas, and other crops. The panoramas are awe inspiring, especially once you reach the lighthouse. Even though the path along the edge is fairly even, it's not suitable for the elderly, very

Sculpting Cayman

A Brac sculptor who is known only as Foots (after his size-16 feet) fantasized of re-creating Plato's lost city of Atlantis. Four decades later, he fulfilled that dream by creating, then sinking mammoth sculptures 45 feet off the Brac's north shore. The resulting artificial reef is an astounding artistic achievement and engineering feat with more than 100 pieces covering several acres.

An architect-contractor who was fascinated by ruins and mythology, Foots found his niche restoring historic buildings, including churches in Germany, Austria, and Iran. To secure permits, Foots submitted a video of his ideal site and a 140-page environmental impact report to the Department of the Environment, noting the goodwill and revenue it would generate in the scuba and tourism industries. "I have money, I just need your blessing," Foots wrote.

He's sunk thousands of dollars ("What price making a dream come true?") and years of his life into the project, which launched officially in 2005, when 150,000 pounds of sculpture were submerged. Specially constructed barges help position the pieces by cranes, lift bags, and drag floats. The technical marvel encompasses nearly 300,000 pounds. The scale is immense, but, as Foots says, "Hopes and dreams make the world livable.... I'm promoting new life and marine growth through art that will last an eternity."

The story starts at the Archway of Atlantis (its two bases weigh 21,000 pounds each). The Elders' Way, lined with 5-foot temple columns, leads to the Inner Circle of Light, centering a 2,600-pound sundial. Two 50,000-pound pyramids tower 20 feet with eight swim-throughs. One ambitious project, the Colossus, a toppled 30-foot statue broken into pieces like 7-foot-long feet and a scepter, will suggest the Lost City's destruction.

Foots modeled the statues after actual people who have contributed to Cayman. He fashions exact plaster of paris molds of their faces (and sometimes hands), then casts in limestone-based cement. Copper piping and doorknobs ingeniously replicate papyrus scrolls; apothecary bottles complete the Medicine Men.

The vision for the entire project has continually evolved inside Foots's head since childhood, without architectural renderings: "I invent so many phases I'd never live long enough to finish.... Atlantis will only end when I do."

Great (Tenson) Scott!

Quite the character, Tenson Scott will regale you with fishing tales, tall and otherwise. Ask him how to catch wahoo without a hook—if he doesn't volunteer this "dynamite, power-packed information" first. Don't blame him if you try it unsuccessfully: He explains, "It's like watching a good love story that turns into Rambo; every fish is different." Another tangent might be a discourse on booby eggs collected from the cliff face for egg punch, "our version of egg nog.... Why go? Man eats the eggs for a month, it improves his performance.... I'm not Spiderman, just a normal Caymanian, but don't go over the cliff just to get nature's Viagra."

You might also hear the story of when he went "fishering" at 14, stopping for fresh rainwater by a hulking boulder known as Slaughterhouse on the southeast coast (he states the name derives from the reputed habit of pirates to spill blood as if consecrating spots where they bury their booty—and the wind-sculpted image of a skull). Tenson tried digging for the long-rumored gold but hit what he thought was a rock. A few years later, some Brackers used a metal detector and sure enough found buried treasure. "I'd have spent it all by now anyway," he shrugs.

---

young, or infirm due to high winds (don't venture onto the dramatic bleached limestone outcroppings: A sudden gust could send you hurtling into the air with the brown boobies that nest in ledges and caves here). It's a compellingly desolate, eerie area, as if future spacefarers were terraforming the moon with hardy "maypole" cacti, century plants, aloes, and wind-lashed silver thatch palms bowing almost as if in deference to nature.

Brac Tourism Office. Free printed guides to the Brac's many heritage and nature trails can be obtained from the Brac Tourism Office; you can also get the guides at the airport or at your hotel. Traditional routes across the Bluff have been cleared and marked; trailheads are identified with signs along the road. It's safe to hike on your own, though some trails are fairly hard going (wear light hiking boots) and others could be better maintained. ⊠ *West End Community Park, west of airport, Cayman Brac* ☎ *345/948–1649.*

Christopher Columbus Gardens. For those who prefer lessstrenuous walking, Christopher Columbus Gardens has easy trails and boardwalks. The park showcases the unique natural flora and features of the Bluff, including two cave mouths. This is a peaceful spot dotted with gazebos and wooden bridges that traverse several ecosystems from cacti to mahogany trees. ⊠ *Ashton Reid Dr. [Bluff Rd.], just north of Ashton Rutty Centre, Cayman Brac.*

Sister Islands District Administration. The administration arranges free, government-sponsored, guided nature and cultural tours with trained local guides. Options include the Parrot Reserve, nature trails, wetlands, Lighthouse/ Bluff View, caving, birding, and heritage sites. You just supply the wheels and spirit of adventure. ⊠ *Cayman Brac* ☎ *345/948–2222.*

ROCK CLIMBING

Aficionados consider the Brac among the world's leading exotic climbing destinations. If you are experienced and like dangling from ropes 140 feet above a rocky, churning sea, the Brac is the place for you. Unfortunately, if you want to learn the ropes, no organization promotes climbing or rents equipment such as ropes and safety gear—you need to bring your own. Through the years, climbers have attached permanent titanium bolts to the **Bluff** face, creating some 70 routes in seven prime regions around the East End, most notably the Spot Bay Areas, the North Wall, the East Wall, and the South Wall. Access is often via private property, so be respectful (though most Brackers will just invite you in for cold drinks and stimulating conversation). The number is still growing as aficionados create new ascents. Difficulty is high; the "easiest" routes are graded 5.8 by the Yosemite Decimal system; most are rated 5.10 to 5.12, though many experienced climbers argue some approach the dizzying 5.14 range, especially around the sheer, "pumpy" (rock-speak for adrenaline-flowing) Northeast Point. This is steep, gnarly terrain of varying stability, suitable only for experienced climbers. Most of the Bluff's faces are hard vertical to overhanging; many walls vault abruptly, if exhilaratingly, to the savage sea.

Climbing the Brac is rocking, but precautions are vital. Sturdy hiking boots are mandatory, since you'll traverse a wide variety of terrain just accessing routes. Leather gloves are also recommended, as most of the high-quality limestone is smooth but has sharp and jagged areas. Two ropes are necessary for many climbs, the longest of which requires 19 quickdraws. Gear should include ascending

devices like prusiks and Tiblocs and shoulder-length slings with carabiners. Don't attempt climbs alone, and you're on your own even in teams should disaster occur. Agree upon rope tug signals, since the wind, waves, and overhangs make hearing difficult. Always analyze surf conditions and prevailing winds (which are variable) before rappelling, and double-check rap setup, anchors, and harnesses. Though titanium glue-ins replaced most of the old stainless steel bolts, many are deteriorating due to stress corrosion cracking; avoid any old bolts.

The Cayman Breakers condo complex has route maps and descriptions *(⇨ see Where to Stay)*. Several world-renowned climbers have built (second) homes on the Brac, including Liz Grenard, John Byrnes, and Ian Stewart.

READ ABOUT THE BRAC. Ian Stewart wrote a fine article on Brac climbing for the website of the Sister Islands Department of Tourism (⊕ *www.caymanbrac.com/islandattractions/climbing. html*). The J. W. Harper blog also contains useful links (⊕ *www. skipharper.com*). Though some of these articles and trip reports were written a few years ago, they're still pertinent.

SPELUNKING

Residents and geologists are still discovering "new" caves and sinkholes in the Brac's 25- to 30-million-year-old dolomite rock. Most of these caves were formed when the sea receded after the last Ice Age as rainwater dissolved the carbonate rock over millennia through cracks made by plants rooting in the limestone. Mineral deposits fashioned fanciful formations in many caves, as well as more typical pillars, stalagmites, and daggerlike stalactites.

Buccaneers (supposedly including Henry Morgan and Edward "Blackbeard" Teach) of the 17th and 18th centuries stopped like most mariners at the Cayman Islands to restock stores of water, wood, and turtles. Many locals still believe buried treasure lies deep within the recesses of the Bluff. But more vitally, the caves served as shelter during the fearsome storms of the first part of the 20th century.

Most caves are closed to the public—even to experienced spelunkers—but several are easily accessed and considered safe. If you plan to explore Cayman Brac's caves, wear good sneakers or hiking shoes, as some paths are steep and rocky and some entrances reachable only by ladders.

Peter's Cave offers a stunning aerial view of the picturesque northeastern community of Spot Bay. The climb is easier from atop the Bluff; the other access is steep, and purchase isn't always easy even with railings. The chambers feature few formations but some pretty multihued striations. **Great Cave**, at the island's southeast end, has numerous chambers and photogenic ocean views. It's the least accessible yet most impressive. You won't fund Bruce Wayne or his Boy Wonder in the **Bat Cave**, but you may see Jamaican fruit bats hanging from the ceiling (try not to disturb them), as well as nesting barn owls. The bats play a crucial role in the ecosystem's food chain because they devour overripe fruits, thereby pollinating plants, disseminating seeds, and reducing insect pests. There are some whimsical formations, and sections cracked and crawling with undergrowth, trees, and epiphytes. **Rebecca's Cave** poignantly houses the graveside of an 18-month-old child who died during the horrific hurricane of 1932. A plaque commemorates her short life ("Daughter of Raib and Helena 'Miss Missy' Bodden"), and people still leave flowers. It's actually a ¼-mile (½-km) hike inland along a well-marked trail called the Saltwater Pond Path, which continues to the North Side. Today it's a prime bird-watching walk lined with indigenous flora like red birch, jasmine, silver thatch palms, agave, dildo cactus, balsam, cabbage trees, duppy bushes, and bull hoof plants.

CAYMANITE. Found only in the crevices of the Bluff, this stone is actually an amalgam of several metals and minerals, including magnesium, iron, calcium, sodium, copper, nickel, phosphorus, and more: practically a quarter of the periodic table. Its striations supposedly represent different geologic eras, ranging from russet to white; no two pieces are identical. Special tools including diamond-tipped cutting wheels and grinders hone the extremely hard rock to a dazzling marble-like finish.

SHOPPING

Shopping is limited on the Brac; there are few small stores, though many local ladies sell their wares from home. You'll also find a boutique at the Brac Reef Beach Resort. The prize craft specialties are woven thatch items and caymanite jewelry.

Kirk Freeport. This is a miniature version of its ritzy Grand Cayman sister outposts, offering a smattering of upscale duty-free items from Waterford to Wedgwood, scents, watches, and jewelry from international to local designers. ⊠ *Next to the museum, Stake Bay, Cayman Brac* ☎ *345/948–2612.*

★ **NIM Things.** Artist and raconteur Tenson Scott fashions exquisite jewelry from caymanite (he climbs down from the lighthouse without ropes to chisel the stone), triton shells, sea eggs, and more unusual materials—hence the name, which stands for Native Island Made. His wife, Starry, creates delicate works from sea urchins, hardening the shell with epoxy: cute turtles, bud vases, and planters decorated with minuscule shells. ⊠ *Northeast Bay Rd., Spot Bay, Cayman Brac* ☎ *345/948–0582, 345/939–5306.*

Treasure Chest. Treasure Chest carries simple resort wear, T-shirts, bonnets, handbags (usually with the Brac logo), and black coral and caymanite jewelry, as well as a small selection of books, including pamphlets on local birds and fish. ⊠ *Tibbetts Sq., West End, Cayman Brac* ☎ *345/948–1333.*

NIGHTLIFE

Divers are notoriously early risers, but a few bars keep things hopping if not quite happening, especially on weekends, when local bands (or "imports" from Grand Cayman) often perform. Quaintly reminiscent of *Footloose* (without the hellfire and brimstone), watering holes are required to obtain music and dancing permits. Various community events including talent shows, recitals, concerts, and other stage presentations at the Aston Rutty Centre provide the rest of the island's nightlife.

Edd's Place. Edd's Place is a combination restaurant (the specialties are burgers and chop suey) and sports bar, known for its joyous happy hours as well as occasional live music. It tends to attract a rowdier, more local crowd, and features a friendly rivalry with Bussy's for "best" jerk on island. You can't miss the colorful mural of revelers splashed across the exterior. ⊠ *West End Rd., West End, Cayman Brac* ☎ *345/926–0376.*

★ **La Esperanza.** Also known as Bussy's, La Esperanza overflows with drinks, good cheer, and seemingly half the island on weekends, when Bussy fires up the grill and does a huge beach jerk barbecue. You can shoot pool and the breeze in the indoor lounge or head outside for the sensational

Thatch Weaving

"Laying rope" is an old-time tradition that originated so that women could support themselves while the men were away at sea, often for months at a time. The Brac was particularly noted for the method of stripping silver thatch palm leaves and drying them in the sun, both creating a labor-intensive twisted hemplike rope that was exported to Jamaica, usually in barter, and various baskets for carrying sand (for gardens) and provisions from little farms atop the Bluff.

You can visit the home-studio/-shop of the craft's foremost practitioner, **Annelee Ebanks** (⊠ 35 White Bay Rd., West End ☎ 345/948–1326), whose skill is such that the Ritz-Carlton commissions her to create pieces as gifts, decorative accents, towel hampers, and waste baskets. Miss Annelee began more than half a century ago at 13 watching her father make traditional baskets. She enjoyed it and "decided as the years went on to start new patterns. I dream at night, sketch the idea, then go back to sleep."

The stripped dried thatch "strings" have several gradations in hue from silvery mint to buff; bunches are tied off in places to ensure the sun doesn't bleach out all the color. She also uses darker brown dried stripped coconut leaves to create multicolored pieces: placemats with matching coasters and napkin rings, hats, baskets, purses, sandals, hand fans, even brooms and switches ("for bad boys"), since thatching originally served utilitarian purposes. It takes her three days to create one beach bag: one day to weave, a second to line and stitch, another to decorate (she uses Magic Marker and spray paint, as well as raffia from Jamaica for binding and decorative curlicues).

Amazingly nimble, she'll gladly demonstrate the process but might recruit you if you prove adept. A bunch (usually two to eight strands) is tied at the bottom; use the thumb and index finger to hold and weave, pleating in and out. "Bend and crease it good at the bottom, then you be the boss of it."

---

sunsets (and drinks in matching colors). The music, heavy on the reggae with the occasional salsa tune thrown in, blares, encouraging everyone to sway along. ⊠ *The Creek, Stake Bay, Cayman Brac* ☎ *345/948–0591.*

Tipsy Turtle Pub. The only spot open until midnight or later nightly, Tipsy Turtle Pub overflows with good cheer and strong drinks. The mudslides are particularly potent, and there are usually some good Cubanos. The alfresco bar serves excellent pub grub (jerk chicken pizza, Caesar salad wrap, portobello-and-Swiss cheeseburger, messy marvelous spare ribs, tempura shrimp) for around $10. Popcorn and Ping-Pong are free. It's the kind of casual congenial hangout where almost everyone ends up buying a round at some point ("What are you drinking?" might elicit a response like "Oh, a little bit of everything"). Depending on your tastes, stop by for Wednesday karaoke on the outside patio, which attracts large, enthusiastic crowds. ⊠ *Brac Reef Beach Resort, West End, Cayman Brac* ☎ *345/948–1323.*

Little Cayman

WORD OF MOUTH

"I have stayed at Little Cayman Beach Resort a few times . . . it is low-key and very safe with decent food. They have bicycles for roaming around . . . although there is little to see. The scuba is fantastic."

—Ronalds

By Jordan Simon

THE SMALLEST AND MOST TRANQUIL of the three Cayman Islands, Little Cayman has a full-time population of only 170, most of whom work in the tourism industry; they are easily outnumbered by iguanas and rare birds. This 12-square-mile (31-square-km) island is practically pristine and has only a sand-sealed airstrip, sharing its "terminal" building with the fire department and a few other vehicles. The grass runway was finally paved with blacktop a few years ago, and locals no longer have to line up their cars at night to guide emergency landings in by headlight. But some things don't change. The speed limit remains 25 mph, as no one is in a hurry to go anywhere. In fact, the island's population of resident iguanas uses roads more regularly than residents; signs created by local artists read "Iguanas have the right of way."

With little commercial development, the island beckons ecotourists seeking wildlife encounters, not urban wild life. It's best known for its spectacular diving in world-renowned Bloody Bay Marine Park, including Bloody Bay Wall and adjacent Jackson Wall. The ravishing reefs and plummeting walls encircling the island teem with more than 500 different species of fish and more than 150 kinds of coral. Fly-, lake-, and deep-sea fishing are also popular, as well as snorkeling, kayaking, and biking. And the island's certainly for the birds. The National Trust Booby Pond Nature Reserve is a designated wetland of international importance, which protects around 20,000 red-footed boobies, the Western Hemisphere's largest colony. It's just one of many superlative spots to witness avian aerial acrobatics.

Secluded beaches, unspoiled tropical wilderness and wetlands, mangrove swamps, lagoons, bejeweled coral reefs—Little Cayman practically redefines "hideaway" and "escape." Yet aficionados appreciate that the low-key lifestyle doesn't mean sacrificing the high-tech amenities, and some of the resorts cater to a quietly wealthy yet unpretentious crowd.

Which isn't to say Little Cayman lacks for lively moments. Halloween parties and Mardi Gras festivities bring out wildly imaginative costumes and floats. It's just one of those rare places that attract more colorful types who are in search of privacy, not just the ardently eco-centric. One of the largest private homes was built and owned by the late actor Burgess Meredith; island rumors persist to this day of planes full of high-school cheerleaders visiting his digs for

TOP EXPERIENCES

■ **Wall-to-Wall Fun.** Divers can't miss the hallowed Bloody Bay, lauded by every Cousteau worth his sea salt.

■ **Booby Watching.** Even if you're not a birder, learning about the rare red-footed booby from its fanatics at the National Trust and spying them through telescopes are more fun than you'd think.

■ **Beachcombing.** A jaunt to Owen Island or Point o' Sand rewards you with practically virgin strands, breathtaking views, and scintillating snorkeling.

■ **Pirates Pointing.** A meal with Gladys Howard at her peerless little resort is memorable not only for the food but the company.

■ **Something Fishy.** The deep-sea fishing is superior, but the light-tackle option should lure any angler.

weeks at a time. Then there's a local who allegedly grew marijuana. The island's two bobbies (who do a four-year stint from Great Britain and learn when to look the other way) caught him with a joint. "But it can't be mine," he protested, "'cuz I woulda smoked it by now." The plants were impounded and placed in a tub in the jail's only cell, while the accused went free.

That doesn't provide a license for misbehavior on this beautiful, idiosyncratic landfall. But this is definitely a place to mellow out; drugs won't be needed. As one regular cackles, "If the island were any more laid-back, it'd be double-jointed."

ORIENTATION AND PLANNING

ORIENTATION

Little Cayman is bracketed by lighthouses at the West and East Ends, whose terrain couldn't be more different. The semiarid East End has a remote, end-of-the-world feel: Limestone sinkholes called karst stitched with xeric shrub give it a pitted moonlike appearance. The West End is much greener. But beaches, snorkeling, nature trails, and bird-viewing areas embroider the entire island. One main road, mostly paved, essentially circumnavigates the coast. Several packed-dirt side roads crisscross the island, often accessing the more remote beaches. These can become muddy and almost impassable in heavy rain.

PLANNING

WHEN TO GO

Though diving and fishing excel in summer as well, the traditional high-season months of December through April apply to Little Cayman, as they do to hotels in much of the Caribbean. Most of the small resorts shut down September through most of October, during the height of hurricane season.

GETTING HERE AND AROUND

BY AIR

Interisland service between Grand Cayman, Cayman Brac, and Little Cayman is provided several times daily by Cayman Airways. Edward Bodden Airfield still has an almost provisional feel, a long grassy stretch that accommodates only STOL craft.

BY CAR

Bikes, usually offered for free by the resorts, are the preferred way of getting around the island; dive operations will pick you up, and the hotels also provide airport transfers. A car is suggested only if you rent one of the more isolated villas or if you plan to explore the farther-flung part of the island on a regular basis. Parking is rarely a problem. Another flexible touring option is a moped. McLaughlin Rentals offers mopeds ($54) and SUVs ($80–$100).

Information **McLaughlin Rentals** ☎ *345/948–1000.*

BY TAXI

Resorts offer airport transfers. Two companies offer land tours (in addition to fishing, kayaking, and other options). Island tours are usually $50 per person (though each additional person is generally discounted, as are children). LCB Tours has a safari bus for larger groups. Maxine McCoy's MAM's Tours can accommodate up to 15 passengers in two minivans, though she's often off-island.

Information **LCB Tours** ✉ *Little Cayman Beach Resort, Blossom Village, Little Cayman* ☎ *345/948–1642, 345/948–1033.* **MAM's Tours** ✉ *65 Mahogany Bay, Candle Rd., West End, Little Cayman* ☎ *345/926–0104, 345/917–4582* ⊕ *www.mamstour.ky.*

RESTAURANTS

The main resorts' dining rooms accept reservations from nonguests pending availability. Otherwise, there are two full-fledged restaurants, both affiliated with villa/condo properties. The choices are limited, with seafood obviously reigning supreme, but the caliber of the few kitchens is generally high.

HOTELS

Accommodations are mostly in small lodges, almost all of which offer meal and dive packages. The chefs in most places create wonderful meals despite often-limited resources. You won't find any independent restaurants, but if you are staying in a villa or condo you can usually have dinner at one of the resorts (be sure to call ahead). Dive packages represent exceptional savings. Most resorts prefer a five- to seven-night stay in high season, but the minimum isn't always strictly enforced. Still, rooms for shorter stays may not become available until two to three weeks prior to your trip dates.

HOTEL AND RESTAURANT PRICES

Prices in the restaurant reviews are the average cost of a main course at dinner or, if dinner is not served, at lunch; taxes and service charges are generally included. Prices in the hotel reviews are the lowest cost of a standard double room in high season, excluding taxes, service charges, and meal plans (except at all-inclusives). Prices for rentals are the lowest per-night cost for a one-bedroom unit in high season.

VISITOR INFORMATION

There is no visitor center on Little Cayman, but each hotel, hotelier, and staffer overflows with information and suggestions. You can also consult the websites of the **Sister Islands Tourism Association** (⊕ *www.itsyourstoexplore.com*) for information on Little Cayman.

EXPLORING LITTLE CAYMAN

Little Cayman isn't much for man-made sights and attractions; those that are here essentially serve to explain and promote nature preserved in all her finery, especially underwater, throughout the island. If you're exploring on your own, pick up the *Little Cayman Heritage Sites and Trails* brochure, available at the hotels and National Trust; it lists all the major points of interest.

WHAT TO SEE

Little Cayman Museum. The museum displays relics and artifacts, including a new wing devoted to maritime memorabilia, that provide a good overview of this tiny island's history and heritage. ⊠ *Across from Booby Pond Nature Reserve, Blossom Village, Little Cayman* ☎ *345/948–1033 for Little Cayman Beach Resort* ☎ *Free* ☉ *Thurs. and Fri. 3–5, by appointment only.*

★ **Fodor's Choice Little Cayman National Trust.** This traditional Caymanian cottage overlooks the Booby Pond Nature Reserve; telescopes on the breezy second-floor deck permit close-up views of their markings and nests, as well as the other feathered friends. Inside you'll find shell collections, panels and dioramas discussing endemic reptiles, models "in flight," and diagrams on the growth and life span of red-footed boobies, frigate birds, egrets, and other island "residents." The shop sells exquisite jewelry made from caymanite and spider-crab shells, extraordinary duck decoys and driftwood carvings, and great books on history, ornithology, and geology. Mike Vallee holds an iguana information session and tour every Friday at 4 pm. The cheeky movie *Calendar Girls* inspired a local equivalent: Little Cayman women, mostly in full, ripe maturity, going topless for an important cause—raising awareness of the red-footed booby and funds to purchase the sanctuary's land. Nicknamed, appropriately, "Support the Boobies," the calendar is tasteful, not titillating: the lasses strategically hold conch shells, brochures, flippers, tree branches, etc. Thanks to chairperson Debbi Truchan's baking skill, this is *the* spot for cappuccino, herb tea, cinnamon buns, and scrumptious homemade ice cream (guava, rum raisin, lemongrass, ginger)—a fantastic place to mingle with residents and visitors. ⊠ *Blossom Village, Little Cayman* ⊕ *www.nationaltrust.org.ky* ☉ *Mon.–Sat. 9–noon and 2–6.*

★ **Little Cayman Research Center.** Near the Jackson Point Bloody Bay Marine Park reserve, this vital research center supports visiting students and researchers, with a long list of projects studying the biodiversity, human impact, reef health, and ocean ecosystem of Little Cayman. Its situation is unique in that reefs this unspoiled are usually far less accessible; the National Oceanic and Atmospheric Administration awarded it one of 16 monitoring stations worldwide. The center also solicits funding through the parent U.S. non-profit organization Central Caribbean Marine Institute; if

Little Cayman

KEY

- Beaches
- Dive Sites
- **1** Restaurants
- **1** Hotels

Restaurants
Blue Lagoon, **1**
Hungry Iguana, **2**
Pirates Point, **3**

Hotels
The Club, **3**
Conch Club, **2**
Little Cayman Beach Resort, **4**
Paradise Villas, **5**
Pirates Point Resort, **6**
Southern Cross Club, **1**

Caribbean Sea

East Pt.

Point of Sand

Snipe Pt.

Mary's Bay

EASTERN BLUFF

Crawl Bay

Charles Bight Pond

Charles Bight

Rosetta Flats

LITTLE CAYMAN

Lower Spot Bay

Tarpon Lake

Wearis Bay

Grape Tree Bay

Jacksons Pt.

Little Cayman Research Centre

Little Cayman National Trust

Booby Pond Nature Reserve

Owen Island

Jackson Wall

Bloody Bay

Bloody Bay Wall

Little Cayman Museum

Spot Bay

South Town

Booby Pond

Blossom Village Park

Edward Bodden Airfield

2 **5**

1

2

3

4

Anchorage Bay

West End Lighthouse

West End Pt.

Preston Bay

Westerly Ponds

3 **6**

0   1 mi

0   1 km

Pirates Point resort

you value the health of our reefs, show your support on the website. Chairman Peter Hillenbrand proudly calls it the "Ritz-Carlton of marine research facilities, which often are little more than pitched tents on a beach." Tours explain the center's mission and eco-sensitive design (including Peter's Potty, an off-the-grid bathroom facility using compostable toilets that recycle fertilizer into gray water for the gardens); sometimes you'll get a peek at the upstairs functional wet labs and dormitories. To make it layperson-friendlier, scientists occasionally give talks and presentations. The Dive with a Researcher program (where you actually help survey and assess environmental impact and ecosystem health, depending on that week's focus) is hugely popular. ⊠ *North Side, Little Cayman* ☎ *345/948–1094* ⊕ *www.reefresearch. org* ☉ *By appointment only.*

WHERE TO EAT

★ **Fodors**Choice ✕ **Pirates Point.** *Eclectic.* Irrepressible Gladys
$$$$ Howard offers Texas-style and Texas-size hospitality at her ravishing little resort. Guests have first privilege, but the kitchen can usually accommodate an extra couple or two. Advance reservations are both a must and a courtesy on this island, where nearly everything is imported at great cost and effort. The resort gardens provide mangoes, key limes, basil, lemongrass, and other herbs. Gladys wears many hats on island (indeed, if you stumble upon her at a special

Iggin Out

An estimated 2,000 prehistoric-looking Little Cayman rock iguanas roam the island, by far the largest population in Cayman. Gladys Howard, former chair of the Little Cayman committee of the nonprofit National Trust for the Cayman Islands, has taken the good fight for the boobies and applied it to the "iggies." Visitors can feed these large (up to 5 feet), fierce-looking but docile vegetarians by hand at the residential Mahogany Bay neighborhood, where the creatures' preferred delica-cies—fruit trees and flowers from bananas and papayas to hibiscus—flourish. But Gladys hopes to purchase more coastal land to serve as a nesting sanctuary. She knows it's a crucial component of ecotourism and, noting how the same species has all but disappeared on the Brac (while the blue iguana still faces extinction on Grand Cayman), says, "We want to avoid that fate. We must preserve them because so few of that species remain on our planet."

occasion, she may be wearing a bear mask, bobby cap, or crab pincers). Her lighthearted antics belie the serious food. Gladys trained with Julia Child, James Beard, and Jacques Pépin, and at the legendary Cordon Bleu in Paris; she still supervises everything with an eagle eye. Memorable three-course prix-fixe dinners (wine but not tip included), served on Wedgwood, could feature anything from filet mignon with a Cabernet reduction and garlic-whipped potatoes to ahi tuna pepper steak with saffron beurre blanc, scallion-infused udon noodles, cucumber-seaweed salad, baby bok choy, and roasted cauliflower. Wildly popular sushi nights feature ultrafresh fish in eye-catching presentations. It all comes with heaping helpings of bon mots and bonhomie. S *Average main: $40* ⊠ *Pirates Point, Preston Bay, Little Cayman* ☎ *345/948–1010* ⚭ *Reservations essential* ⊙ *Closed Sept.–mid-Oct. No lunch.*

8

$$ ✕**Blue Lagoon.** *Caribbean.* This little waterfront hangout is daubed in edible colors from its lime-and-blueberry facade to salmon-and-mint walls hung with little driftwood signs espousing its philosophy ("Yeah Man," "Chillin," "Relax"). Picture windows afford wondrous views of Kingston Bight, especially when the setting sun triggers a laser show across the bay as smooth and finely hued as Murano glass. The Bight is the island's only truly safe harbor, and everyone has moorings here, so the BL is filled with

Art Dive

The bar at Pirates Point typifies the fun, funky sensibility of the dive set, who adorn their favorite resorts with painted stones and driftwood. Here you'll find an idiosyncratic, imaginative gallery of mobiles, painted sandals, coconut fronds, and found art. An old oar fashioned into the likeness of a Caymanian lizard might read "Texas Roadkill Dive Club"; sculpted penguins say "We don't know how we got here but we know we're not leaving." Owner Gladys Howard has created an annual competition for best creation, with prizes including free stays. She provides brushes, paints, and a hot glue gun; guests canvas for raw materials on the shore. One recent winner was a lionfish created from palm fronds and sea sponges.

character and characters. Food is incidental but more than serviceable (though half the extensive menu usually isn't available). Fish-and-chips (fresh catch), lasagna, red-bean soup, chicken tikka masala, turtle steak, and pepper-crusted tuna are usually reliable. ⑤ *Average main: $20* ⊠ *Kingston Bight, Little Cayman* ☎ *345/948–1065, 345/948–0117* ⊙ *No dinner Sun.*

$ ✕ **Hungry Iguana.** *Eclectic.* The closest thing to a genuine sports bar and nightclub on Little Cayman, the "Iggy" caters to the aquatically minded set with a marine mural, wood-plank floors, mounted trophy sailfish, lots of fishing caps, and yummy fresh seafood. Conch fritters are near definitive, while corn-crusted calamari with Scotch bonnet salsa are mouth and eye watering. It's a great hangout for (relatively) cheap eats; prix-fixe theme nights between CI$18 and CI$40 offer fine value: pizza, fajitas, curry, and more. Drink in the smashing sunset views on the delightful patio overlooking the water, and also drink of the house specialty Iguana Punch (rum, rum, more rum, and coconut rum with orange and pineapple juices). ⑤ *Average main: $24* ⊠ *Paradise Villas, Blossom Village, Little Cayman* ☎ *345/948–0001* ⊙ *No dinner Sun.*

WHERE TO STAY

Accommodations are mostly in small lodges, many of which offer meal and dive packages. The meal packages are a good idea; the chefs in most places create wonderful dishes with often limited resources.

For expanded reviews, facilities, and current deals, visit Fodors.com.

PRIVATE VILLAS

A few private villas on Little Cayman can be rented, most of them basic but well maintained, ranging from one to four bedrooms. There are also three condo complexes and one villa resort on island. Rental fees are reasonable, and normally the price for extra couples in the larger units is only $200 per week, representing substantial savings for families or couples traveling together, while the kitchen helps reduce the price of dining out. In addition, government tax and often a service fee are sometimes included in the quoted rate (be sure to verify this). As a general rule of thumb, properties are thoroughly cleaned before your arrival; you must pay extra if you want daily maid service. Rates are sometimes discounted in the off-season. Most villa owners mandate a three- to seven-night minimum stay in high season, though this is often negotiable. Unless otherwise noted, properties have landline phones; local calls are usually free, but phones are generally locked for international calls.

8

RECOMMENDED HOTELS AND RESORTS

$$ 🏨 **The Club.** *Rental.* These ultramodern, luxurious, three-bedroom condos are Little Cayman's newest and nicest units, though only five are usually included in the rental pool. **Pros:** luxurious digs; lovely beach; hot tub. **Cons:** housekeeping not included; rear guest bedrooms dark and somewhat cramped; handsome but heavy old-fashioned decor. 🟑 *Rooms from: $311* ✉ *South Hole Sound, Little Cayman* ☎ *345/948–1033, 727/323–8727, 800/327–3835* ⊕ *www.theclubatlittlecayman.com* 🛏 *8 condos* ⭕ *No meals.*

$$ 🏨 **Conch Club.** *Rental.* The handsome oceanfront development ⚙ ment grafts Caribbean-style gingerbread onto New England maritime architecture with gables and dormers. **Pros:** splendid views; gorgeous beach; complimentary airport transfers; beachfront hot tub; complimentary bicycles and kayaks. **Cons:** long walk to nearby restaurants; dated decor; housekeeping surcharge. 🟑 *Rooms from: $350* ✉ *Blossom Village, Little Cayman* ☎ *345/948–1026, 345/925–2875*

Southern Cross Club

⊕ *www.conchclubcondos.com* ⇘ *18 2-bedroom condos, 2 3-bedroom condos* ⦿ *No meals.*

$$$ ⊺ **Little Cayman Beach Resort.** *Resort.* This two-story hotel,
★ the island's largest, offers the most options for fun seekers
☾ and modern facilities yet a boutique vibe. **Pros:** extensive
facilities; fun crowd; state-of-the-art technology; glorious LED-lighted pool. **Cons:** less intimate feel than other island resorts; tiny patios; fee to rent bikes. ⑤ *Rooms from: $395* ⊠ *Blossom Village, Little Cayman* ☎ *345/948–1033, 800/327–3835* ⊕ *www.littlecayman.com* ⇘ *40 rooms* ⦿ *Multiple meal plans.*

★ **Fodor's Choice** ⊺ **Pirates Point Resort.** *Resort.* The large repeat
$$$$ clientele attests that everything from the comfortable rooms to the fine cuisine lives up to the billing at this hideaway nestled between sea grape and casuarina pines on a sparkling sweep of palapa-dotted sand. **Pros:** fabulous food; fantastic beach; dynamic dive program; fun-loving staff and owner. **Cons:** everyone respects honeymooners' privacy, but this isn't a resort for antisocial types; tasteful rooms are fairly spare; occasional Internet problems. ⑤ *Rooms from: $484* ⊠ *Pirates Point, Little Cayman* ☎ *345/948–1010* ⊕ *www. piratespointresort.com* ⇘ *11 rooms* ⊘ *Closed Sept.–mid-Oct.* ⦿ *Multiple meal plans.*

★ **Fodor's Choice** ⊺ **Southern Cross Club.** *Resort.* Little Cayman's
$$$$ first resort was cofounded in the 1950s as a private fishing club by the CEO of Sears-Roebuck and CFO of General Motors, and its focus is still on fishing and diving. **Pros:**

barefoot luxury; complimentary use of kayaks and snorkel gear; splendiferous beach; international staff regales you with globe-trotting exploits. **Cons:** not child-friendly (though families can rent a separate cottage); Wi-Fi promised but still not available in some rooms, with spotty signal otherwise. ⑤ *Rooms from: $617 ⊠ South Hole Sound, Little Cayman ☎ 345/948–1099, 800/899–2582 ⊕ www. southerncrossclub.com ⊅ 11 rooms, 3 suites, 1 2-bedroom cottage ⊗ Closed mid-Sept.–mid-Oct.* ⓘ *All meals.*

$ ⊤ **Paradise Villas.** *Rental.* The cozy, sunny, one-bedroom units have beachfront terraces and hammocks and are simply but immaculately appointed with rattan furnishings, marine artwork, painted driftwood, and bright abstract fabrics. Stylish contemporary touches include flat-screen TVs. **Pros:** good value; friendly staff; frequent online-only deals in addition to good dive packages. **Cons:** noisy some weekend nights in season; poky beach; now a (minimal) charge for bike use; dive shop no longer on-site (though the contracted operation runs smoothly). ⑤ *Rooms from: $195 ⊠ South Hole Sound, Little Cayman ☎ 345/948–0001, 877/322–9626 ⊕ www.paradisevillas.com ⊅ 12 1-bedroom villas ⊗ Closed mid-Sept.–late Oct.* ⓘ *No meals.*

BEACHES

The southwest part of the island seems like one giant beach; this is where virtually all the resorts sit, serenely facing Preston Bay and South Hole Sound. But there are several other unspoiled, usually deserted strands that beckon beachcombers, all the sand having the same delicate hue of Cristal Champagne and just as apt to make you feel giddy.

Blossom Village Park. Developed by the local chapter of the National Trust, this site of the first, albeit temporary, Cayman Islands settlement in the 1660s is lined with traditional cottages; bricks are dedicated to old-time residents and longtime repeat guests. There are picnic tables, a playground, and a dock. The beach is small but has plenty of shade trees, good snorkeling, and calm water. ⊠ *Little Cayman.*

★ **Fodor'sChoice Owen Island.** This private, forested island can be reached by rowboat, kayak, or an ambitious 200-yard swim. Anyone is welcome to come across and enjoy the deserted beaches and excellent snorkeling. Nudity is forbidden as "idle and disorderly" in the Cayman Islands, though that doesn't always stop skinny-dippers (who may

not realize they can be seen quite easily from shore on the strands facing Little Cayman). ⊠ *Little Cayman*.

★ Fodor'sChoice **Point of Sand.** Stretching over a mile on the easternmost point of the island, this secluded beach is great for wading, shell collecting, and snorkeling. On a clear day you can see 7 miles (11 km) across to Cayman Brac. It serves as a green- and loggerhead turtle nesting site in spring, and a marvelous mosaic of coral gardens blooms just offshore. It's magical, especially at moonrise, when it earns its nickname, Lovers' Beach. There's a palapa for shade but no facilities. The current can be strong, so watch the kids carefully. ⊠ *Little Cayman*.

SPORTS AND THE OUTDOORS

Little Cayman is a recreational paradise on land and especially underwater, with world-class diving, light-tackle angling, and bird-watching the star attractions. Befitting an eco-centric destination, nature owns the island, and you're strictly cautioned about dos and don'ts. But lectures are given with a smile, and then you're free to explore this zoo without cages, and aquarium without tanks.

BIRD-WATCHING

National Trust. The website of the National Trust and the **Sister Islands Tourism Authority** has information on bird-watching. ⊠ *Little Cayman* ⊕ *www.itsyourstoexplore.com*.

★ **Booby Pond Nature Reserve.** The reserve is home to 20,000 red-footed boobies (the largest colony in the Western Hemisphere) and Cayman's only breeding colony of magnificent frigate (or man-of-war) birds; other sightings include the near-threatened West Indian whistling duck and vitelline warbler. The RAMSAR Convention, an international treaty for wetland conservation, designated the reserve a wetland of global significance. Near the airport, the sanctuary is open to the public, and has a gift shop and reading library. ⊠ *Little Cayman*.

BIRD-WATCHING SITES
Grape Tree Ponds. This splendid wetland spot on the North Side is great for observing West Indian whistling ducks and has some lovely shore walks. ⊠ *Little Cayman*.

Bloody Bay Wall

Jackson's Pond. This is a vast mangrove-fringed body of water offering excellent viewing of herons, ducks, rails, stilt, plovers, and sandpipers. ⊠ *Little Cayman.*

Tarpon Lake. There's more here than just fishing. A long deck extends into the writhing tangle of red mangrove roots where white herons, ospreys, and whistling ducks dive-bomb for fiddler crabs and mosquito fish skittering through the brackish water alongside sun-silvered pirouetting tarpon. ⊠ *Little Cayman.*

West End Lighthouse. West End Lighthouse offers magnificent sunset views and serves as arrivals check-in for migrant shorebirds. ⊠ *Little Cayman.*

Westerly Ponds. These shallow wading pools in the ironshore by Preston Bay are lined by low buttonwood trees and herbaceous vegetation where killdeer, willet, black-necked stilt, and American coot perform an aerial ballet. ⊠ *Little Cayman.*

DIVING AND SNORKELING

A gaudy, voluptuous tumble of marine life—lumbering grouper to fleet guppies, massive manta rays to miniature wrasse, sharks to stingrays, blue chromis to Bermuda chubs, puffers to parrotfish—parades its finery through the pyrotechnic coral reefs like a watery Main Street on Saturday night. Gaping gorges, vaulting pinnacles, plunging walls, chutes, arches, and vertical chimneys create a virtual underwater city, festooned with fiery sponges and sensuously waving gorgonians draped like come-hither courtesans over limestone settees.

Expect to pay around $95 for a two-tank boat dive and $25–$30 for a snorkeling trip. The island is small and susceptible to wind, so itineraries can change like a sudden gust.

DIVE AND SNORKEL SITES

Snorkelers will delight in taking Nancy's Cup of Tea or "scaling" Mike's Mountain, as well as enjoying Eagle Ray Roundup, Three Fathom Wall, and Owen Island. The areas around the East End are difficult to access from shore due to the jagged ironshore (boats are often preferable) but are worthwhile: Mary's Bay, Snipe Point, and Lighthouse Reef (which has stunning Brac vistas).

Among the many superlative dive sites are the Great Wall, the Meadows, the Zoo, Coconut Walk Wall, School Bus Stop, Sarah's Set, Black Hole, Mixing Bowl, Charlie's Chimneys, and Blacktip Boulevard.

★ **Fodor'sChoice** **Bloody Bay Wall.** This beach, named for having been the site of a spectacular 17th-century sea battle, has been declared one of the world's top three dive sites by no less than the *maîtres* Jacques and Philippe Cousteau and forms part of a protected marine reserve. It plunges dramatically from 18 to 6,000 feet, with a series of staggeringly beautiful drop-offs and remarkable visibility. Even snorkelers who are strong swimmers can access the edge from shore, gliding among shimmering silver curtains of minnows, jacks, bonefish, and more. The critters are amazingly friendly, including Jerry the Grouper, whom dive masters joke is a representative for the Cayman Islands Department of Tourism. ⊠ *Little Cayman.*

★ **Jackson Wall.** Adjacent to Bloody Bay, Jackson Wall and reef are nearly as stunning. Conditions are variable, the water now glassy, now turbulent, so snorkelers must be strong swimmers. It's renowned for Swiss-cheese-like swimthroughs; though it's not as precipitous as Bloody Bay, the more rugged bottom results in astonishing rock formations whose tunnels and crevices hold pyrotechnic marine life. ⊠ *Little Cayman.*

RECOMMENDED OPERATORS

Conch Club Divers. This is a personable, experienced outfit that often customizes trips on its 42-foot *Sea-esta*. ⊠ *Little Cayman* ☎ *345/948–1026* ⊕ *www.conchclubcondos.com.*

Pirate's Point Dive Resort. This popular resort has fully outfitted 42-foot Newtons with dive masters who excel at finding odd and rare creatures, and encourage computer diving so you can stay down longer. ⊠ *Little Cayman* ☎ *345/948–1010* ⊕ *www.piratespointresort.com.*

Reef Divers. Little Cayman Beach Resort's oufitter also offers a full-service photo and video center; their custom boats' state-of-the-art outfitting includes AEDs (defibrillators). ⊠ *Little Cayman* ☎ *345/948–1033* ⊕ *www.littlecayman.com.*

Southern Cross Club. The Southern Cross Club limits each of its boats to 12 divers and has its own dock. It's particularly good with specialty courses and mandates computer diving. ⊠ *Little Cayman* ☎ *345/948–1099, 800/899–2582* ⊕ *www. southerncrossclub.com.*

FISHING

Bloody Bay is equally celebrated for fishing and diving, and the flats and shallows including South Hole Sound Lagoon across from Owen Island, Tarpon Lake, and the Charles Bight Rosetta Flats offer phenomenal light-tackle and fly-fishing action: surprisingly large tarpon, small bonefish, and permit (a large fish related to pompano) weighing up to 35 pounds. Superior deep-sea fishing is available right offshore for game fish including blue marlin, dolphin, wahoo, tuna, and barracuda.

Little Cayman Fishing Club. Walter Rhyan, longtime resident, can often be seen relaxing at the gazebo on his gorgeous dock, headquarters for Little Cayman Fishing Club, opposite Owen Island. Captain Steve Pace commandeers the 37-foot Hatteras *Donna Lorraine* (after Walter's sister's and mother's names), which was specially rigged to navigate Little Cayman's shallower waters while offering big-time comfort for up to six anglers. The cabin is air-conditioned, with an L-shaped couch, refrigerator, TV/DVD, CD player, microwave, electric toilet, and four separate bunks for overnight trips. Nonalcoholic drinks, snacks, and tackle are provided; the cost is $700 for up to five hours; smaller boats are $350 per half day. You can also go bonefishing ($220) in the sound on a 17-foot Boston Whaler that can accommodate two to three anglers with Captain Jeremy Loercher, who's also a crackerjack fly-fishing instructor. ⊠ *Head O' Bay, Little Cayman* ☎ *345/948–0038, 345/925–2921, 345/926–8452.*

MAM's Tours. This reliable company is run by energetic local Maxine McCoy, who comes from fishing royalty of sorts (she, her mum, dad, and five brothers ran McCoy's Diving and Fishing Resort). Deep-sea fishing costs $125 per hour for up to four people; those angling for tarpon and bonefish pay $50 per hour ($75 per couple). Maxine also runs snorkeling trips to Owen Island and will take you conching in season. She's spending more time on the Brac, so call in advance to ensure she'll be on island. ⊠ *65 Mahogany Bay, Candle Rd., West End, Little Cayman* ☎ *345/926–0104, 345/917–4582* ⊕ *www.mams.ky.*

Southern Cross Club. The Southern Cross Club offers light-tackle and deep-sea fishing trips. ⊠ *Little Cayman* ☎ *345/948–1099, 800/899–2582* ⊕ *www.southerncrossclub.com.*

HIKING

Flat Little Cayman is better suited to biking, but there are a few jaunts, notably the **Salt Rocks Nature Trail,** where you pass ancient mule pens, abandoned phosphate mines, and the rusting tracks of the original narrow-gauge railway now alive with a profusion of flowering cacti and scrub brush.

Travel Smart
Cayman Islands

WORD OF MOUTH

"The island is small. I would suggest renting a car. We did for the entire week we were there. It was not expensive at all. And worth it."

—CaribbeanChick

GETTING HERE AND AROUND

Grand Cayman is a relatively small island, and the longest distance you can travel should take no more than a couple of hours. You can get by on Grand Cayman using a combination of tours and local buses (especially if you are staying in the Seven Mile Beach area), but if you want to explore on your own, it's easier with a rental car. Although driving is on the left, British style, Grand Cayman's well-paved road system makes independent travel fairly easy, though signage is not always clear. Cayman Brac and Little Cayman are even tinier and can be navigated by bike or moped.

▌ AIR TRAVEL

Several carriers offer frequent nonstop or direct flights between North America and Grand Cayman's Owen Roberts Airport. Flying time from New York is about four hours, just over an hour from Miami. Only small STOL propeller aircraft serve Cayman Brac and Little Cayman.

AIRPORTS

Grand Cayman's Owen Roberts Airport (GCM) is a modern facility located in the western, busier section of the island, roughly 2 miles (3 km) east of George Town. The current multimillion-dollar expansion and general upgrade (to meet the projected increase in arrivals over the next two decades) should be completed by late 2012.

The airport is about 15 minutes from hotels situated along Seven Mile Beach, about 30 to 45 minutes from the East End and West Bay lodgings, and 10 minutes from George Town. Cayman Brac's Gerrard Smith Airport (CYB) can accommodate smaller jets, while Little Cayman's Edward Bodden Airstrip can only accommodate prop aircraft due to runway limitations.

Airport Information Owen Roberts Airport ✉ *GCM, Grand Cayman* ☎ *345/943-7070.* **Gerrard Smith International Airport** ✉ *CYB, Cayman Brac* ☎ *345/948-1222.* **Edward Bodden Airstrip** ✉ *LYB, Little Cayman* ☎ *345/948-0021.*

GROUND TRANSPORTATION

In Grand Cayman, ground transportation is available immediately outside the customs area of the airport. Taxis aren't metered, but fares are government-regulated (about $15–$30 to resorts along Seven Mile Beach, $60 to the East End). Be sure, however, to confirm the fare before getting into the taxi and whether the price quoted is in U.S. or Cayman dollars.

Round-trip airport transfers are generally included (or at least offered) by hotels on the Sister Islands, where most accommodations sit within 10 minutes' drive of the airports.

Taxis are always available at Grand Cayman's airport. They

don't dependably meet flights on the Sister Islands, so make sure your resort or villa company has made arrangements.

FLIGHTS

All nonstop and direct air service is to Grand Cayman, with connecting flights to Cayman Brac and Little Cayman on a small propeller plane. Cayman Airways offers nonstops from several destinations, including Miami, New York–JFK, and Tampa. All operate several times weekly except Miami, which is daily. American offers nonstop daily service from Miami. Delta flies weekly from Detroit, Minneapolis, and New York–JFK, and several times weekly from its Atlanta hub. United flies weekly from Washington Dulles and Newark, and daily from Houston. U.S. Airways offers daily nonstop service from Charlotte and weekly flights from Boston and Philadelphia. Cayman Airways also flies to both Cayman Brac and Little Cayman. Canadian carrier WestJet flies nonstop three times weekly from Toronto. There's also interisland charter service on Island Air.

Airline Contacts American Airlines/American Eagle ☎ 345/949–0666. **Cayman Airways** ☎ 345/949–2311. **Delta** ☎ 345/945–8430. **Island Air** ☎ 345/949–5252 ⊕ www.islandair.ky. **United** ☎ 800/241–6522 ⊕ www.united.com. **US Airways** ☎ 345/949–7488. **WestJet** ☎ 888/937–8538 ⊕ www.westjet.com.

▮ BIKE AND MOPED TRAVEL

When renting a motor scooter or bicycle, remember to drive on the left and wear sunblock and a helmet. Bicycles ($15 a day) and scooters ($50 a day) can be rented in George Town when cruise ships are in port. On Cayman Brac or Little Cayman your hotel can make arrangements for you (most offer complimentary bicycles for local sightseeing).

Rental Companies Island Scooter Rentals ⊠ George Town, Grand Cayman ☎ 345/949–2046.

▮ BUS TRAVEL

On Grand Cayman, bus service is efficient, inexpensive, and plentiful, running roughly every 15 minutes. Minivans marked "Omni Bus" are mostly independently operated (there are 38 buses and 24 owners) and run from 6 am to midnight from West Bay to Rum Point and the East End. All routes branch from the George Town terminal adjacent to the library on Edward Street and are described in the phone book; color codes denote the routes. The one-way fare from George Town to West Bay via Seven Mile Beach is CI$1.50, to East End destinations CI$2, and from West Bay and northern Seven Mile Beach to East End CI$3. Some bus stops are well marked; others are flexible. Respond to an approaching bus with a wave; then the driver toots his horn to acknowledge that he has seen you.

▮ CAR TRAVEL

Driving is easy on Grand Cayman, albeit on the left (British style). Most visitors, especially if they're staying along Seven Mile Beach, are content taking taxis or a one-day tour to see the sights rather than renting a car. Traffic on the road from Seven Mile Beach to George Town then onto Bodden Town in Grand Cayman is terrible, especially during the 7 to 9 am and 4:30 to 6:30 pm commuting periods, despite construction of a bypass road. Fortunately, roads are generally well marked and well maintained. One major coastal highway circumnavigates most of the island (remember that no shortcuts divide the extensive East End), though you can get lost in the tangle of side roads in primarily residential West Bay. Exploring Cayman Brac on a scooter is fun and straightforward. You won't really need a car on Little Cayman, though there are a limited number of Jeeps for rent; bikes are the preferred mode of transport.

GASOLINE

In Grand Cayman, you can find gasoline stations in and around George Town, the airport, and Seven Mile Beach. Although times vary, most open daily with hours that extend into the evening; a few remain open 24 hours a day. There are two gasoline stations on Cayman Brac and one on Little Cayman. Prices are exorbitant, even compared to those in the United States and most of the Caribbean, especially on the Sister Islands.

PARKING

Park only in approved parking areas. Most hotels offer free parking. Many airport, Camana Bay, George Town, and Seven Mile Beach parking lots are free, but increasing development has prompted some major shopping centers to charge a fee if you park for more than 15 minutes (about $2.50 per hour); however, if you purchase something, parking should be validated and free. There is limited street parking, but watch for signs indicating private parking (in lots as well). Private enforcement companies are employed to discourage interlopers, placing a boot on the wheel and charging CI$75 for removal.

ROAD CONDITIONS

Grand Cayman has well-paved roads that follow the coastline. A network of main highways and bypasses facilitates traffic flow into and out of George Town. Small signs tacked to trees and poles at intersections point the way to most attractions, and local people are helpful if you get lost. Remote roads are in good repair, yet lighting can be poor at night—and night falls quickly at about 6 pm year-round.

Cayman Brac has one major road that skirts the coast, with a shortcut (Ashton Reid Drive) climbing the Bluff roughly bisecting the island. Little Cayman also provides a coastal route; unpaved sections in less-trammeled areas can become almost impassable after heavy rain. Other than that, goats, chickens, cattle, and the occasional iguana have the right of way.

ROADSIDE EMERGENCIES

Each car-rental agency has a different emergency-assistance provider. In the event of theft, accidents, or breakdowns, call your car-rental agency and follow instructions.

RULES OF THE ROAD

In the Cayman Islands, drive on the left, British style. Be mindful of pedestrians and, in the countryside, occasional livestock walking on the road. When someone flashes headlights at you at an intersection, it means "after you." Be especially careful negotiating roundabouts (traffic circles). Observe the speed limit, which is conservative: 30 mph (50 kph) in the country, 20 mph (30 kph) in town. George Town actually has rush hours: 7 to 9 am and 4:30 to 6:30 pm. Park only in approved parking areas. Always wear your seat belts—it's the law!

CAR RENTAL

To rent a car in The Cayman Islands, you must have a valid driver's license and major credit card. Most agencies require renters to be between 21 and 70 years of age, though the minimum age may be 25. Those over 75 may need a certified doctor's note indicating a continuing ability to drive safely. A local driver's permit, which costs $7.50, is obtained through the rental agency. Several dozen agencies rent cars, 4WD vehicles, and SUVs; rates are expensive—ranging from $40 to $95 per day (or $250 to $600 or more per week) in high season, depending on the vehicle and whether it has air-conditioning. Many firms offer significant discounts in low season, as well as reduced three-day rates. The rental generally includes insurance, pickup and delivery service (or shuttle service to your hotel or the airport), maps, 24-hour emergency service, and unlimited mileage. Car seats are usually available upon request.

The major agencies have offices to the left as you depart from the airport terminal in Grand Cayman; the closest, Andy's, is to the right. All require that you walk outdoors for a hundred yards. Make sure your luggage is portable, because there's no shuttle; if there are two of you, one can watch the bags while the other gets the car. Many car-rental firms have free pickup and drop-off along Seven Mile Beach (or second branches) so you can rent just on the days you want to tour. Consider security when renting a Jeep that cannot be locked. Midsize cars here often mean subcompact, so you may end up with a car that you wear unless you check the model.

Grand Cayman Agencies
Ace Hertz ☎ *345/949–2280, 800/654–3131* ⊕ *www. acerentacarltd.com.* **Andy's Rent a Car** ☎ *345/949–8111* ⊕ *www.andys. ky.* **Avis** ☎ *345/949–2468* ⊕ *www. aviscayman.com.* **Budget** ☎ *345/ 949–5605, 800/527–0700* ⊕ *www. budgetcayman.com.* **Coconut Car Rentals** ☎ *345/949–4037, 345/949– 7703, 800/941–4562* ⊕ *www. coconutcarrentals.com.* **Dollar** ☎ *345/949–4790* ⊕ *www.dollarlac. com.* **Economy** ☎ *345/949–9550* ⊕ *www.economycarrental.com.ky.* **Thrifty** ☎ *345/949–6640, 800/367– 2277* ⊕ *www.thrifty.com.*

Cayman Brac Agencies B&S Motor Ventures ☎ *345/948–1646* ⊕ *www.bandsmv.com.* **CB Rent-a-Car** ☎ *345/948–2424, 345/948–2847* ⊕ *www.cbrentacar.com.* **Four D's Car Rental** ☎ *345/948–1599.*

Little Cayman Agencies McLaughlin Rentals ☎ *345/948–1000.*

CAR INSURANCE

If you own a car, your personal auto insurance may cover a rental to some degree, though not all policies protect you abroad; always read your policy's fine print. If you don't have auto insurance, then seriously consider buying the collision- or loss-damage waiver (CDW or LDW) from the car-rental company, which eliminates your liability for damage to the car.

Some credit cards offer CDW coverage, but it's usually supplemental to your own insurance and rarely covers SUVs, minivans, luxury models, and the like. If your coverage is secondary, you may still be liable for loss-of-use costs from the car-rental company. But no credit-card insurance is valid unless you use that card for *all* transactions, from reserving to paying the final bill. All companies exclude car rental in some countries, so be sure to find out about the destination to which you are traveling.

▌ TAXI TRAVEL

On Grand Cayman, taxis operate 24 hours a day; if you anticipate a late night, however, make pickup arrangements in advance. Call for a cab to be dispatched,

as you generally cannot hail one on the street except occasionally in George Town. They carry up to three passengers for the same price. Fares aren't metered; the government sets rates, and they're not cheap, so ask ahead. The tariff increases with the number of riders and bags. To travel in style by limo, you can call A.A. Transportation or Elite Limousine Services. Drivers are courteous and knowledgeable; most will narrate a tour at an hourly rate of about $25 for up to three people. Be sure to settle the price before you start off and agree on whether it's quoted in U.S. or Cayman dollars.

Taxis are scarcer on the Sister Islands; rates are also fixed and fairly prohibitive. Your hotel will provide recommended drivers.

Taxi Companies A.A. Transportation Services ☎ *345/926–8294* ⊕ *www.burtons.ky.* **Charlie's Super Cab** ☎ *345/949–4748* ⊕ *www.charliescabs.net.* **Elite Limousine Services** ☎ *345/949–5963* ⊕ *www.elitelimo.ky.*

▌ ACCOMMODATIONS

Grand Cayman offers a wide range of lodgings in all price categories (though it ranks as one of the more expensive Caribbean destinations). You'll find luxury resorts, hotels both large and intimate, fully equipped condos, stylish individual villas, B&Bs, and more affordable locally run guesthouses. Quality, professionalism, high-tech conveniences, and service all rank among the region's best. With a few notable exceptions, condo resorts rule Seven Mile Beach (most hotels lie across the coastal "highway"). These are particularly attractive family options, as they include kitchen facilities. Cayman Brac and Little Cayman accommodations emphasize function above glitz and glamour (though most lack neither character nor characters), befitting the Sister Islands' status as topnotch scuba-diving destinations. Both have villas, condo resorts, and small hotels that often run on an all-inclusive or meal-plan basis and simple, family-run inns.

▌ COMMUNICATIONS

INTERNET

In Grand Cayman most hotels and resorts provide Internet access—either free or for a small fee—for their guests; wireless is increasingly prevalent, including at the airport in Grand Cayman. You'll also find Internet cafés in George Town. Rates range from $2.50 for 15 minutes to $10 per hour. Several restaurants also advertise free Wi-Fi hotspots. Although there are no cybercafés on the Sister Islands, most of the small hotels have high-speed access in rooms and/or public spaces. Those lacking Wi-Fi or high-speed Internet connections in rooms usually have a public computer or permit use of the office facilities. A few individual villas offer Wi-Fi.

PHONES

The area code for the Cayman Islands is 345.

CALLING WITHIN THE CAYMAN ISLANDS

In the Cayman Islands local calls are free from private phones; some hotels charge a small fee. For directory assistance, dial 411; international directory assistance is 010. Calls from pay phones cost CI¢25 for five minutes. Prepaid phone cards, which can be used throughout Cayman and other Caribbean islands, are sold at shops, attractions, transportation centers, and other convenient outlets.

CALLING OUTSIDE THE CAYMAN ISLANDS

From the Cayman Islands, direct dialing to the United States and other countries is efficient and reasonable, but always check with your hotel to see if a surcharge is added. Some toll-free numbers cannot be accessed, especially on the Sister Islands. To charge your overseas call on a major credit card or U.S. calling card without incurring a surcharge, dial 800/225–5872 (1-800/CALL-USA) from any phone.

The country code for the United States is 1.

Information AT&T ☎ 800/872–2881. **LIME** ☎ 345/949–7800 in Grand Cayman.

CALLING CARDS

LIME phone cards, which can be used for both local and international calls, are available for purchase in various denominations at many retail outlets, including supermarkets and gas stations. They can be used from any touch-tone telephone (including pay and cell phones) in the Cayman Islands. The rates on island are competitive with those of online servers and more reliable.

MOBILE PHONES

If you're bringing your own mobile phone and it's compatible with 850/1900 Mhz GSM network or TDMA digital network, you should be able to make and receive calls during your stay, especially from Grand Cayman. Be sure, however, to check with your home provider that you have roaming service enabled, and note that charges can be astronomical depending on your calling plan. Renting a cell phone if you're planning an extended vacation or expect to make a lot of local calls may be a less expensive alternative than using your own. Mobile-phone rental is available from LIME (formerly Cable & Wireless) and Digicel; you can stay connected for as little as CI$5 per day plus the cost of a calling card (denominations range from CI$10 to CI$100). International per-minute rates usually range from CI¢35 to CI¢60. You can rent phones for use on-island from either LIME or Digicel.

Mobile Phone Companies
LIME ✉ Anderson Square Bldg., Shedden Rd., George Town, Grand Cayman ☎ 345/949–7800 ⊕ www.time4lime.com ✉ Galleria Plaza, West Bay Rd., Seven Mile Beach, Grand Cayman ⊕ www.time4lime.

com/ky. **Digicel** ✉ Leeward One, Regatta Office Park, 1158A West Bay Rd., Seven Mile Beach, Grand Cayman ☎ 345/623–3444 ⊕ www.digicelcayman.com.

ESSENTIALS

▪ CUSTOMS AND DUTIES

**Contacts Cayman Islands
Customs** ☎ 345/949–4579
🌐 *customs.gov.ky.*

▪ EATING OUT

Obviously seafood reigns supreme in the Cayman Islands, where it's served everywhere from tiny family-run shanties to decadently decorated bistros. But befitting Grand Cayman's reputation as a sophisticated, multinational destination (with residents from 113 countries at last count), you can find a smorgasbord of savory options from terrific Tex-Mex to Thai to Italian. Menus could highlight by-the-book bouillabaisse or barbecue, kebabs or cannelloni, ceviche or sushi. This is one destination where larger resorts generally have excellent restaurants. Two must-try local delicacies are conch, particularly fritters and chowder, and turtle (protected but farmed); the latter is stewed or served like a steak. Many restaurants offer kids' menus, and vegetarians should find acceptable options. *For information on food-related health issues, see ⇨ Health.*

MEALS AND MEALTIMES

Most restaurants serve breakfast from 7 to 10 am, lunch from 12 to 3 pm, and dinner from 6 to 11 pm. But these hours can vary widely, especially at remote resorts on Grand Cayman's East End and West Bay, as well as on the Sister Islands, which have few independent eateries. Every strip mall along Grand Cayman's Seven Mile Beach has at least one restaurant open late (often doubling as a lounge or nightclub); many beachfront bars also offer late dining, especially on weekends. Restaurants are likeliest to shutter on Sundays, especially in the less-trafficked areas. Since most markets also close, prepare for contingencies, especially if you're staying at an individual villa or condo. If you arrive on Saturday, when most villa and condo rentals begin, make sure you do your grocery shopping that afternoon. Most grocery stores will be closed on Sunday.

Unless otherwise noted, the restaurants listed in this guide are open daily for lunch and dinner.

PAYING

Major credit cards are widely accepted, even on the Sister Islands, though some smaller local establishments only accept cash.

For guidelines on tipping, see ⇨ Tipping.

RESERVATIONS AND DRESS

Grand Cayman is both cosmopolitan and conservative, so scantily clad diners are frowned upon or downright refused seating. Many tonier establishments require long pants and collared shirts for gentlemen in the evening (lunch is generally more casual). Footwear and something to cover bathing suits (a sarong or sundress for women, T-shirt and shorts for men) are required save at some beachfront bars. The Sister Islands are far more casual. Reservations are strongly recommended for dinner at most restaurants throughout the islands.

We mention dress only when men are required to wear a jacket or a jacket and tie.

BEER, WINE, AND SPIRITS

Beer, wine, and spirits are readily available at most restaurants. Some pricier restaurants take great pride in their wine lists. Aficionados of local products may want to try the refreshing Caybrew beers (the nutty, smoky dark amber pairs well with many foods) and Tortuga rum (the 12-year-old is a marvelous after-dinner sipper in place of Cognac or single-malt Scotch).

▮ ELECTRICITY

Electric current on the Cayman Islands is 110 volts–60 cycles, U.S. standard. Hotels generally have plug adapters and transformers available for guests who bring appliances from countries that operate on 220-volt current.

WORD OF MOUTH

Was the service stellar or not up to snuff? Did the food give you shivers of delight or leave you cold? Did the prices and portions make you happy or sad? Rate restaurants and write your own reviews in Travel Ratings or start a discussion about your favorite places in Travel Talk on ⊕ www.fodors.com. Your comments might even appear in our books. Yes, you, too, can be a correspondent!

▮ EMERGENCIES

Emergency Services Ambulance ☎ 911. **Fire** ☎ 911. **Police** ☎ 911.

Foreign Consulates U.S. Consular Agency ⊠ Cayman Centre, Unit B1, 118 Dorcy Dr., George Town, Grand Cayman ☎ 345/945-8173 ⊕ travel.state.gov/travel/cis_pa_tw/cis/cis_1084.html.

Hospitals George Town Hospital ⊠ 1 Hospital Rd., George Town, Grand Cayman ☎ 345/949-8600. **The Brac Clinic** ⊠ Tibbetts Sq., West End, Cayman Brac ☎ 345/949-1777. **Cayman Clinic** ⊠ Grand Cayman ☎ 345/949-4234. **Faith Hospital** ⊠ Stake Bay, West End, Cayman Brac ☎ 345/948-2243.

Pharmacies Cayman Drug ⊠ Kirk Freeport Centre, George Town, Grand Cayman ☎ 345/949-2597. **Foster's Pharmacy** ⊠ Foster's Food Fair, Airport Rd., George Town, Grand Cayman ☎ 345/949-0505 ⊕ www.fosters-iga.com. **Health Care Pharmacy** ⊠ Photo-Pharm Centre, Walkers Rd., George Town, Grand Cayman

☎ 345/949–0442. **Kirk Pharmacy** ✉ Kirk Supermarket, Eastern Ave., George Town, Grand Cayman ☎ 345/949–7180.

Diving Emergencies
Cayman Hyperbaric ✉ Hospital Rd., George Town, Grand Cayman ☎ 345/949–2989.

▮ HEALTH

Health concerns are minimal in the Cayman Islands, and Grand Cayman offers some of the Caribbean's finest medical facilities. Though there have been isolated cases of dengue fever (one or two annually, contracted elsewhere), the last on-island outbreak was in 2005. Airlift to Miami for serious emergencies is available. Physicians are highly qualified and speak English. Be sure to pack prescription medications; consider wearing a MedicAlert ID tag if you suffer from such chronic conditions as diabetes, epilepsy, or heart disease. Though many hospitals offer reciprocity with U.S. insurers, you can also purchase medical-only insurance (see ⇨ Trip Insurance under Things to Consider in Before You Go). Tap water is perfectly safe to drink throughout all three islands. Be sure to wash fruit thoroughly or, better yet, peel it before eating. The subtropic sun can be fierce, especially at midday. Be sure to wear sunglasses and a hat, and use high-SPF sunscreen (most U.S. brands are available). Beware of dehydration and heat stroke; take it easy the first couple of days. Insects can be a real nuisance during the wet season (July–November); bring along repellent to ward off mosquitoes and sand flies. Shops also stock numerous name brands.

MEDICAL INSURANCE AND ASSISTANCE

Consider buying trip insurance with medical-only coverage. Neither Medicare nor some private insurers cover medical expenses anywhere outside the United States. Medical-only policies typically reimburse you for medical care (excluding that related to pre-existing conditions) and hospitalization abroad and provide for evacuation. You still have to pay the bills and await reimbursement from the insurer, though.

Another option is to sign up with a medical-evacuation assistance company. A membership in one of these companies gets you doctor referrals, emergency evacuation or repatriation, 24-hour hotlines for medical consultation, and other assistance. International SOS Assistance Emergency and AirMed International provide evacuation services and medical referrals. MedjetAssist offers medical evacuation.

Medical Assistance Companies
AirMed International ⊕ www.airmed.com. **International SOS Assistance Emergency** ⊕ www.internationalsos.com. **MedjetAssist** ⊕ www.medjetassist.com.

Health Information National Centers for Disease Control & Prevention (CDC). ☎ 877/394–8747 international travelers' health line ⊕ www.cdc.gov/travel. **World Health Organization** (WHO). ⊕ www.who.int.

**Medical-Only Insurers
International Medical Group**
☏ *800/628–4664* ⊕ *www.imgglobal.
com.* **International SOS** ⊕ *www.
internationalsos.com.* **Wallach
and Company** ☏ *800/237–6615,
540/687–3166* ⊕ *www.wallach.com.*

■ HOURS OF OPERATION

Banks in the Cayman Islands are
generally open Monday through
Friday from 9 to 3. Post offices
are open weekdays from 8:30 to
4 and Saturday from 9 to 1. Shops
are usually open weekdays from 9
to 5; in outer shopping plazas they
are open from 10 to 5. Shops are
usually closed Sunday except in
hotels or when cruise ships are visiting. Pharmacy hours vary, most
opening between 7 and 9 am, closing between 6 and 10 pm.

HOLIDAYS

In the Cayman Islands public holidays include New Year's Day, Ash
Wednesday (46 days before Easter), Good Friday (Friday before
Easter), Easter Sunday (usually
March or April), Discovery Day
(May 19), Queen's Birthday (June
16), Constitution Day (July 7),
Remembrance Day (November
17), Christmas, and Boxing Day
(December 26). The last refers to
boxing extra presents for charity,
not prizefighting!

■ MAIL

Sending a postcard to the United
States, Canada, other parts of the
Caribbean, or Central America
costs CI25¢. An airmail letter is
CI75¢ per half ounce. To Europe
and South America, rates are

CI25¢ for a postcard and CI80¢
per half ounce for airmail letters. When addressing letters to
the Cayman Islands, be sure to
include the new postal codes that
have been introduced. You can
find them at ⊕ *www.caymanpost.
gov.ky* or on leaflets at any of the
islands' post offices. The main
post office lies at the intersection of Edward Street and Cardinal Avenue in downtown George
Town. There is no home delivery;
instead, all mail is delivered to
numbered post-office boxes. For
faster and reliable service to the
United States, Federal Express,
UPS, and DHL all have locations
in the downtown area. Airmail can
take two weeks to be delivered to
farther-flung areas, including Australia and New Zealand.

■ MONEY

You should not need to change
money in Grand Cayman, since
U.S. dollars are readily accepted,
though you may get some change
in Cayman dollars. ATMs accept-
ing MasterCard and Visa with Cir-
rus affiliation are readily available
in George Town; you usually have
the option of U.S. or Cayman dollars. The Cayman dollar is pegged
to the U.S. dollar at the rate of
approximately CI$1.25 to $1, and
divided into a hundred cents, with
coins of 1¢, 5¢, 10¢, and 25¢ and
notes of $1, $5, $10, $25, $50,
and $100. There's no $20 bill.
Traveler's checks and major credit
cards are widely accepted. Be sure
you know which currency is being
quoted when making a purchase.

Prices throughout this guide are given for adults and unless otherwise indicated are in U.S. currency. Substantially reduced fees are almost always available for children, students, and senior citizens.

ATMS AND BANKS

There are more than 600 banks on the Cayman Islands; practically every major international financial operation is represented. ATMs are available 24 hours a day at bank branches, transportation centers, shopping centers, gas stations, and other convenient spots throughout the island. Those at banks usually dispense both Cayman and U.S. dollars.

CREDIT CARDS

The following abbreviations are used: **AE**, *American Express;* **D**, *Discover;* **DC**, *Diners Club;* **MC**, *MasterCard; and* **V**, *Visa.*

It's a good idea to inform your credit-card company before you travel, especially if you're going abroad and don't travel internationally very often. Otherwise, the credit-card company might put a hold on your card owing to unusual activity—not a good thing halfway through your trip. Record all your credit-card numbers—as well as the phone numbers to call if your cards are lost or stolen—in a safe place, so you're prepared should something go wrong. Both MasterCard and Visa have general numbers you can call (collect if you're abroad) if your card is lost, but you're better off calling the number of your issuing bank, since MasterCard and Visa usually just transfer you to your bank; your bank's number is usually printed on your card.

If you plan to use your credit card for cash advances, you'll need to apply for a PIN at least two weeks before your trip. Although it's usually cheaper (and safer) to use a credit card abroad for large purchases (so you can cancel payments or be reimbursed if there's a problem), note that some credit-card companies *and* the banks that issue them add substantial percentages to all foreign transactions, whether they're in a foreign currency or not. Check on these fees before leaving home, so there won't be any surprises when you get the bill.

▌ PASSPORTS AND VISAS

All visitors to the Cayman Islands must have a valid passport and a return or ongoing ticket to enter the Cayman Islands. A birth certificate and photo ID are *not* sufficient proof of citizenship.

▌ SAFETY

Though crime isn't a major problem in the Cayman Islands, take normal precautions. Lock your room, and don't leave valuables—particularly passports, tickets, and wallets—in plain sight or unattended on the beach. Use your hotel safe. Don't carry too much money or flaunt expensive jewelry on the street. For personal safety, avoid walking on the beach or on unlit streets at night. Lock your rental car, and don't pick up hitchhikers. Using or trafficking in illegal drugs is strictly prohibited in the Cayman Islands. Any offense is punishable by a hefty fine, imprisonment, or both.

▪ TAXES AND SERVICE CHARGES

At the airport, each adult passenger leaving Grand Cayman must pay a departure tax of $25 (CI$20), payable in either Caymanian or U.S. currency. It may be included in cruise packages as a component of port charges; it isn't usually added to airfare—check with your carrier—and must be paid in cash by each traveler prior to entering the secure area of the airport.

A 10% government tax is added to all hotel bills. A 10% service charge is often added to hotel bills and restaurant checks in lieu of a tip. There is no VAT or comparable tariff on goods and services.

▪ TIME

U.S. Eastern Standard Time (EST), five hours behind Greenwich Mean Time (GMT-0500), is in effect year-round on all three islands; daylight saving time is not observed.

▪ TIPPING

At large hotels a service charge is generally included and can be anywhere from 6% to 10%; smaller establishments and some villas and condos leave tipping up to you. Although tipping is customary at restaurants, note that some automatically include 10%–15% on the bill—so check the tab carefully. At your discretion, tip another 5% or more to recognize extraordinary service. Taxi drivers expect a 10%–15% tip. Bellmen and porters expect $1 per bag, more in luxury hotels (especially if you bring lots of luggage). Tip the concierge (if your resort has one) anywhere from $10 to $100, depending on services rendered and length of stay. Tips are not expected simply for handing out maps and making the occasional dinner reservation. Spa personnel should receive 15%–20% of the treatment price (but verify that a service fee wasn't already added).

▪ TOURS

GUIDED TOURS

A sightseeing tour is a good way to get your bearings and to experience Caymanian culture. Taxi drivers will give you a personalized tour of Grand Cayman for about $25 per hour for up to three people. Or you can choose a fascinating helicopter ride, a horseback or mountain-bike journey, a 4x4 safari expedition, or a full-day bus excursion. The prices vary according to the mode of travel and the number and kind of attractions included. Ask your hotel to help you make arrangements.

Costs and itineraries for island tours are about the same regardless of the tour operator. Half-day tours average $40–$50 a person and generally include a visit to Hell and the Turtle Farm at Boatswain Beach adventure park in West Bay, as well as shopping downtown. Full-day tours ($60–$80 per person) add lunch, a visit to Bodden Town (the first settlement), and the East End, where you stop at the Queen Elizabeth

II Botanic Park, blowholes (if the waves are high) on the ironshore, and the site of the wreck of the *Ten Sails* (not the wreck itself—just the site). The pirate graves in Bodden Town were destroyed during Hurricane Ivan, and the blowholes were partially filled. As you can tell, land tours here are low-key. Children under 12 often receive discounts.

A.A. Transportation Services offers taxis and tour buses. Ask for Burton Ebanks. B.A. McCurley, owner of McCurley Tours, is a free-spirited, freewheeling midwesterner who's lived in Cayman for 24 years and knows everything and everyone on the East End. Not only is she encyclopedic and flexible, she also offers car rentals and transfers for travelers staying on the East End; don't be surprised if she tells you what to order at lunch, especially if it's off the menu.

Majestic Tours caters mostly to cruise-ship and incentive groups but also offers similar options to individuals and can customize tours; it's particularly good for West Bay, including Boatswain's Beach and Hell.

Tropicana Tours offers several excellent Cayman highlights itineraries on its larger buses, including Stingray City stops, as well as reef-runner adventures across the North Sound through the mangrove swamps.

Your hotel or villa agent can recommend and organize drivers for tours of the Sister Islands.

Contacts A.A. Transportation Services ☎ 345/949–6598, 345/926–8294, 345/949–7222 ⊕ www.burtons.ky. **Majestic Tours** ☎ 345/949–7773 ⊕ www. majestic-tours.com. **McCurley Tours** ☎ 345/947–9626, 345/916–0925 ✑ mccurley@cwhiptop.com. **Tropicana Tours** ☎ 345/949–0944 ⊕ www.tropicana-tours.com.

SPECIAL-INTEREST TOURS

Cayman Custom Cycles' Harley Davidson tours allow you to go hog wild, wind in your face, exploring the East End and playing Hells Angels in Hell. Tours run $125–$250 (the full-day option includes lunch). Additional passengers can hitch a ride for 50 smackers.

Cayman Island Helicopters offers exhilarating eagle-eye views on three itineraries: $75 for a flyover of Seven Mile Beach; $115 for a trip adding Stingray City; and $295 for a thrillingly panoramic island-wide aerial tour (discounts are available if you book via the company's website, and shuttle service is free). Though the island is flat and mostly arid, the sight of waters rippling from turquoise to tourmaline is exciting enough.

Cayman Safari hits the usual sights but emphasizes interaction with locals, so you learn about craft traditions, folklore, and herbal medicines.

Contacts Cayman Custom Cycles Harley Davidson Tours ☎ 345/916–0088, 345/916–8319 ⊕ www.caymancustomcycles. com. **Cayman Island Helicopters** ☎ 345/943–4354, 345/926–6967

⊕ www.caymanislandshelicopters. com. **Cayman Safari** ☎ 345/925–3001, 866/211–4677 ⊕ www. caymansafari.com.

▮ TRIP INSURANCE

Comprehensive trip insurance is valuable if you're booking a very expensive or complicated trip (particularly to an isolated region) or if you're booking far in advance. Comprehensive policies typically cover trip cancellation and interruption, letting you cancel or cut your trip short because of illness or, in some cases, acts of terrorism in your destination. Such policies might also cover evacuation and medical care. (For trips abroad you should have at least medical-only coverage *(see ➪ Medical Insurance and Assistance under Health)*. Some also cover you for trip delays because of bad weather or mechanical problems as well as for lost or delayed luggage.

Another type of coverage to consider is financial default—that is, when your trip is disrupted because a tour operator, airline, or cruise line goes out of business. Generally you must buy this when you book your trip or shortly thereafter, and it's available to you only if your operator isn't on a list of excluded companies.

Always read the fine print of your policy to make sure that you're covered for the risks that most concern you. Compare several policies to be sure you're getting the best price and range of coverage available.

Insurance Comparison Sites
Insure My Trip ☎ 800/487–4722 ⊕ www.insuremytrip.com. **Square Mouth** ☎ 800/240-0369 ⊕ www.squaremouth.com.

Travel Insurers Access America ☎ 800/284–8300 ⊕ www. accessamerica.com. **AIG Travel Guard** ☎ 800/826–4919 ⊕ www. travelguard.com. **CSA Travel Protection** ☎ 800/711–1197 ⊕ www. csatravelprotection.com. **Travelex Insurance** ☎ 800/228–9792 ⊕ www. travelex-insurance.com. **Travel Insured International** ☎ 800/243–3174 ⊕ www.travelinsured.com.

▮ VISITOR INFORMATION

The Cayman Islands has tourist offices in the United States, where you can get brochures and maps in advance of your trip. There are also tourism offices on the islands for on-site help.

Cayman Islands Department of Tourism ☎ 305/599–9033 *in Miami*, 847/678–6446 *in Chicago*, 212/889–9009 *in New York City*, 713/461–1317 *in Houston*, 877/422–9626, 213/738–1968 *in Los Angeles* ⊕ www. caymanislands.ky.

Department of Tourism ✉ *Regatta Office Park Windward 3, West Bay Rd., Seven Mile Beach* ☎ 345/949–0623 ✉ *Owen Roberts Airport, Grand Cayman* ☎ 345/949–3603 ✉ *West End Rd., North Side, Cayman Brac* ☎ 345/948–1649.

ON-LINE RESOURCES

Brac And Little. *Brac And Little* is a useful, privately run adjunct to the official Sister Islands websites, offering lots of local news and gossip, photos, and often faster updates. ⊕ *www. bracandlittle.com.*

Caymanian Compass. *Caymanian Compass,* the online version of the national newspaper, offers news, occasionally provocative commentary, event listings, weather reports, currency converter, photo galleries, interactive map, and the CaymanEye live webcam. ⊕ *www. compasscayman.com.*

Cayman Islands Destination Magazine. *Cayman Islands Destination Magazine* provides information on everything from airlines to accommodations, restaurants to real estate, with useful links. ⊕ *www. destination.ky.*

Cayman Islands Vacations and Business Directory. *Cayman Islands Vacations and Business Directory,* funded by private-sector businesses, functions as a de facto Chamber of Commerce adjunct, with extensive transportation, lodging, dining, recreational, bar-hopping, and shopping write-ups, as well as information on everything from marine conservation to culture, weather to weddings. ⊕ *www.gocayman.ky.*

Cayman Net News Online. Cayman Net News Online provides all the daily local news that's fit to cyber-print, with a helpful weekly Sister Islands supplement titled *The Bracker and Little Caymanian.* ⊕ *www.caymannetnews.com.*

Cayman Observer. *Cayman Observer* is a weekly business-oriented newspaper with intriguing news items and editorials taking the current pulse of the islands. ⊕ *www.caymanobserver. com.*

Cayman Restaurant Guide. Cayman Restaurant Guide is a fairly comprehensive listing of eateries with sample menus, maps, reviews, even recipes. ⊕ *www. caymanrestaurants.com.*

Good Taste. Good Taste bills itself as "Cayman's definitive dining and entertainment guide," dishing out menus for dozens of restaurants, alongside articles on local cuisine and charts detailing which eateries offer children's portions, alfresco dining, water views, and more. ⊕ *www.caymangoodtaste.com.*

Key to Cayman. Key to Cayman is the online version of a thick, stylish quarterly with particular focus on shopping, real estate, heritage, attractions, and crafts. ⊕ *www. keytocayman.com.*

National Trust for the Cayman Islands. National Trust for the Cayman Islands is an admirable nonprofit institution dedicated to preserving the cultural, historic, and environmental heritage of the Cayman Islands. Its informative website includes information on programs, maps, events, and more. ⊕ *www.nationaltrust.org.ky.*

Nature Cayman. Nature Cayman details the Sister Islands' rich flora and fauna on land and underwater, along with detailed coverage of Cayman Brac and Little Cayman history and culture. ⊕ *www.naturecayman.com.*

Sister Islands Tourism Association. Sister Islands Tourism Association is the website of a business group that publicizes its member establishments on Cayman Brac and Little Cayman. ⊕ *www.sisterislands.com.*

Tourism Attraction Board. Tourism Attraction Board runs several of Grand Cayman's leading attractions and events, including Pedro St. James historical site, Queen Elizabeth II Botanic Park, and November's annual Pirates Week Festival. ⊕ *www.tab.ky.*

▌ WEDDINGS

Getting married in the Cayman Islands is a breeze, and each year many couples tie the knot here. Most choose to say their vows on lovely Seven Mile Beach, with the sun setting into the azure sea as their picture-perfect backdrop. Underwater weddings in full scuba gear with schools of fish as impromptu witnesses are also possible (kissing with mask on optional). Cathy Church can photograph your underwater wedding *(see ⇨ Shopping in Chapter 2).* You can literally leave things up in the air, getting hitched while hovering in a helicopter ("I do; Roger and out," responded one blushing bride over the propeller noise). A traditional church wedding can even be arranged, after which you trot away to your life together in a horse-drawn carriage.

Documentation can be prepared ahead of time or in one day while on the island. There's no on-island waiting period. In addition to the application, you need proof of identity and age (those under 18 must provide parental consent), such as an original or certified birth certificate or passport; a Cayman Islands international embarkation/disembarkation card; and certified or original copies of divorce decrees/death certificates if you have been married before. You must list a marriage officer on the application, and you need at least two witnesses; if you haven't come with friends or family, the marriage officer can help you with that, too. A marriage license costs CI$200 (US$250).

The best way to plan your wedding in the Cayman Islands is to contact a wedding coordinator (resorts such as the Reef, Westin Casuarina, and Ritz-Carlton have one on staff), who will offer a wide variety of packages to suit every taste and budget. All the logistics and legalities will be properly handled, giving you time to relax and enjoy the wedding of your dreams. The Cayman Islands Department of Tourism keeps a list of wedding coordinators. Or you can order the brochure "Getting Married in the Cayman Islands" from Government Information Services. Vernon Jackson, of Cayman Weddings, is a wonderful marriage officer with a soft accent and a kind heart. You can choose from many different styles of services or rewrite one as you wish.

Information Cayman Weddings ☎ *345/949–8677* ⊕ *www.caymanweddings.com.ky.* **Deputy Chief Secretary** ✉ *Government Administration Bldg., 3rd Floor, George Town, Grand Cayman* ☎ *345/949–7900, 345/914–2222.* **District Commissioner's Office** ✉ *District Administration Bldg., Stake Bay, Cayman Brac* ☎ *345/948–2222, 345/948–2506.* **Government Information Services** ✉ *Cricket Sq., George Town, Grand Cayman* ☎ *345/949–8092.* **Heart of Cayman** ☎ *345/949–1343, 345/916–2576* ⊕ *www.heartofcayman.com.*

INDEX

PHOTO CREDITS

1, SuperStock/age fotostock. 2, Stuart Pearce / age fotostock. 3 (top), Burrard-Lucas Photography/Cayman Islands Department of Tourism. 3 (bottom), Mark Narsanski/Cayman Islands Department of Tourism. 4 (top left), Allister Clark/iStockphoto. 4 (top right), Pirates Point Resort. 4 (bottom), J & C Sohns / age fotostock. 5, Lawson Wood/Cayman Islands Department of Tourism. 6, Stephen Frink Collection / Alamy. 7 (top left), Zach Stovall/Bonnier Corporation. 7 (top right), Martyn Poynor. 7 (bottom), RENAULT Philippe / age fotostock. 8 (top left), Rohit Seth/Shutterstock. 8 (top right), Shimon & Tammer. 8 (bottom), Lawson Wood / age fotostock. 11, FLPA/age fotostock. Chapter 1: Experience Cayman Islands: 12-13, Anne Flinn Powell/age fotostock. 15, JodiJacobson /istock. 15, (bottom), Cayman Islands Department of Tourism. 19, Allister Clark/iStockphoto. 20, Dan McDougall/Cayman Islands Department of Tourism. 21, Cayman Islands Department of Tourism. 23 (left), Christian Wheatley/Shutterstock. 23 (right), Michael Macsuga/Shutterstock.Chapter 2: Exploring Grand Cayman: 25, Cayman Islands Department of Tourism. 28, allyclark /istock. 32, Cayman Islands Department of Tourism. 37, SSImages Collection/iStockphoto. 39, 41, and 50-51, Cayman Islands Department of Tourism. Chapter 3: Where to Eat in Grand Cayman: 59 and 63, Ortanique. 70, Mark Wieland. 73, Starwood Hotels & Resorts. Chapter 4: Where to Stay in Grand Cayman: 89, Courtney Platt. 94, aceshot1/Shutterstock. 96, Caribbean Club. 98-99. PixAchi/Shutterstock. 100, The Ritz-Carlton, Grand Cayman. 102, Dan McDougall/Cayman Islands Department of Tourism. 106, Courtney Platt. 109, Dan McDougall/Cayman Islands Department of Tourism. 110, Robert Smith/age fotostock. Chapter 5: Grand Cayman Nightlife and the Arts: 111, Angelo Cavalli/age fotostock. 117, MCHart/Flickr. 119, Danita Delimont/Alamy. Chapter 6: Grand Cayman Sports and Outdoor Activities: 127, Kevin Panizza/iStockphoto. 130-131, Jan Greune/age fotostock. 137, Peter Heiss/iStockphoto. 141, Corbis. 150 and 152-53, Cayman Islands Department of Tourism. 162-63, Ronald J. Manera/iStockphoto. Chapter 7: Cayman Brac: 165, Greg Johnston/age fotostock. 174, J & C Sohns/age fotostock. 179, Jan Greune/age fotostock. 184-185, RENAULT Philippe/age fotostock. 186, Kevin Panizza/iStockphoto. 190-91, Greg Johnston/age fotostock. Chapter 8: Little Cayman: 197, Karen & Ian Stewart/Alamy. 204, Dan McDougall/Cayman Islands Department of Tourism. 208, Cayman Islands Department of Tourism. 210-11, RENAULT Philippe/age fotostock. 213, Chris A. Crumley/Alamy.

NOTES

NOTES

FODOR'S INFOCUS CAYMAN ISLANDS

Editor: Douglas Stallings, *series editor*

Editorial Contributor: Jordan Simon

Production Editor: Elyse Rozelle

Maps & Illustrations: David Lindroth and Mark Stroud, *cartographers*; Rebecca Baer, *map editor*; William Wu, *information graphics*

Design: Fabrizio La Rocca, *creative director*; Tina Malaney, Chie Ushio, Jessica Ramirez, *designers*; Melanie Marin, *senior picture editor*

Cover Photo: Stephen Frink/The Image Bank/Getty Images

Production Manager: Angela L. McLean

COPYRIGHT

3rd Edition

ISBN 978-0-89141-963-1
ISSN 1941–0220

SPECIAL SALES

This book is available for special discounts for bulk purchases for sales promotions or premiums. Special editions, including personalized covers, excerpts of existing books, and corporate imprints, can be created in large quantities for special needs. For more information, write to Special Markets/Premium Sales, 1745 Broadway, MD 3-1 New York, NY 10019, or e-mail specialmarkets@randomhouse.com.

AN IMPORTANT TIP & AN INVITATION

Although all prices, opening times, and other details in this book are based on information supplied to us at press time, changes occur all the time in the travel world, and Fodor's cannot accept responsibility for facts that become outdated or for inadvertent errors or omissions. **So always confirm information when it matters,** especially if you're making a detour to visit a specific place. Your experiences—positive and negative—matter to us. If we have missed or misstated something, **please write to us.** Share your opinion instantly through our online feedback center at fodors. com/contact-us.

PRINTED IN CHINA
10 9 8 7 6 5 4 3 2 1

ABOUT OUR WRITER

Jordan Simon worked in various aspects of the entertainment industry, from actor to director, before defecting to journalism. He's served as food and/or wine editor for *Atlanta Homes & Lifestyles, Hamptons, Second Home, Snow Country,* and *Ski Impact*; contributing editor for *TAXI, I-MI,* and *Shermans Travel*. He oversaw development of *Wine Country International* as founding editor-in-chief. He's currently contributing travel editor for *Nikki Style,* columnist for AOL Travel, and lifestyle editor for *Caribbean Living*. He's beach-combed for many magazines and websites, including *Caribbean Travel & Life, Condé Nast Traveler, Town & Country, Modern Bride, Diversion,* ShermansTravel.com, Jetsetter.com, *Cooking Light, Interval, Art & Antiques, USAir Magazine, TravelAge,* and *American Way*.

He's written several guidebooks, including the original editions of *Fodor's Colorado* and *Fodor's Branson: The Official Travel & Souvenir Guide*. He co-wrote *The Celestial Seasonings Cookbook: Cooking with Tea* with Mo and Jennifer Siegel; *Astronumerology: Your Key to Empowerment Using Stars & Numbers* with Pam Bell; and *Edge Atlanta* with Jeff Clark, et al.